ManagingNonprofits.org

WILEY NONPROFIT LAW, FINANCE, AND MANAGEMENT SERIES

The Art of Planned Giving: Understanding Donors and the Culture of Giving by Dougles E. White

Beyond Fund Raising: New Strategies for Nonprofit Investment and Innovation by Kay Grace

Budgeting for Not-for-Profit Organizations by David Maddox

Careers in Fund-Raising by Lilya Wagner

The Complete Guide to Fund Raising Management by Stanley Weinstein

The Complete Guide to Nonprofit Management by Smith, Bucklin & Associates

Critical Issues in Fund Raising edited by Dwight Burlingame

Cultural Diversity in Fund-Raising by Janice Glow Pettey

Developing Affordable Housing: A Practical Guide for Nonprofit Organizations, Second Edition by Ben Hecht

Faith-Based Management: Leading Organizations that are Based on More than Just Mission by Peter Brinckerhoff

Financial and Accounting Guide for Not-for-Profit Organizations, Sixth Edition by Malvern J. Gross, Jr., Richard F. Larkin, John H. McCarthy, PricewaterhouseCoopers LLP

Financial Empowerment: More Money for More Mission by Peter Brinckerhoff

Financial Management for Nonprofit Organizations by Jo Ann Hankin, Alan Seidner, and John Zietlow

The First Legal Answer Book for Fund-Raisers by Bruce R. Hopkins

Fund-Raising Fundamentals: A Guide to Annual Giving for Professionals and Volunteers by James M. Greenfield

Fundraising Cost Effectiveness: A Self-Assessment Workbook by James M. Greenfield

Fund-Raising Regulation: A State-by-State Handbook of Registration Forms, Requirements, and Procedures by Seth Perlman and Betsy Hills Bush

Grantseeker's Budget Toolkit by James A. Quick and Cheryl S. New

Grantseeker's Toolkit: A Comprehensive Guide to Finding Funding by Cheryl S. New and James A. Quick

Grant Winner's Toolkit: Project Management and Evaluation by James A. Quick and Cheryl S. New

High Impact Philanthropy: How Donors, Boards, and Nonprofit Organizations Can Transform Nonprofit Communities by Kay Sprinkel Grace and Alan L. Wendroff

High Performance Nonprofit Organizations: Managing Upstream for Greater Impact by Christine W. Letts, William P. Ryan, and Allen Grossman

Improving the Economy, Efficiency, and Effectiveness of Nonprofits: Conducting Operational Reviews by Rob Reider

Intermediate Sanctions: Curbing Nonprofit Abuse by Bruce R. Hopkins and D. Benson Tesdahl

International Fund Raising for Nonprofits by Thomas Harris

International Guide to Nonprofit Law by Lester A. Salamon and Stefan Toepler & Associates

Joint Ventures Involving Tax-Exempt Organizations, Second Edition by Michael I. Sanders

The Law of Fund-Raising, Second Edition by Bruce R. Hopkins

The Law of Tax-Exempt Healthcare Organizations, Second Edition by Thomas K. Hyatt and Bruce R. Hopkins

The Law of Tax-Exempt Organizations, Seventh Edition by Bruce R. Hopkins

The Legal Answer Book for Nonprofit Organizations by Bruce R. Hopkins

A Legal Guide to Starting and Managing a Nonprofit Organization, Third Edition by Bruce R. Hopkins

The Legislative Labyrinth: A Map for Not-for-Profits edited by Walter Pidgeon

Managing Affordable Housing: A Practical Guide to Creating Stable Communities by Ben Hecht, Local Initiatives Support Corporation, and James Stockard

ManagingNonprofits.org: Dynamic Management for the Digital Age by Ben Hecht and Rey Ramsey

Mission-Based Management: Leading Your Not-for-Profit in the 21st Century, Second Edition by Peter Brinckerhoff

Mission-Based Management: Leading Your Not-for-Profit in the 21st Century, Second Edition, Workbook by Peter Brinckerhoff

Mission-Based Marketing: How Your Not-for-Profit Can Success in a More Competitive World by Peter Brinckerhoff

Nonprofit Boards: Roles, Responsibilities, and Performance by Diane J. Duca

Nonprofit Compensation and Benefits Practices by Applied Research and Development Institute International, Inc.

The Nonprofit Counsel by Bruce R. Hopkins

The Nonprofit Guide to the Internet, Second Edition by Michael Johnston

Nonprofit Investment Policies: A Practical Guide to Creation and Implementation by Robert Fry, Jr.

The Nonprofit Law Dictionary by Bruce R. Hopkins

Nonprofit Compensation, Benefits, and Employment Law by David G. Samuels and Howard Pianko

The Nonprofit Handbook, Third Edition: Management by Tracy Daniel Conners

The Nonprofit Handbook, Third Edition: Fund Raising by James M. Greenfield

The Nonprofit Manager's Resource Dictionary by Ronald A. Landskroner

Nonprofit Organizations' Business Forms: Disk Edition by John Wiley & Sons, Inc.

Planned Giving: Management, Marketing, and Law, Second Edition by Ronald R. Jordan and Katelyn L. Quynn

The Private Foundation Answer Book by Bruce Hopkins and Jody Blazek

Private Foundations: Tax Law and Compliance by Bruce R. Hopkins and Jody Blazek

Program Related Investments: A Technical Manual for Foundations by Christie I. Baxter

Reengineering Your Nonprofit Organization: A Guide to Strategic Transformation by Alceste T. Pappas

Reinventing the University: Managing and Financing Institutions of Higher Education by Sandra L. Johnson and Sean C. Rush, PricewaterhouseCoopers LLP

The Second Legal Answer Book for Nonprofit Organizations by Bruce R. Hopkins

The Second Legal Answer Book for Fund Raisers by Bruce R. Hopkins

Social Entrepreneurship: The Art of Mission-Based Venture Development by Peter Brinckerhoff

Special Events: Proven Strategies for Nonprofit Fund Raising by Alan Wendroff

Starting and Managing a Nonprofit Organization: A Legal Guide, Third Edition by Bruce R. Hopkins

Strategic Communications for Nonprofit Organizations: Seven Steps to Creating a Successful Plan by Janel Radtke

Strategic Planning for Nonprofit Organizations: A Practical Guide and Workbook by Michael Allison and Jude Kaye, Support Center for Nonprofit Management

Streetsmart Financial Basics for Nonprofit Managers by Thomas A. McLaughlin

A Streetsmart Guide to Nonprofit Mergers and Networks by Thomas A. McLaughlin

Successful Marketing Strategies for Nonprofit Organizations by Barry J. McLeish

Successful Corporate Fund Raising: Effective Strategies for Today's Nonprofits by Scott Sheldon

The Tax Law of Colleges and Universities by Bertrand M. Harding

Tax Planning and Compliance for Tax-Exempt Organizations: Forms, Checklists, Procedures, Third Edition by Jody Blazek

The Universal Benefits of Volunteering: A Practical Workbook for Nonprofit Organizations, Volunteers, and Corporations by Walter P. Pidgeon, Jr.

Trade Secrets for Every Nonprofit Manager by Thomas A. McLaughlin

Values-Based Estate Planning: A Step-by-Step Approach to Wealth Transfers for Professional Advisors by Scott Fithian

Also by Ben Hecht:
Developing Affordable Housing: A Practical Guide for Nonprofit Organizations, Second Edition
Managing Affordable Housing: A Practical Guide for Building Stable Communities

ManagingNonprofits.org

Dynamic Management for the Digital Age

Ben Hecht and Rey Ramsey

John Wiley & Sons, Inc.

Library of Congress Cataloging-in-Publication Data:

Hecht, Bennett L., 1959–
   Managingnonprofits.org: dynamic management for the digital age/Bennett L. Hecht and Rey Ramsey.
      p. cm.
   Includes index.
   ISBN 0-471-39527-7 (cloth : alk. paper)
      1. Nonprofit organizations—Management. 2. Nonprofit organizations—Management—Computer Network Services. 3. Web sites.   I. Ramsey, Rey
II. Title.

HD62.6 .H43 2001
658'.048—dc21   2001045361

ISBN 0-471-39527-7

Printed in the United States of America.

10 9 8 7 6 5 4 3 2 1

Joseph C. and Phyllis Hecht

BH

Felix and Janice Ramsey

Elizabeth A. Peiffer

RR

Contents

Foreword

One of the core values at Cisco Systems is customer success. We drive customer success by listening to our customers, taking whatever steps are necessary to meet their needs, and sharing with them the gains we have experienced through the use of our own Internet-based applications. That is a key ingredient to success—for customer success transcends to organizational success.

The question we ask ourselves is—how does this translate into the nonprofit world? This is a task we have set for ourselves at Cisco: leverage the Internet and technology to extend innovation to and for the use of nonprofit organizations.

There are many parallels to be drawn between the organizational development and management of corporations and that of nonprofits. Although the end user or customer may be different, the operational challenges and opportunities are quite similar—"product" development and delivery, administration, finance, human resources, benefits, talent recruitment, staff development and training, internal and external communications. . . . The size and scale of an operation varies in both corporations and nonprofits, but the solutions for addressing these issues can be adapted across sectors. Many of these challenges have been addressed through the Internet.

The relationships between businesses, consumers, governments, nations, and individuals have been forever altered by the Internet revolution. It has democratized the power of one-to-many and many-to-one relationships by enabling equal access and equal participation. However, this has also posed the threat of greater opportunity divides between those organizations who have access and those who don't. There is really no practical reason why the nonprofit sector should not be in lock step with the opportunities and innovations enjoyed by the corporate and government sectors. The main difference is that corporations and governments have made Internet technology a priority and budget for this annually. They view it as a strategic investment and a critical success factor.

Nonprofits should also consider Internet technology as a key element in their ability to better deliver services to their customers. For an example of how the Internet investment can provide value to nonprofit organizations, one need only to look to the applications that are currently leveraged. For instance, the Cisco Network Academy is a comprehensive, 8-semester, 560-hour curriculum that trains students and in-transition workers how to design, build, and maintain computer networks. Employing an e-learning model, the Networking Academy Program delivers Web-based educational content, on-line testing, student performance tracking, hands-on labs, and instructor training and support. The curriculum, developed by education and networking experts, is offered at secondary schools, technical schools, colleges, universities, and other educational programs around the world. This has enabled schools and community-based organizations in their training and workforce development programs—both for those newly entering the workforce, as well as the workforce in transition (going from industrial type jobs to technology-based jobs).

In addition to training, there exists a huge opportunity to leverage communications and public relations about a nonprofit organization (NPO) in attracting new donors and furthering advocacy. The Internet enables nonprofits to become more "customer" centric and reach out to new constituencies, and to create strong relationships between the NPO, the donors, government organizations, and communities of interest.

This book by Ben Hecht and Rey Ramsey makes a compelling statement about the "strategic inflection points" facing nonprofits. However, the good news is that many corporations, foundations, governmental organizations, and individuals are committed to the success of nonprofits during this period. We, at Cisco, have a commitment to the success of the nonprofit sector. We believe that the best role we can play is to support the work of community organizations via our technology, financial resources, and the application of best practices learned across all sectors.

The book does an excellent job of teeing up many of the key issues NPOs are facing as they enter a period of rapid change, much of it brought on by the Internet Revolution. Technology is both the catalyst of change and the vehicle for mastering it. I wish you well as you launch into the new world of the digital age.

John P. Morgridge,
Chairman of the Board, Cisco Systems

Preface

ManagingNonprofits.org is a book about people and the power of ideas. It is about building a twenty-first century nonprofit organization that uses technology and the best management thinking to create a digital culture or a place that caters to customers, where people want to work and where ideas are the currency of choice. Digital culture is less about hardware and software and more about mindset. An organization with a digital culture has an ethos of learning, rewards innovation and risk-taking, puts its people first, and looks for ways in which technology can help do things in new and different ways. This book will help you build that culture into your own organization.

More importantly, however, we hope this book will help you to thrive on change and become a better leader. If we have learned anything in the past 10 years, it is that the Digital Age is about change. Leaders who flourish in today's environment do so because they have developed a dynamic process of self-reflection and have a willingness to do things differently. They reflect constantly upon their individual and organizational efforts and are not afraid to reposition themselves in order to embrace change, capture market opportunities, and serve customers. We call this process of continual reflection and repositioning "Dynamic Management" and provide you with a map to help you make it part of who you are and how you manage.

Use this book to harness the power of technology to strengthen your organization, to provide new and value-added products and services to an expanding customer base, and to adapt the best management and leadership practices to your efforts. We look forward to being with you as you begin your journey toward dynamic management. Visit us regularly at www.managingnonprofits.org to learn about the trends in the field and to be a part of a new wave of nonprofit organizations.

Ben Hecht

Rey Ramsey

Acknowledgments

The authors want to thank and acknowledge all the people who helped us to make this book a reality. Ricki Baker, Alec Ross, David Saunier, Rob Bole, Phillip Hughes, Rachel Jackson, Greg May, and Adam Richman for their research, editing, hunting, and gathering. Peg Cunningham for her administrative support. All of the nonprofits who opened their doors to us and spent time explaining and detailing their efforts including Fred Krupp, Environmental Defense, Denise Joines, ONE/Northwest, David Prendergast, America's Second Harvest, Ned Rimer, Citizens Schools, Kelly Fitzsimmons, New Profit, Inc., Steven Marine, Roger Guard, NetWellness, BB Otero and Jomo Graham, Calvary Bilingual Multicultural Learning Center, Billy Shore, Share Our Strength, Susan Herman, National Center for Victims of Crime, Rebecca Wodder, American Rivers, John Ball, Kristin Wolff, Worksystems, Inc., Darrell Hammond, Kaboom!, Kevin Smith, Fannie Mae Foundation, Sarah Holloway, MOUSE, Michael Bodaken, National Housing Trust, Judy Stein and Charlie Quatt, Quatt & Associates. We also want to thank Mario Morino, Jed Emerson, Joan Fanning, Mark Weinheimer, and Carol Berde for their insights into the future of the nonprofit movement.

Special thanks to our original editor at John Wiley & Sons, Martha Cooley, whose enthusiasm, support, and advocacy for this book made it happen and to Susan McDermott who took over for Martha midstream and made sure we had a great final product. Ben Hecht wants to acknowledge his wife, Lynn Leibovitz and his children, Eliza and Sam, for their love, patience, and support as he worked on this book, as well as his other less time-consuming endeavors. Rey Ramsey wants to acknowledge his entire family for their faith and inspiration throughout.

About the Authors

Ben Hecht is an experienced nonprofit executive, author, and teacher. In 2000, he and Rey Ramsey founded One Economy Corporation, a national nonprofit dedicated to maximizing the power of technology to help low-income people to improve their quality of life and get out of poverty. He currently serves as One Economy's President and Chief Operating Officer. From 1996 to 2000, he was with The Enterprise Foundation; he last served as Senior Vice President for Program Services. In that capacity, he led the organization's efforts beyond housing—building well-respected programs in child care, workforce development, and economic development. He also increased the organization's revolving loan fund, from $30 million to $200 million.

Mr. Hecht has written two books, *Developing Affordable Housing: A Practical Guide for Nonprofit Organizations* (2nd Edition, 1999) and *Managing Affordable Housing: A Practical Guide for Building Stable Communities* (1996), both published by John Wiley & Sons. He also has written law review articles on place-based housing and economic development and contributed chapters on state historic preservation laws and the use of partnerships and syndications in *Historic Preservation: Law and Taxation* (Bender, 1986).

Mr. Hecht received his Juris Doctorate from Georgetown University Law Center and his CPA from the State of Maryland. For 10 years, he taught at Georgetown University Law Center and built the premier housing and community development clinical program in the country. In 1992, with Congressional support, Mr. Hecht founded the National Center for Tenant Ownership at Georgetown, a program facilitating affordable housing development by nonprofits and tenant groups nationwide.

Prior to his work at Georgetown, Mr. Hecht worked for the public accounting firm of Coopers & Lybrand in Washington and served as counsel to the nonprofit National Rural Development and Finance Corporation. He has been an adjunct professor of law at Georgetown University Law Center for 12 years, teaching accounting concepts for lawyers. Over the years, Mr. Hecht has served on the boards of non-profit housing organiztions in Portland, Oregon, Cleveland, Ohio, and New York City and on the national boards of the National Center for Lead Safe Housing and the Consensus Organizing Institute. He lives in Washington, D.C., with his wife, Lynn Leibovitz, and two children.

Rey Ramsey is a seasoned executive and social entrepreneur. He currently serves as Chief Executive Officer and Board Chair of One Economy, a nonprofit organization that he founded together with Ben Hecht. From 1996 to 2000, he was the President and Chief Operating Officer of The Enterprise Foundation. As President, Mr. Ramsey played an instrumental role in the dramatic growth and programmatic impact of the organization. He was also publisher of that organization's first online magazine. Mr. Ramsey also drove the Foundation's development of quality information resources and the use of technology to help community development organizations. Mr. Ramsey joined Enterprise in 1993.

At age 29, the Governor of Oregon appointed Mr. Ramsey to serve as the state's Director of the Department of Housing. Mr. Ramsey worked with the state legislature to create Oregon's first housing trust fund and merged two state agencies to create a combined Housing and Community Services Department.

Mr. Ramsey holds a BA in political science from Rutgers University and a Juris Doctorate from University of Virginia Law School. After law school, Mr. Ramsey moved to Oregon where he practiced law before becoming the state economic development officer for eight central Oregon counties.

Mr. Ramsey serves on many boards including Habitat for Humanity International and the Advisory Board of the Brookings Insitution Center on Urban and Metropolitan Policy.

CHAPTER ONE

Nonprofits and the Digital Age

The 21st century will be a time of immense change for the nonprofit industry. In the coming years, the digital age will hit us in full force. Technology and the Internet will increasingly cause the same types of chaotic changes and market disruptions in the nonprofit industry that it continues to cause in the for-profit industry. Customers, who will become increasingly "wired," used to comparison shopping on Web sites, and accustomed to overnight delivery, will demand more products and services in more convenient ways. Dramatic infusions of new money from government devolution and philanthropy will foster unprecedented consolidation and competition in the industry.

Simply put, business will not continue as usual. At times like this, certain fundamentals about the way the nonprofit industry has operated will change. At a strategic inflection point, Intel chairman Andy Grove argues, the forces of change are so great that they can be fatal if not attended to. At those times, organizations that understand and anticipate these fundamental changes and learn how to operate in new ways will thrive. Those who maintain the status quo are unlikely to survive intact. This book is designed to provide a framework to help you navigate through the strategic inflection point when it hits your part of the industry and to build an organization that thrives on change.

UNDERSTANDING THE FORCES OF CHANGE

The fundamental forces of change facing the nonprofit industry fall into five related but distinct categories: technology, customers, money, competition, and choice. Although these factors have all been at work over the past decade to various degrees, most sectors of the industry have not had to face or have chosen not to face the consequences of these forces to date.

Technology

Leading nonprofits in the 21st century will require applying lessons learned from the dot.com world's use of technology and the Internet as a communications tool that efficiently moves information to fundamentally reshape old ways of doing business. What is this likely to look like?[1] Nonprofits will scale their operations in ways never seen before. They will use their organization's information assets, often as the first-mover in their sector, to get to a lot of customers—both old and new—fast. They will be able to be both a "high-tech" and "high-touch" organization by combining physical qualities and information/digital assets. This approach will give them both a distinct competitive advantage and the capacity to act as a broker with traditional and new customers.

Nonprofits will embrace strategic alliances with value-added partners. Working with former competitors, friends, and even new for-profit and nonprofit organizations, they will build mechanisms to share information and knowledge with each other to enhance their collective competitive advantages. From these relationships, some existing organizations will likely become obsolete and replaced with new infomediaries who are able to play an enormous role in a particular sector by mining customer data and making customization of that data possible.

Technology and the Internet will enable organizations to redesign themselves from the inside out by creating new business processes and systems. With the Internet as their communications backbone, the knowledge required for innovation will flow freely from one employee to the next regardless of position within the organization.

Customers

Customer-led applications of technology and the Internet will force nonprofits to change if they want to attract, interact with, and retain their customers. Simply put, customers are fast becoming part of the Internet culture. Results from the U.S. Department of Commerce's most recent report on the digital divide[2] show that computers and the Internet are rapidly becoming a part of every American's way of life. The data show that the overall level of U.S. digital inclusion is rapidly increasing. The share of households with Internet access soared by 58 percent, rising from 26.2 percent in December 1998 to 41.5 percent in August 2000. More than half of all households (51.0 percent) have computers, up from 42.1 percent in December 1998. There were 116.5 million Americans online at some location in August 2000, 31.9 million more than there were only 20 months earlier. The share of individuals using the Internet rose by 35.8 percent, from 32.7 percent in December 1998 to 44.4 percent in August 2000. If growth continues at that rate, more than half of all Americans will be using the Internet by the middle of 2001.

The rapid uptake of new technologies is occurring among most groups of Americans, regardless of income, education, race or ethnicity, location, age, or gender. Groups that have traditionally been digital "have nots" are now making dramatic gains. The gap between households in rural areas and households nationwide that access the Internet narrowed from 4.0 percentage points in 1998 to 2.6 percentage points in 2000. In rural areas in 2000, 38.9 percent of the households had Internet access, a 75 percent increase from 22.2 percent in December 1998. African-Americans and Hispanics, while still lagging behind other groups, showed impressive gains in Internet access. In 2000, African-American households were more than twice as likely to have home access than they were 20 months before, rising from 11.2 percent to 23.5 percent. Hispanic households also experienced a tremendous growth rate during this period, rising from 12.6 percent to 23.6 percent.[3]

This Internet culture is about more than just access, however; it's about putting that access into action. More Americans are going online to conduct such day-to-day activities as business transactions, personal correspondence, research and information gathering, and shopping. Eighty percent of Internet users report that they regularly use e-mail. Low-income Americans are more likely than higher-income Americans to use the Internet for online coursework and local job searching. In fact, 45 percent of Americans who use the Internet at home and earn $10,000 to $15,000 use it to take online courses; 25 percent use it for local job searching.[4]

What does all of this mean for nonprofits? It means that they will have to build new and different customer-centered relationships with their customers. These relationships will have to reflect where their customers are now, not where they have been in the past. The quantity and quality of communications will have to increase through creative and compelling applications of e-mail, instant messaging services, list serves, and Web sites. Products and services will have to be available where and when customers want them. Customers will want their interactions customized to fit their unique circumstances.

Money

An unprecedented amount of money has become available for investment in the nonprofit industry over the past decade. The devolution of power from centralized government at the federal and state level to local communities has literally flooded some sectors of the nonprofit industry with new money. Billions of dollars annually are being delegated to the local level to implement reforms of education, health care, energy conservation, affordable housing, and transportation. More often than not, government units are ill-prepared or too thinly staffed to do this work. This situation has left nonprofits as the only viable vehicle for change. Nowhere is this more obvious than in the way that the United States has implemented its approach to welfare reform. After more than 30 years of telling states and poor people what they had to do to fight poverty, the federal government has thrown out all the rules, granted large sums of money to the states, and told them to figure out how to get the job done. In turn, state legislatures, wary of failed government programs, are relying on local nonprofit organizations to solve seemingly intractable problems. They are now looking to nonprofits to help get people to work, find and keep a good job, and pay for quality child care.

These recent opportunities, however, have the potential of being dwarfed by what the future holds. Despite periodic stock market fluctuations, the economic boom of the past 20 years has created an astonishing amount of individual and foundation wealth in America. That funding combined with the $4.8 trillion that will be transferred from parents to children in the next 20 years—the so-called intergenerational transfer of wealth—is likely to create the largest pool of money dedicated to making positive social change in the history of humankind. Add the growing interest in venture phil-anthropy to this mix and you have a formula for financing truly innovative approaches to solving many of the world's problems.

Competition and Choice

The availability of technology and new resources has spurred growth in the industry. In fact, the sheer number and scope of non-profits has grown more in the past decade than it had in the pre-ceding 20 years.[5] Every area of public life has been impacted by this change, from institutions like schools, universities, and muse-ums to groups advocating for environmental, human, and women's rights. This rising tide, however, has not necessarily raised all the boats. For example, organizations that have been unable to "scale up" their programs to meet funder or government demands or to withstand outside scrutiny have been losing out to other nonprofit or for-profit groups that can answer these chal-lenges. In some cases, additional funds have so severely taxed antiquated internal accounting and reporting systems that these issues have overwhelmed senior management's energies and par-alyzed organizations.

Competition has also come from unexpected places, especially where the amount of money in play is significant. In Dallas, Texas, for example, the city awarded its welfare-to-work program man-agement contract to Lockheed Martin, the large defense contractor with a track record of managing complex databases and being a fierce competitor for business, not a nonprofit workforce develop-ment organization. For all intents and purposes, the nonprofit workforce development sector has been shut out of this work. This example alone illustrates both the promise and pitfalls that non-profits will face more often in the 21st century.

Finally, wired customers will increasingly demand more choices, driving both competition and consolidation. For example, many nonprofits who stick only to high-touch in a limited geographic area inevitably will be driven out of business or forced to compete with an organization that can deepen the customer experience with high-tech, customized interactions online as well. Nonprofits will have to provide their customers with flexible choices, delivered directly or through other strategic relationships to compete in the marketplace.

FORCES OF CHANGE AT WORK

You don't have to look far to see these forces of change at work. Ten years ago, nonprofit and university research hospitals were everywhere; today, there are 50 percent fewer of them. The nonprofit health care system faced a strategic inflection point—a tsunami of change involving technology, money, customers, consolidation, and competition—and was simply wiped out by the force of it. In fact, Intel Chairman Andy Grove would probably say that this part of the sector has been through its strategic inflection point and has already come out on the other side. Unfortunately, not many nonprofit hospitals are still standing.

As we have traveled throughout the country, we see many nonprofits that have not yet focused on these forces of change or begun positioning themselves to adapt to them. This inaction often results from one or more of the following syndromes:

- Business discipline is bad, especially if it leads to profits.
- Doing good means never having to say you're sorry.
- I don't need to worry about my staff because I have God on my side.
- Don't fix it if it ain't broke.

Business Discipline Is Bad, Especially if It Leads to Profits

Some nonprofits still view money as a bad thing, profits even worse, and the idea of "business discipline" as antithetical to the mission of their organization. This notion could not be further from the truth. In fact, some of the best nonprofits and the happiest nonprofit managers are those that embrace profits and creativity and have back-end systems that can go toe-to-toe with the business operations of many for-profit corporations. Two of our favorites are Pioneer Human Services in Seattle, Washington, which grosses $40 million a year making sheetmetal for Boeing and running the

Starbucks cafeteria, and New Community Corporation in Newark, New Jersey, with an annual budget of more than $200 million and more than $500 million in real estate investments. Both organizations make a lot of money and use that money to help thousands of people each year. They make their money the hard way: They are entrepreneurial; they sell a huge amount of products and services; and they watch their "double bottom line," helping people and making money.

Doing Good Means Never Having to Say "I'm Sorry"

Some people might call it "righteous indignation" or "the arrogance of good." Either way, the result is the same: A nonprofit organization gets so carried away with its own self-worth that it forgets why it was really started in the first place. This often manifests itself in several ways. One way is it stops leading—no longer setting out a vision for what the world should be and how the organization can help it get there. One national organization that we know, facing a change in senior management, proudly announced that it was putting "a moratorium on creativity." Somehow it decided that the organization was so inherently worthwhile that its own internal problems were more important than the problems of the people and organizations that it was serving.

The other way a nonprofit gets carried away is to stop paying attention to its customers and markets—it takes these things for granted. One of the best examples of losing touch with customers is the birth and growth of the charter school movement in public education. Although most public schools in America provide a quality education, some schools and school boards acted as if they had a captive audience. They were certain that no matter how bad the teachers were or how unresponsive the administrators were, parents would keep sending their kids there because they had no choice. All of a sudden when parents realized they could have a choice through vehicles like charter schools, the parents voted with their feet and walked.

I Don't Need to Worry about My Staff because I Have God on My Side

In the rush to make a difference, nonprofits of all sizes sometimes forget that they are only effective because they have extraordinary employees working for them. These people need, and deserve, care and attention. You need to feed both their hearts and their heads. They want to be a part of an organizational culture that is something special and to make a difference in people's lives. Most importantly, they want to feel like they are working in an environment that is giving them the chance to reach their full potential.

We coined the name of this syndrome from an experience we had with a faith-based nonprofit organization. This group had had some quick successes but had fallen on tough times. Things were not getting done and people were leaving the organization in droves. No matter how hard we tried, the Executive Director refused to accept our arguments that the organization's lack of productivity was directly tied to the fact that he no longer could attract and keep quality staff to do the work. Finally, after we continued to push on this issue, he blurted out, "You may be right, but all I can do is rely on God to make things right." Divine intervention will always help, but creating the right working environment and supporting your staff will bring even more consistent and sustainable results.

Don't Fix It if It Ain't Broke

This may be the single most dangerous syndrome of all because it gives nonprofits the right to maintain the status quo. If we have learned one thing from our work, it is that a nonprofit organization is always "broke" to some extent and must work to improve itself continuously. It must always be working to be a place where people want to work. It must set out its vision and preserve its values for its employees and customers. It must work to understand its customers and its markets; hire and retain the best people; and build a culture and environment that thrives on change.

Nowhere is this more important than in the area of products and services. Nonprofits that are content with how and what they deliver to customers are the most at risk. We have repeatedly seen organizations go one of two ways: (1) become marginalized because they refused to evaluate and change their products and services, or (2) become a powerhouse by being willing to challenge long-held assumptions about their products and services and make fundamental changes where necessary.

St. Vincent DePaul of Lane County, Oregon (SVDP) is a great example of a nonprofit that constantly challenges its assumptions about products and services. Part of a national, loosely affiliated network of nonprofit, second-hand stores, SVDP started out selling the used clothing and furniture that it collected from donors around Eugene, Oregon. By talking to its customers and paying attention to sales, they saw an unmet demand for bureaus. With an initial donation of scrap wood from pulp and paper companies in the Northwest, SVDP began a furniture manufacturing business. This business has since turned SVDP into a major manufacturer/remanufacturer of products made from reused materials. Annually, SVDP earns more than $20 million from sales of used appliances, wood furniture, and even the export of rags to Thailand. The company's 200 employees all earn more than minimum wage with full benefits. SVDP has built a sophisticated distribution system for its products that includes its seven stores in the Eugene area and strategic sales relationships with other SVDP affiliates throughout the nation.

Technology and the Internet only heighten the importance of having an organization that always thinks something needs to be fixed. The Pet Shelter Network is a great example of an organization on the cutting edge of managing change. Only a few years ago, a family with a lost dog had to call countless shelters in hopes of finding their lost pet. Now, because of the Internet and enlightened management, any family anywhere in the United States and Canada at any time of the day or night, can log onto www.petshelter.com, type in a description of their animal, and automatically search shelters throughout their area. If The Pet Shelter Network hadn't thought anything was broken, they never would have fixed this problem.

LEARNING TO OPERATE IN NEW WAYS

Obviously, as The Pet Shelter Network example shows, some nonprofits have made extraordinary efforts to understand these forces of change and to learn how to operate in new ways. Many of them, like Environmental Defense, America's Second Harvest, and The Exploratorium Museum, are highlighted throughout this book. As we worked together over the past five years, we were committed to overcoming these syndromes in our own organization, to anticipating the changes that were about to occur in our part of the industry, and to learning to operate in new ways. We found that we had to focus on the following six things to make this happen:

1. *Our corporate culture.* We needed to build and sustain a culture through our vision, values, and a focus on our people. People want and deserve to have a clear vision for the future, but vision alone will not attract the best people to an organization or get them to stay there. That requires a "people first" attitude with fair pay and benefits, opportunities for personal and professional growth, and a quality work environment.

2. *Our business model.* We needed to clearly define our business model and bring a business discipline to everything we were doing. This meant being customer-centered and understanding our customers (who we serve), including how we access them and how they access us. We had to regularly evaluate our content (what we do)—the products and services that we were delivering and how we were delivering them. We had to work to see that we had the infrastructure necessary to support the culture we built. We had to stay aligned, keeping all the parts working together or focused toward a shared vision.

3. *Best new management and leadership thinking.* We needed to be on top of the best thinking so we could adapt it to our own organization.

4. *Technology and the Internet.* We needed to harness the power and potential of technology and the Internet in everything we did.

5. *Reflection and repositioning.* We needed to constantly reflect on our individual and organizational efforts and be prepared to reposition ourselves to meet and embrace change, capture market opportunities, and serve customers.

6. *Dynamic renewal.* We had to accept, and help the organization accept, the fact that our work would never be done—that building and managing an effective organization is a dynamic and continuous process. Change should be embraced, not feared.

BUILDING THE DYNAMIC MANAGEMENT MAP: THRIVING ON CHANGE

We built a model, the Dynamic Management Map, that helped us to meet these goals (see Exhibit 2.1 on page 15). The map looks at issues through an inverted pyramid, always addressing the biggest issues first, creating a dynamic process for reflecting on where you currently are, and then repositioning your organization so you can make the changes you need to go where you need to go.

We used the map, which is described fully in Chapter 2, to help our organization evolve into a dynamic, vibrant, and vital place that thrived on change. We call this a "dynamic organization." That experience, which led to our new venture, One Economy Corporation, detailed in Chapter 9, and the keen interest in our work expressed by other nonprofit leaders, convinced us that we had to share what we have learned more broadly—to help more organizations become dynamic organizations ready for the digital age.

It is not too late to start understanding the forces of change that your organization is facing and to begin learning how to operate in different ways. Follow the map, as we define and describe it over the next few chapters. Use it to navigate through your own strategic inflection point. Take small steps if necessary, but whatever you do, take action. You will come out on the other side of your strategic inflection point better, stronger, and more vibrant than ever—a dynamic organization for the digital age.

NOTES

[1]Sendil Ethiraj, Isin Guler, and Harbir Singh, www.knowledge@ wharton.edu, from the Wharton School of Business, University of Pennsylvania, developed this general framework. We have taken great liberties with the authors' language so it would be more applicable to the nonprofit community, but we are greatly indebted to them for establishing the framework.

[2]U.S. Department of Commerce, *Falling Through the Net IV* (October 2000), 1.

[3]Ibid., 2.

[4]Ibid., 2.

[5]*The Independent Sector*, www.independentsector.org, "The New Nonprofit Almanac IN BRIEF."

CHAPTER TWO

Dynamic Management and Dynamic Organizations

The Dynamic Management Map will help you build an organization that thrives on change and learns to operate in new ways. In this chapter, we further define Dynamic Management and the work of the Dynamic Manager. We walk through the map in detail, explain the Dynamic Management process, and remind you that Dynamic Management is a journey, not a destination in itself.

DYNAMIC MANAGEMENT DEFINED

Dynamic Management is the continual process of organizational self-reflection and dynamic repositioning that enables the organization to embrace change, capture market opportunities, and serve customers. Dynamic Managers use the map to confront the forces of change around them. The map enables them to harness the power of technology to strengthen the organization, provide value-added products and services to an expanding customer base, and adapt the best new management and leadership practices to their own efforts.

The map also helps Dynamic Managers to integrate elements of what we call a "digital culture" into their corporate culture. An organization with a digital culture is continually learning, rewarding innovation and risk taking, communicating with customers, putting its people first, and looking for ways that technology can help improve operations and provide products and services in new and different ways. We talk much more about culture in Chapter 4.

What Is the Dynamic Management Process?

The Dynamic Management process calls for managers to continually reflect and reposition.

Reflect on the following aspects of the organization:

- Its current state and the state of the nonprofit industry in which it operates
- The culture—primarily the state of the vision, values, and the people who work there
- Its business model—primarily the customers and content offered to them
- The infrastructure—the supports needed to sustain the culture and deliver the content
- The alignment—the matching of people and resources to priorities and needs

Reposition the organization to operate in new or better ways by adapting, to its own use, successful methods, approaches, and technologies used by other nonprofit or for-profit organizations.

This idea of continual reflection and repositioning is at the core of Dynamic Management. Ben Hecht learned it from the Jesuits when he worked at Georgetown University, and Rey Ramsey learned it from his own personal spiritual and professional journey. But we've both seen it work in real life . . . and we've done it together. The organization that believes that it is good but is always looking to do better, actually does better. Collins and Porras, authors of *Built to Last*, one of our favorite books, and one that had a great influence on us professionally, believe the following:

A highly visionary company displays a powerful mix of self-confidence combined with self-criticism. Self-confidence allows a visionary company to set audacious goals and make bold and daring moves, sometimes flying in the face of industry conventional wisdom or strategic prudence; it simply never occurs to a highly visionary company that it can't beat the odds, achieve great things, and become something truly extraordinary. Self-criticism, on the other hand, pushes for self-induced change and improvement before the outside world imposes the need for change and improvement; a visionary company thereby becomes its own harshest critic. As such, the drive for progress pushes from within for continual change and forward movement in everything that is not part of core ideology.[1]

DYNAMIC MANAGEMENT MAP

The road to Dynamic Management is a never-ending journey. We have created the Dynamic Management Map (see Exhibit 2.1) to help guide managers on this journey—to structure the process for organizational self-reflection in particular. The chapters that follow describe each element of the process.

Each chapter also offers guidance on positioning or repositioning the organization to embrace change, meet new market opportunities,

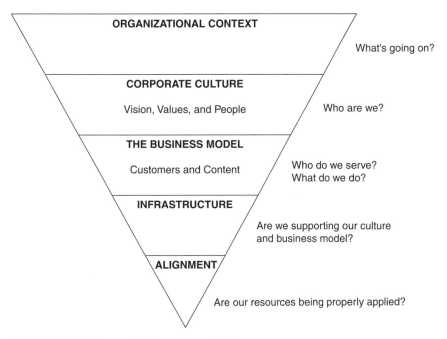

Exhibit 2.1 Dynamic Management Map

and better serve customers. Wherever possible, we try to summarize trends in a given area and provide real-life stories that illustrate broad principles that can be easily adapted to the circumstances of any nonprofit organization. In short, we expect the map to help structure your reflection and the examples and principles in each chapter to help guide your repositioning. To make the Dynamic Management process easier, at the end of each chapter we highlight the key points to consider when reflecting and repositioning the organization, as well as a set of guiding principles.

USING THE MAP

The map starts with the big picture or general issues first and moves down to the specific. In the beginning, that means asking the general question "What's going on?" This step sets the stage and provides internal and external context to your work. It requires the Dynamic Manager to take the organization's pulse, looking inward (holding a mirror up to yourself and the organization) and outward (taking a closer look at the sector in which the organization functions) to spot issues, events, or conditions that could inform your decision to reposition the organization's culture, business model, and infrastructure. Chapter 3 provides guidance on taking the pulse.

The map then moves from context to an evaluation of the corporation's culture and the questions "Who are we?" and "Is that who we want to be?" During this process, we examine whether the vision and values are appropriate for the times and if they are compelling to those people who are most important to the organization. We make sure we are valuing our people and putting them first. In every organization, the vision, values, and people must carry the most weight. Everything that is done—from selecting programs to designing the infrastructure—must build on the organization's vision and values and on the people who are expected to make that vision a reality. They shape all that follows. Chapter 4 focuses on corporate culture.

Chapters 5 and 6 help the Dynamic Manager reflect on the organization's business model by asking three questions: "Whom do we serve?" "What do we do?" and "How do we do it?" Answering these questions requires a thorough understanding of the organization's competitive environment, customer relationships, products, and services. Nowhere is technology having more of an impact on how nonprofits can reposition themselves than in the nonprofit's business model and the ways it delivers its products and services.

The map then examines the infrastructure that supports the culture and business model. Chapter 7 assists the Dynamic Manager in answering the question, "Are we appropriately supporting our culture and business model?" by providing a framework for looking closely at senior management, available resources, and information technology. Promising methods for repositioning the organization to strengthen the infrastructure are discussed.

Finally, the map addresses alignment, "Are the organization's financial and human resources applied in a way that is consistent with the vision, values, people, and business priorities set out in the business model?" Chapter 8 provides the Dynamic Manager with tools for keeping the organization in alignment, from planning and measuring performance to budgeting and organizational structure.

WHAT IF YOU DON'T INVERT THE PYRAMID?

As we discussed in Chapter 1, over the years, the inverted pyramid has helped us solve all kinds of problems, large and small. It forces you to identify and think through the big issues first (the top of the inverted pyramid) and then to develop strategies to get you there (the details that constitute the lower portion of the inverted pyramid). In other words, the top of the inverted pyramid is the forest, and the bottom is the trees. More often than not, by returning to the top of the inverted pyramid, you are forced to take a fresh look at what you are trying to accomplish. This frees you to design new solutions or gives you a chance to reaffirm your initial approach. Either way, if you don't invert the pyramid, you spend most of your time with the micro issues, either unable to see the whole picture or only the negatives.

Applying these principles to Dynamic Management is no different. The Dynamic Management Map allows you, as manager, to identify the issues, develop solutions, and engage talent in applying solutions. It helps you stop and think about issues that are as broad as the world around you (corporate context) and as narrow as the design of your Web site (infrastructure). The culture must be able to give birth to the business model. The business model must be supported by the infrastructure. It reminds you that success comes only when all of the tiers of the map are aligned and working toward a common purpose. In the digital age, only dynamic organizations led by Dynamic Managers will overcome the forces of change and thrive.

IMPLEMENTING DYNAMIC MANAGEMENT

Becoming a Dynamic Manager costs no money and requires no new systems or staff; it only requires you to change or adjust your mind-set. Whether you are dealing with a big issue (going after new customers or expanding your presence on the Internet) or a small issue (outsourcing your information technology functions), the Dynamic Management Map can bring clarity, best practices, and structure to influence your thinking.

We hope this book will help by providing inspiration along the way. We also know that by the time this book is published, more state-of-the-art repositioning strategies and practices will be being used throughout the nonprofit industry. Therefore, we urge readers to visit our Web site, www.managingnonprofits.org, to get the latest information on Dynamic Management.

IS DYNAMIC MANAGEMENT REALLY POSSIBLE?

Dynamic Management is being incorporated more and more into nonprofit organizations every day. In writing this book, we interviewed dozens of nonprofit organizations and leaders around the country who are positioning their organizations to thrive in the digital age. Many of them are highlighted in this book. We are seeing many corporate cultures becoming more digital. American Rivers (VA), Calvary Bilingual Multicultural Learning Center (DC), and Worksystems, Inc. (OR) have been building digital cultures in their own organizations for some time now. Business models are changing rapidly. Organizations are aggressively seeking out new customers and working to retain their current ones. The Exploratorium Museum in San Francisco recently increased its customers from 1 million to 7 million because of its extraordinary Web site. ONE/Northwest (Seattle, WA) conducts e-mail classes and hosts an advisory group every month to keep current with its customers.

No area is changing more than content. Nonprofits are expanding their existing customer relationships by adding an online component (Mayo Clinic), letting go of information and Web-enabling their knowledge (NetWellness), making technology a part of their products and services (MOUSE), and collaborating virtually in ways never before possible (Bay Area Homeless Alliance).

Organizations are working diligently to ensure that their infrastructure can support their culture, their customers, and their content. They are defining the environment that they want senior management to create—an environment that enables people to perform at their best and the organization to be "Net ready." Organizations as diverse as Share Our Strength, the national hunger organization, and the Fremont Public Association, a small community organization in Washington State, are expanding their funding bases with individuals, corporations, foundations, venture philanthropy, earned-income opportunities, and even through the Internet.

Technology is adding value to business processes, such as at the animal shelter in Phoenix, Arizona, that puts the pictures of all its stray animals online and quickly matches pets with old and new owners. Technology is also helping organizations create an ethos of learning through 24-7 access to continuing education classes and customer feedback. Technology is becoming the common thread that ties the entire organization together.

Few organizations have done more to become a dynamic organization than Environmental Defense, based in New York. Environmental Defense has used technology to transform its organization dramatically and to deepen its content and impact. Founded in 1967 to fight the use of the pesticide DDT in one Long Island, New York community in court, it has become a national organization with nearly 200 scientists, economists, attorneys, and other professionals in eight regional offices. Over the past 15 years, its Executive Director Fred Krupp has championed what he terms "the third stage of environmentalism": increased attention to proposing positive solutions to problems, increased use of market-oriented incentives, and the building of new coalitions, even "coalitions of former enemies."[2]

As the rare environmental organization with more scientists than attorneys, Environmental Defense has been well positioned to lead this "third stage" and has done so. In 1989, Environmental Defense approached McDonald's Corporation with a proposal to collaborate on new ways to reduce waste. Within a year, McDonald's had accepted all 42 recommendations of the joint task force and took the first steps by replacing foam-plastic hamburger boxes with less-bulky wraps and increasing its use of recycled material. Many of McDonald's competitors have followed suit, leading to the establishment of the Alliance for Environmental Innovation, a partnership with The Pew Charitable Trusts, to work with companies on improving environmental performance.

Similarly, to break a Congressional impasse on acid rain, Environmental Defense found a way to harness the power of the marketplace to reduce power-plant emissions of sulfur dioxide, a major cause of acid rain. The old "second stage" method was to tell each plant owner how much pollution to cut and how to cut it. The "third stage," advocated by Environmental Defense and written into the 1990 Clean Air Act, requires that sulfur emissions be cut in half nationwide, but allows each company to decide how to do it. Companies could also be rewarded for reducing emissions more than the law requires. Under this market-based plan, sulfur emissions have gone down faster—and at far lower cost—than predicted.

To move the "third stage" even further, Environmental Defense has become a dynamic organization. It has built an internal digital culture and has integrated technology into its content so thoroughly that it can never revert back to delivering its products and services the "old way."

Building the Digital Culture and the Right Environment Internally

Fred Krupp credits the following four things with expediting the culture change:

- The vision of some of his "insurgent" employees, particularly Bill Pease, who saw how technology could fundamentally change the group's products and services and who was willing to take risks to make it happen.

- An advisory group of technology leaders (including Scott Cook at Intuit, Brook Byers of Kleiner Perkins, Nick Nicholas, formerly of *Time*, and Shelby Bonnie at CNET), who helped senior management appreciate the power and practical application of technology to programs.

- His own willingness to get out of the insurgents' way and let them innovate, raise money to support their efforts, and "talk up" their work throughout the organization. (In fact, two of their past three national staff meetings have featured the Web-based products and services.)

- The fact that constituents are actually using the new technology-based content: "We demonstrated the power, not simply preached the power [of technology]."[3]

Krupp summarizes the group's new vision this way, "We look at the whole world through the Web, not Web sites. We ask ourselves, "How can we use the Internet to power every part of our organization? Are there new tools and capabilities that the Internet provides that will allow us to do more?"[4]

Providing Cutting-Edge Content

This new world view within Environmental Defense has led to remarkable results. The organization is using technology to dramatically expand its reach. It is reaching out to new audiences, building specialized databases to share its information, providing content not possible without the Internet, bringing similarly minded organizations together, and actually working to change personal behaviors. In Krupp's words, "We are fundamentally changing the way that we interact with the public—giving them information that is directly relevant to them."[5]

Scorecard. Scorecard (www.scorecard.org) is a geographically indexed Web site that allows users to type in their zip codes, click "go," and follow interactive maps and emission data as well as relevant background on health issues in their own neighborhoods (see Exhibit 2.2). Users learn who is polluting, the types of pollutants at issue, and the chemical effects of these pollutants. From the Web site, people who are directly affected by pollutor's actions can send faxes at no charge to major polluters and government agencies. Users can personalize the site to stay current on developments of specific interest to them. The site not only informs people, but it also provides them with the ammunition to take action. Although Environmental Defense's home page links directly to Scorecard, Environmental Defense deliberately built and promotes Scorecard as a stand-alone site with a unique, narrowly focused purpose.

Action Network. Environmental Defense recognizes that the environmental movement has changed significantly over the past 10 years. Recently, local environmental groups have proliferated, and groups dedicated to other causes have begun taking positions on environmental questions. These groups include civil rights organizations, hunting and fishing groups, labor unions, public health advocates, and religious organizations. One Environmental Defense staff member, Bill Roberts, presents a compelling view of

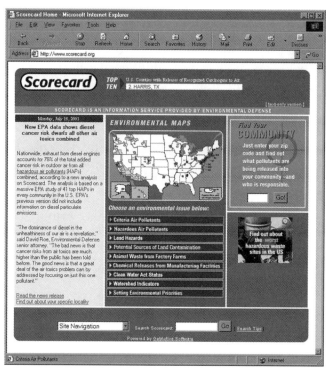

Exhibit 2.2   Scorecard Home Page

building a "neutral platform"—a place where technology but not editorial content is managed by Environmental Defense for all in the industry to use—for these diverse groups by using technology.

Environmental Defense's e-mail Action Network (www.action-network.org) has enrolled literally hundreds of thousands of activists who contact each other, Congress, and other opinion leaders on fast-breaking issues (see Exhibit 2.3). As they migrated these activities from a PC to the Web, membership in Environmental Defense's Action Network increased from 4,000 to well over 100,000. The Web has dramatically reduced the organization's transaction costs to reach this key constituency and to enlist them to take action in a timely fashion.

Like Scorecard, the Action Network is a stand-alone site built as a resource for environmental activists anywhere in the country. Environmental Defense automatically e-mails anyone who joins the network when key issues come up. These "action alerts" tell mem-

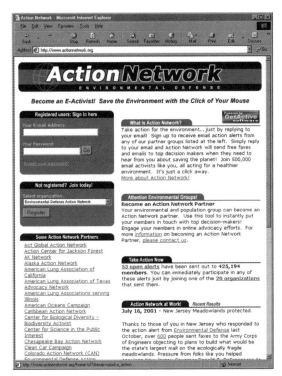

Exhibit 2.3 Action Network Home Page

bers exactly how to respond quickly to stop a bill, regulation, or policy that is harmful to the environment or to advocate for a good one. The organization has now launched efforts to expand recruitment of members for this action network further, especially in the states where it has regional offices.

Consumer Behavior. Neither Environmental Defense nor other environmental groups has devoted much attention to the underlying causes of environmental damage, among which are population growth and burgeoning consumer demand. Despite its work analyzing the role of population growth in climate change and its campaign to promote recycling and waste prevention, Environmental Defense believes that consumption patterns are treated too often as if they were outside human control. They cite the fact that rising shrimp consumption has done severe damage both to endangered sea turtles, which are snared and drowned at sea, and to tropical mangrove forests and other ecosystems that are degraded by improperly managed shrimp farms. Although methods to protect the turtles during shrimping are being proposed, no one has developed a strategy to reduce the per capita consumption of shrimp in favor of other sources of protein whose harvest would have fewer adverse consequences for the environment.

Environmental Defense, using much of what it has learned about the power of technology through its Scorecard and Action Network sites, is now building a Web site with other groups to help influence consumer behavior to reduce environmental harms and offer practical ways to live that are consistent with its views on protecting the environment. The group has also received permission from the AdCouncil to expand its recycling campaign into a range of consumer issues, like seafood choice and energy use.

REFLECT AND REPOSITION

- Do you have a system for continually confronting the forces of change around you?
- Are you working toward integrating elements of a digital culture into your corporate culture?

GUIDING PRINCIPLES

- Reflection and repositioning are at the core of Dynamic Management.
- Inverting the pyramid forces you to think through the big issues first before you develop strategies to get you where you want the organization to go.
- Dynamic Management requires no new money, systems, or staff, only a change or adjustment in mindset.

NOTES

[1]James C. Collins and Jerry I. Porras, *Built to Last: Successful Habits of Visionary Companies* (New York: Harper Business, 1994), 84.

[2]In an interview with Fred Krupp, Krupp states that the first stage is "represented by President Theodore Roosevelt and the early Sierra Club, who reacted to a truly rapacious exploitation of nat-

ural resources in the wake of the Industrial Revolution." This stage led to the creation of the National Forest and National Parks system. Krupp believes that the second stage was triggered by Rachel Carson's *Silent Spring* in 1962 and led to a focus on air and water, dangerous pesticides, and hazardous wastes.

[3]Ibid.

[4]Ibid.

[5]Ibid.

CHAPTER THREE

Organizational Context: Taking the Pulse

The Dynamic Manager must take the pulse of the organization before considering steps that would alter existing systems or business models. At the top of the map, you must ask "What's going on?" What's going on in your own mind? In the organization's operations? In the industry? And in society in general? This pulse-taking process requires you to look inward (holding a mirror up to yourself and your organization) and outward (looking closely at the trends in the sector and society in which your organization functions) to spot issues, events, or conditions that could shape how you reflect on and reposition the organization's culture, business model, and infrastructure later in the map.

We talk a lot in this chapter about the Dynamic Manager's personal inner journey. We have found that there is no more important pulse to take at this stage in the map than that of the leader. More often than not, if the leader is not ready to lead the organization into the digital age, then the organization is not ready to go there either. We share what we have learned from our own journeys toward self-improvement and provide examples from two organizations, MOUSE and the National Center for Victims of Crime—organizations that have used their own pulse-taking journey to build a customized Dynamic Management Map for the future.

WHY ASK "WHAT IS GOING ON?"

You must regularly ask this question for several important reasons. First, it helps you continually improve and challenge yourself. As with many things discussed in this book, your modeling of self-reflection and self-improvement set the example for others in the organization. The process further reinforces the "ethos of learning," a cornerstone of the digital culture discussed in the next chapter.

This step also helps you formally identify and acknowledge that the forces of change are at work around you. We are often too engrossed in the day-to-day operations to observe changes and how they may impact on how we do business. We fly blind and can miss opportunities. We may fail to see danger signs, such as new competitors and new ways of doing business, that may divert our customers from us. It is our belief based on experience that Dynamic Managers cannot afford to skip this vital step.

HOLDING THE MIRROR UP TO YOURSELF: CHECKING YOUR OWN PULSE

Pulse taking should always start by looking inside yourself. We firmly believe that an organization's ability to improve is directly tied to the leader's capacity for self-improvement. In fact, there is a significant body of scholarship that connects self-improvement with organizational development. We adapt some of this knowledge to our own use in the following pages. This process of looking within yourself requires a level of courage and openness not universally encouraged or rewarded in corporate structures; however, it is absolutely essential to the success of Dynamic Management. Reduced to its core, Dynamic Management is about self-improvement. When you reflect and then reposition, you improve through change—changing what you are doing and how you are doing it. You also grow the ability to know and trust yourself—a critical skill when facing the forces of change impacting on your organization.

Inner Journey

Stephen Covey, Peter Senge, and Kevin Cashman have all written extensively about leadership and self-improvement. Covey refers to "principle-centered" leaders as "being constantly educated by their [own] experiences . . . the more they know, the more they realize they do not know." His books provide a course for improving personal and interpersonal effectiveness and "leadership by [internal] compass or natural laws that are self-evident and self-validating."[1] Peter Senge, author of *The Fifth Discipline*, advocates for the discipline of personal mastery—"a process of continually focusing and refocusing on what one truly wants, on one's visions.[2] Kevin Cashman describes all of this as "leadership from the inside out."[3] He believes that you "Grow the person and grow the leader."[4]

We call this approach to self-improvement the inner journey. The inner journey begins with the Dynamic Manager making a deeply personal commitment to self-improvement. This commitment is made real by reflection; a structured, ongoing approach to learning about yourself; and a willingness to take action for the better, when necessary.

Commitment

Committing to improve yourself means committing to change. That often involves overcoming those things that have been holding you back, such as emotions and bad habits. Covey talks about being grounded to bad habits by three forces: (1) appetites and passions; (2) pride and pretension; and (3) aspiration and ambition.[5] Once you deal with the habits of old, you can commit to the present and the future.

Reflection

Most people we talk to about personal mastery and self-improvement are quick to share their own experiences with personal reflection. By design or default, these people have found the time to explore themselves. Cashman and others have it right when they say that our externally focused culture is "designed perfectly to avoid genuine contact with the deeper levels of ourselves."[6] Despite being committed to change, the inner journey cannot happen unless you take the time to silence some of these outside noises. As Thoreau said, "Each person must rather be careful to find out and pursue his own way and not his father's or his mother's or his neighbor's. Take the time to reflect and keep it simple."[7]

Reflection is best when it centers on who you are and where you want to go. It helps you to understand your weaknesses and appreciate your strengths. For many of us, it also involves connecting with our beliefs. Cashman says, "As you believe, so shall you lead,"[8] and we agree. "Reflection helps you connect with your beliefs, surface them and, in many cases, reconcile them."[9] When we look at our beliefs, we often see that we are trained to think things about others or ourselves that are not aligned with our beliefs. Reflection is the starting point for dealing with these internal conflicts, for being honest with ourselves.

Reflect on yourself by asking yourself questions such as the following:

- Am I still inspired by my work and the organization's vision?
- What are my beliefs?
- Are my actions consistent with these beliefs?
- Am I growing personally and professionally, and where do I want to go?
- What are the actions I know that I should take but have not taken?
- Am I comfortable in an environment where technology, customers, competition, and change reign? If not, why not?
- What value do I add to the organization?
- How are my relationships with staff? With the board?
- What is working well? What is not working well?
- How can I improve?

Some excellent programs throughout the country help leaders jump start their personal reflection. Some years ago, Rey Ramsey participated in a program sponsored by the American Leadership Forum (ALF), a national nonprofit dedicated to developing leaders, that continues to influence his life today. ALF brings people together from diverse backgrounds for monthly meetings and sessions about cutting-edge topics of leadership. The curriculum was developed and influenced by people like John Gardner, a leadership guru from Stanford University, and Joe Jaworski, author of *Synchronicity*. Topics included valuing diversity, collaborative leadership, and theories of change, but the overarching theme of the entire curriculum was knowing self and self-awareness—creating change from the inside out. There was structured time to reflect, from a weeklong wilderness experience to less formal moments when individuals took it upon themselves to reflect on what they had learned. The participants made the commitment to be there, but the overall ALF program design further taught the importance of reflection. Today the ALF program has literally touched thousands of lives, helping leaders grow and benefiting the organizations they serve along the way.

We also have seen positive results when experienced leaders have been able to secure an extended leave, from six weeks to 12 months, to ponder these types of questions and to reflect on themselves personally and professionally. Programs like the Fannie Mae Foundation's James A. Johnson Fellowship and the Loeb Fellowships at Harvard Graduate School of Design give people a chance to do just that. Bob Boulter, President of the Washington, DC–based Jubilee Enterprise and a Johnson Fellow, said that the experience was a "renewal" for him and gave him time to reexamine himself, the vision and purpose of his work, his organization, and his role in it. In fact, as we write this book, Bob has announced his resignation from Jubilee Enterprise to begin a new faith-based venture. His commitment and ongoing reflection actually led him to take action and gave him the strength to change his course.

Structure

The inner journey often requires some ongoing structure if it is to be truly effective. Senge believes that self-improvement must be approached as a "discipline, as a series of practices that must be applied."[10] Structure can provide that discipline and focus. The key, however, is to find a system or structure that works best for you. Some people learn best in classroom settings or programs like ALF mentioned previously, preferring the discipline that a trainer can provide. Others prefer a more private experience of reading and reflection. Regardless of the methodology, the structure selected must support your need and interest to learn more about yourself. Structured management training can be valuable, but without a structured program to enhance self, the training will be an investment not fully maximized.

Action

Structure helps make the commitment to an inner journey focused and useful, but it does not take the place of action. You must continually put what you have learned about yourself into action. Taking steps to follow your beliefs and to seek your purpose is a powerful thing. The people that we know who commit, continually reflect, and act exhibit a level of confidence, boldness, and daring that we admire. Their organizations are often dynamic, full of other people who know where they want to go and who are in full pursuit of realizing who they really want to be. Action is always easier said than done because true action requires courage and perseverance. It is an ongoing proposition. We urge you to persevere on your inner journey.[11]

A Few Words about Self-Improvement in Your Staff

The choice to take this inner journey belongs to the individual. Despite your best intentions and efforts, you can't force people to make this choice for themselves. What you can do, however, is foster an environment where such journeys are encouraged. Let people know that it is not only okay but also a valued behavior in the organization. Make it safe and comfortable for people to search, find, and challenge themselves and others. Dynamic organizations unleash individuals to spend time on the present and the future and ultimately understand that organizations grow as individuals grow. There are a variety of ways that this can be done, such as sponsoring staff retreats and participating in programs like ALF, but nothing is more important than just "living it." Senior management that lives the example of self-improvement can create or change the environment for the better. Showing people that you are not afraid to learn, letting them see that it is okay to not be perfect, will go a long way toward creating this type of environment. We talk more about building the right environment in Chapter 7.

HOLDING THE MIRROR UP TO YOUR ORGANIZATION AND THE WORLD AROUND YOU

The checklist in Exhibit 3.1 can help you to hold a mirror up to your organization and to look at the world around you. It is meant to jump start your analysis of the state of your organization and the issues facing your industry and society as a whole. The questions are intended to stimulate thinking and help you develop a checklist that meets your personal circumstances. Some leaders move their organizations through this type of review as part of an annual planning process. In other organizations, it serves as a precursor to more formal strategic planning efforts. Either way, it has helped organizations shape their work and has injected a helpful dose of reality in what they hoped to achieve.

HOLDING THE MIRROR UP TO THE ORGANIZATION

☐ What business(es) are we in?

☐ Are we in the right business(es)?

☐ Do we do our work in the best way(s) possible?

☐ Do we really do what we say we do?

☐ Are we a leader in our sector/field?

☐ Are we known to the people who should know us?

☐ Do we have managerial depth?

☐ What elements of a digital culture have taken root in the organization?

☐ Does our staff view us as a People First organization?

☐ Do we have problems retaining staff?

☐ Are we growing/shrinking financially and/or programmatically and should we be? Is it by design?

☐ Are we too reliant on one source of revenue for survival?

☐ Do we integrate technology into operations and program?

☐ Do we have real strategic, value-added partnerships, or do we just talk about them?

☐ Are we comfortable with our base of political support?

☐ Is our board performing as we hoped?

☐ What is our value-added proposition to our customers?

TAKING A LOOK AT THE INDUSTRY/SECTOR

☐ Who are the industry/sector leaders? Our major competitors?

☐ What are the leaders/competitors doing differently from us?

☐ What are the trends in our industry/sector? Are we poised to take advantage of those trends?

☐ What are the key programmatic interests and priorities of the leading funders in our industry/sector?

☐ How is technology impacting on our sector?

TAKING A LOOK AT SOCIETY

☐ What are the current trends in popular culture (music, arts, film)?

☐ What is the current political mood (angry, benevolent, conservative, liberal)?

☐ What is the current state of the economy?

☐ What impact is technology having on society (wireless, handhelds, instant messaging)?

Exhibit 3.1   Holding the Mirror up to the Organization

TWO ORGANIZATIONS THAT TOOK
THEIR PULSE AND CHANGED FOREVER

When done right, this first step, pulse taking, echoes all the way down the Dynamic Management Map. Two organizations that we know well, New York City–based MOUSE (Making Opportunities for Upgrading Schools and Education) and the Washington, DC–based National Center for Victims of Crime, discovered things about themselves and their respective industries while taking their own pulse. What they learned has enabled them to begin aggressively repositioning themselves for the digital age.

MOUSE

MOUSE began taking its own pulse in December 2000. With the help of an outside consulting firm, it began holding a mirror up to itself and looking at the world around it. The organization had been in existence for a little more than three years and, to some extent, was becoming a victim of its own success. What started as a small program that mobilized New York's growing technology sector to help public schools make the most of technology now was at a crossroads. Just within the past year alone, as described in Chapter 5, it merged with another organization, HEAVEN (Helping Educate, Activate, Volunteer and Empower Via the Net), and literally became the sole poster child for New York's technology sector philanthropic interests. Internally, MOUSE had to ask itself, are we an organization that exists to change schools or to impact the lives of young people? Should we be incubating new ideas, expanding old ideas, franchising their approach locally or nationally? MOUSE also took the time to look at its own culture. It asked: What are some core values that we know we have to preserve given the fact that we have a board of 19 opinionated entrepreneurs who abhor the constant chasing of money from foundations that characterizes many nonprofits?

When they stopped to look outside of their organization, MOUSE's leaders saw a world different from the one in which they started their work in 1997. First and foremost was the crash of the technology industry in New York in 2000. MOUSE had been relying on that industry in several ways. Programmatically, MOUSE had been securing commitments from technology companies to accept interns in their IT departments as they finished their training at MOUSE programs. Now, many of the local technology companies could not make future commitments to accept interns in the coming year. Financially, MOUSE had prospered in recent years through the donation of "friends and family" stock from local technology companies that were completing their Initial Public Offerings (IPOs). Conversations with board members and supporters made it clear that this type of financial support would not be forthcoming for the foreseeable future. But MOUSE also found that traditional New York–based Fortune 500 companies on Wall Street and Madison Avenue wanted to be a part of their efforts. In fact, these companies often had even more to offer MOUSE programmatically because they had larger IT departments and existing, formal programs for integrating interns into their work.

MOUSE also looked at its main "partner," the New York City school system. Over the years, it worked hard to navigate this complicated system; however, it asked itself, what can a $2 million a year organization like MOUSE really do to change an $11 billion a year operation like the school system?

Finally, MOUSE also looked at its competitors to make sure that it truly was differentiating itself from other organizations—it liked what it saw. MOUSE was avoiding niches in the education space that were already crowded, such as teacher training, staff development, or specialized software development. They had been working with community technology centers (CTCs) but more as an access point for young people, not as a CTC intermediary.

The process has helped MOUSE shape its future. They have now put the following set of core realities and principles in place to inform the organization as it reflects and repositions its culture, business model, and infrastructure to meet today's realities and opportunities:

- MOUSE is an educational technology company with a competitive advantage over similar organizations because of its ability to improve certain education programs in targeted New York City schools through corporate involvement and to effect positive change in these schools by leveraging MOUSE's corporate relationships.
- MOUSE will continue to be a lean and nimble organization that seeks innovative ways to bring about grassroots, not systemwide, change in the public schools to improve the quality of life for young people.

- MOUSE has the credibility and access to play an important role in education technology policy development in New York and will work to play this role.
- MOUSE will expand its efforts to involve traditional Wall Street companies in their intern and job shadowing programs.

The organizational pulse taking also helped Sarah Holloway, MOUSE's Executive Director, with her own inner journey. Attracted to MOUSE when it was founded in 1997 because of her interest in education, she has realized through this process that MOUSE's strengths and her own interests lie not in changing the education system, but rather in building a stronger community among the people dedicated to improving certain educational programs in their schools or their neighborhoods. For Sarah, what started as a commitment to education reform has become a commitment to building community. This insight has influenced her work, the choices she helps MOUSE staff and board members make, and her own personal growth. Now a first-year graduate student at Columbia University, Sarah is working on Saturdays toward her Masters in Public Policy and Administration with a special focus on finance. Sarah summarized the process well, "We took our organizational pulse at the right time for me and for MOUSE. We took the time to find out about ourselves, our world, and our competition, and we have mobilized our staff and our board for change. We are positioned for the future."

National Center for Victims of Crime

The National Center for Victims of Crime began its pulse-taking process more than three years ago when it was called the National Victim Center. Unlike MOUSE, which seemed to have more opportunities than it knew what to do with, the board of the National Victim Center had a sense that the organization was stagnating, that there were changes on the horizon that they may not be positioned to take advantage of, and that they needed to diversify their funding base. They also had had a series of Executive Directors, each of whom stayed only a year or two. With their new Executive Director, Susan Herman, they held a mirror up to themselves and the world outside.

They started by talking to people outside the organization about the state of the victims movement and their views of the center.

They learned a lot. People viewed the National Victim Center as a place primarily dedicated to local "retail" work—helping local victim services programs to improve operations. This was true. At the time, 75 percent of the center's activities were focused in this area. They also learned that people believed there was no national organization dedicated to doing national, "wholesale" work—advocating for larger systemic changes in the role that victims play in the system and the resources they receive, and that the center was not necessarily interested in developing new initiatives.

The center found that its very name was impeding its mission. When asked to respond to the name National Victim Center, people said several interesting things. First, they said the name suggested a place where individual victims went for help. Second, they admitted that the idea of being focused on "victims" was unappealing. Americans simply don't like to think of themselves or their neighbors as "victims." People were less troubled by the notion of "victims of crimes" because so many of them had experienced crime first-hand.

Based on this information, Susan began repositioning the organization to meet the challenges and opportunities that this pulse taking identified. She started by looking within. She had been active in the victims' services movement for more than a decade, helping victims directly and working with the New York City Police Department to improve their policies and responses to victims. Before joining the center, however, she had worked with us at the Enterprise Foundation and saw the intersection of housing, jobs, child care, safety, and victims' services. She had worked on the "retail" and "wholesale" levels, helping build local programs but also influencing areas of national policy. Susan realized that the center had the potential to become the organization that she wanted to lead and that the industry needed, but she knew that it would take a lot of work. The center would have to do business differently.

Susan and the board started with symbolic changes: the organization's name, mission, logo, and corporate colors. The National Victim Center became the National Center for Victims of Crime. The new name reflected market research on the word *victim* and the center's goal to be a "place for ideas," not just a resource for local victim services programs. Their mission expanded from "a focus on helping individual victims and not tolerating violence" to "forging a national commitment to helping victims to rebuild their lives."

Next, they set out to become an organization aligned with its new mission. That meant having staff members understand the vision for the organization and their role in making it a reality. Susan knew that once this work started, it could never be allowed to stop. She instituted regular communications with staff that continue to this day. All staff members began meeting weekly with their supervisors. A monthly staff meeting and biweekly senior management team meetings were instituted. Every six to eight weeks, she met with administrative staff. Once a year, she met one-on-one with every staff member and asked the same three questions, "How do you like your job? How could your job be better? What suggestions do you have to improve the National Center?"

She also knew that performance expectations had to be clear and supportive of the new vision and mission; otherwise, the organization would continue dedicating 75 percent of its efforts to local "retail." People were now to be reviewed on goals and objectives they set for themselves with input from their supervisors. They could propose changing these goals and objectives as they felt necessary, especially if priorities changed, but they were responsible for keeping them relevant and for meeting them. Sixty percent of their performance evaluation would be based on meeting these goals and objectives, with 40 percent based on working well with others. The previous system did not consider individual goals and objectives when considering performance. All employees would meet with their supervisors twice yearly to gauge progress.

Susan knew that some people would balk at the new system, would be uncomfortable with setting tangible goals and objectives, and would ultimately leave the organization. Early in the process, she met with each staff member to explain the reasons for the new process and how the organization would be changing. She personally invited them to be part of the change.

And change happened. The center, building on existing support, began putting victims' issues on other people's agendas. From working at Enterprise, Susan knew that within communities were nonprofit organizations that built and managed affordable housing. She also knew that local District Attorneys had difficulty finding places to house crime victims, often putting them up in decrepit motels and hotels. The center set out to create a winning strategy: connect the DA's office with these nonprofit housing providers so crime victims get a decent place to live and the nonprofit gets a good tenant and full occupancy. The "new" center didn't just complain about the living conditions of crime victims; it created new solutions to the problems and looked beyond the criminal justice system for answers.

The center also began inserting itself into tough, national issues to help shape solutions with victim concerns in mind. For example, between 500,000 to 700,000 prisoners will be released from U.S. prisons in the next few years. Although a host of issues have been raised about this fact, little attention has been paid to the victims of the crimes. The center has made sure that it now has a seat at the table so it can influence the planning, conditions of release, and level of communication that will take place with the victims about the releases.

To take full advantage of its expanded, national "wholesale" efforts, the National Center knew that it had to do a better job of communicating what it was doing and providing opportunities for people to become involved. Using technology and their Web site, the center began reaching out and putting their knowledge on the Web. Speeches, presentations, papers, and reports were all posted directly to the Web site. Outreach efforts were stepped up to individual victims, organizations that serve them, professionals who work with them, and the victim services organizations and the public. The result? Membership doubled. By developing an affiliated organization, the National Crime Victim Bar Association, and an online database of relevant case law, lawyers representing victims of crimes in civil cases have added a strong voice for victims. Services to victims continue as well. E-mail now complements the traditional toll-free number staffed by the National Center. Work in this area has deepened and grown.

Through all of these efforts, the center began to diversify its funding sources dramatically. The U.S. Department of Justice, Office of Crime Victims, had supported the National Center's work for years, but now other Justice Department programs like the Violence Against Women Office, Community Policing, Bureau of Justice Assistance, and Weed and Seed are also on board. The Department of Education provides support for National Center efforts as well.

Susan Herman summarizes the last three years this way: "We looked at ourselves and saw that we were not what we wanted to be. So we set out a bold vision, began changing so we could live up to that vision, and tried to bring as many different people as possible along with us. We'll never be done, but we've come a long way."

REFLECT AND REPOSITION

- Look inward: Hold up a mirror to yourself and your organization.
- Look outward: Take a closer look at the macro trends in your part of the nonprofit industry and in society.

GUIDING PRINCIPLES

- The Dynamic Manager must regularly ask "What is going on?" It's the only way to improve continually, to challenge yourself, and to force yourself to acknowledge that the world is changing around you—quickly.
- We are often too busy to notice how things are changing and how the changes are having an impact on how we do business.
- There is no more important pulse to take than that of the leader. More often than not, if the leader is not ready to lead the organization into the digital age, the organization is not ready to go there either.
- When you reflect first and reposition second, you improve and grow by changing—what you are doing and how you are doing it. The inner journey helps you know and trust yourself.

NOTES

[1]Stephen R. Covey, *Principle Centered Leadership* (New York: Fireside, 1992), 75.

[2]Peter Senge, *The Fifth Discipline: The Art and Practice of the Learning Organization* (New York: Doubleday, 1990).

[3]Kevin Cashman, *Leadership from the Inside Out* (Utah: Executive Excellence Publishing, 1998).

[4]Cashman.

[5]Covey.

[6]Cashman.

[7]Henry David Thoreau, *Walden* (New York, Walter J. Black, Inc., 1942), xiii.

[8]Cashman.

[9]Cashman, 36.

[10]Senge, 147.

[11]We must not hope to be mowers
And to gather the ripe gold ears,
Unless we have first been sowers
And watered the furrows with tears.

It is not just as we take it,
This mystical world of ours,
Life's field will yield as we make it
A harvest of thorns or of flowers.
    Johann Wolfgang von Goethe

CHAPTER FOUR

Corporate Culture: Vision, Values, and People

Your corporate culture reflects who you are and what you hope to become. In our experience, an organization's culture is a combination of its vision, values, and people. The vision inspires and establishes a north star; the values define core beliefs; and the people, attracted by your vision and values, translate the shared vision and these values into action. The Dynamic Manager must align all three elements simultaneously, keeping them fresh and responsive. Here's why: Vision without values is inauthentic and insincere. Values without vision are devoid of leadership. People without vision and values usually choose to work somewhere else. This chapter helps you reflect on each element of your organization's culture and reposition them, as appropriate, to meet the forces of change in the digital age.

THE IMPORTANCE OF CULTURE

For us, culture is the defining issue to address if you want to lead a truly dynamic organization. Your vision, values, and people must reflect the continual process of organizational self-reflection and dynamic repositioning that Dynamic Management requires. The culture must encourage and reward continual reflection, repositioning, and change. It must provide a compelling vision and common values that buoy the organization during tough times and propel it in times of abundance. Multiple cultures within an organization, however, can keep that from happening. In fact, we have all read about corporate mergers, like Chrysler and Daimler-Benz, that never quite reached their potential because two different cultures failed to come together as one. In our experience, however, culture clashes are not limited to mergers. They occur when Dynamic Managers fail to create or sustain one dominant, authentic culture.

Creating Culture

Our experience has shown that vision, values, and people are the essential elements in creating corporate culture. Rey Ramsey's work in Oregon provides a compelling example. In 1990, Rey had the opportunity to create culture when the Oregon legislature merged The Oregon Housing Agency (as it was then known) with the Community Services Department to create a combined department—Housing and Community Services (HCS). Rey headed the Housing Agency and was later named director of the new HCS by then Governor Barbara Roberts. Needless to say, people on all sides were apprehensive about the change, especially staff from the Community Services Department. This merger brought together different organizations with two different cultures. Stated simply, the housing staff had a "bankers" culture. They financed real estate transactions with complex financing programs. The community services staff had a more "social service" culture. They worked with social service agencies on issues of hunger, jobs, and families. Expectations for HCS were high, but so was the level of scrutiny being applied by staff from both departments to Rey's decisions and actions. The ultimate success of the merger depended on the creation of a culture that worked for everyone.

The first order of business was to deal with the vision issue. The vision had to excite and unify the new department's constituencies yet be realistic about spending. A small, diverse team of staff and customers led by John Blatt and Lynn Schoessler fashioned a vision that was "road tested" with great success. It gave equal billing to the issues of financing affordable housing and alleviating poverty. It positioned HCS to function as a catalyst and intermediary; to be responsible for securing new resources for housing and community services; and to train and assist all community-based organizations so they could both maximize their potential and work with the department as trusted partners. The shared vision unified the two former departments and provided the needed space and time to further the goals of the merger. The vision was directly responsible for the Oregon legislature creating Oregon's first-ever housing trust fund that today still provides valuable resources to both housing development organizations and community services/community action agencies.

In creating culture at HCS, a lot of time was spent on values and people. The first step was to give equal rank and authority to the administrator of community services and the housing administrator. As time passed, several other values, such as diversity, local partnerships, innovation, and customer service, that had been articulated early on by stakeholders, took hold. These values were promoted at every opportunity. In addition, hiring and career advancement decisions were made with these values in mind. Over the course of two years, a new, dominant, and authentic culture was created at HCS.

Sustaining and Repositioning Culture

The exciting thing about culture is that it is not static. HCS, like any nonprofit organization, had to work hard to sustain and reposition the culture to meet the changing times. Rey and later department heads had to keep the vision fresh and relevant. The values had to be instilled throughout the department, and the right people had to be retained and continually attracted to the organization.

Nonprofits use many techniques to strengthen, sustain, and reposition culture. These can often be small but powerful acts such as rituals, customs, and storytelling. We did several things at Enterprise toward this end. Quarterly meetings with all the national staff highlighted the things that we valued most: new employees, new programs that best reflected our vision for the future, and the work of employees who personified the organization's values in their work. We called these "the Spirit of Enterprise Awards." We later expanded this program to recognize staff who had actively helped secure large grants during the previous year. We hoped this would instill the idea that everyone who worked in the organization should see themselves as a fundraiser and advocate for the organization. Finally, we were fortunate to have the organization's co-founder, Patty Rouse, on hand for board and management meetings, at which she would tell stories from the organization's early days. Patty also spoke at new employee orientation about how she and Jim Rouse had created and built the organization.

Similarly, Habitat for Humanity International sustains its culture as a Christian ministry with a short prayer before and after meetings, functions, and events. Although Habitat has expanded into more than 76 countries and serves people of all religions, races and colors, this prayer reflects the organization's core beliefs and reminds people of the importance of providing "a decent place to live for all God's people in need."

Culture requires continuous reflection as well as action. It is easy to allow culture to slip away and have those things you value suddenly become exceptions to the normal course. We try to provide guidance on reflecting and repositioning your culture in the following sections.

Toward a Digital Culture

A word about digital culture. We first raised the idea of *digital culture* in Chapter 2, and you will find it used throughout the book. When we use the term, we are actually talking about values that an organization has to absorb into its existing corporate culture if it wants to be positioned to survive the forces of change, learn how to operate in new ways, and thrive in the digital age. Digital cultures:

- *Embrace digital solutions.* They continually seek ways that technology can help them operate better and provide more products and services.

- *Worship the power of ideas.* They support insurgents; celebrate individuality; reward innovation, risk taking, and failure; and give space for new ideas no matter where they crop up in the organization.

- *Create an ethos of learning.* They make the pursuit and sharing of knowledge paramount.

- *Put their people first.* They create a caring, flexible, diverse, mobile, and fairly compensated workplace.

- *Center on the customer.* They communicate with existing customers, seek new ones, and deepen the customer relationship.

We have found that many of the organizations highlighted in this book share these attributes. They are different in many ways, but they often have these values in common.

VISION

Vision provides inspiration to an organization's culture. Most of us have been lucky enough to be part of a mission or a campaign of some sort, whether it's trying to pass a specific law during a legislative term or meeting an ambitious fundraising goal. You feel exhilarated, exhausted, and inspired, all at the same time. That is the same feeling you get when you work for an organization that has an inspiring vision. Ultimately, you believe that your work is special. You are more than willing to give your time and talent to the cause. Put simply, an inspiring vision is effective because it draws you in and compels you to act.

The Importance of Vision

Vision for us is a mental portrait of success that captures the heart (compelling enough to inspire) and the mind (credible enough to be attained). Many leaders attempt to inspire and lead by mission, not vision. In the nonprofit world, that often means that they fail to lead at all. We recently reviewed the mission statements of more than a dozen nonprofit organizations, large and small, and had a hard time distinguishing one from the other. Essentially, all wanted to improve the well-being of people, in one way or another. So if the missions are similar, what sets those organizations apart from one another? Vision.

Vision is meant to compel people to take action to "stimulate progress toward an envisioned future."[1] Vision often captures goodwill, sustains us when funds are low, keeps us working for modest wages, attracts customers, and entices would-be donors. Nevertheless, the visions of some nonprofits are uninspiring, outdated, or simply unknown. You know that you are in trouble when your employees and board members can't articulate your vision. This is more often than not caused by neglect. Too much time is spent focusing on the trees (such as products and services or even internal systems)—the issues that you'll find lower in the Dynamic Management Map—and not enough time on the forest—the top of the map. Both the trees and the forest must be continually reviewed and renewed.

Some vision-challenged organizations can survive for awhile because of past reputation or political patronage, but they will not be able to thrive and adapt to the digital age without a compelling vision. As Andrew Ditton, now Senior Vice President of Citibank for Global Relations but previously the Chief Operating Officer for Local Initiatives Support Corporation, a national nonprofit inter-mediary organization, said, "Some nonprofit organizations, like old dead redwood trees, can appear to be alive long after they are dead simply based on their past accomplishments or size, but most peo-ple know that inside, they're really dead." That is the plight of a nonprofit organization without a vision.

Some say that vision is overrated. "We know what we need to do, just give us the funds and step back." But as President George Bush found out in the election of 1992, the "vision thing" is far more than just reading lips. It can make or break a campaign and be the dif-ference between winning and losing.

Elements of Vision

The best visions seem to share the following characteristics:

- *Compelling*. Such visions appeal to your desire to win, to serve a higher calling, to make things better for others.
- *Simple and clear*. When Millard and Linda Fuller started Habitat for Humanity International, their vision was and remains to provide "a decent place to live for all God's people in need." Millard is fond of calling this "The Theology of the Hammer." Today, 100,000 homes later, with affiliates in 76 countries, this organization with a simple, easily understood vision is building homes and changing lives all over the world.
- *Inclusive*. To say that we are all individuals and that we live in an increasingly diverse society is an understatement. Therefore, an inspiring vision must in some ways be a "big tent," able to carry the dreams and imagination of people both inside and outside of the organization. Not so big as to be meaningless, but large enough so that a diverse population can be inspired to act on your behalf. A "big tent" vision mobilizes people to assist you and your organization.
- *Personal*. People must be able to find themselves in your vision. A part of who they are and what they believe has to be present if they are to be inspired to act. That includes all the people you are trying to attract: insiders (staff and board) and outsiders (customers and funders). And don't overlook the importance of

vision on your own personal commitment. It must invigorate you as well.

Personal to Staff and Board

Over the years, we have asked hundreds of folks at nonprofit organizations why they work where they do. Nine out of ten answer "vision." When the organization's vision is in sync with the employees' convictions, they tend to be dedicated, passionate, and committed to their work. The vision allows them to truly invest their creative energies, what we call their "psychic energy," into their work. Psychic energy is precious because it is that time at work, at home, or at play where that employee thinks about work and devises and dreams of the positive changes that they can help catalyze. Some call it capturing the heart and mind of a person. Only a vision can inspire this type of activity.

Organizations that capture the psychic energy of staff are typically high-performing organizations. The vision and the excitement of work becomes the supplemental pay for employees. Ben Hecht's father calls this "psychic income," and we think that's right.

We always marveled at how little turnover we had among our local office directors at Enterprise. Every director, in one way or another, talked about the psychic rewards of working for the organization.

The Dynamic Manager has the responsibility to mold, interpret, and articulate the vision so it becomes personal to the staff. Jim Rouse was one of the great Americans of the 20th century. Jim, heralded around the world as an urban visionary, founded The Enterprise Foundation. He was a master at capturing staff's psychic energy by telling stories about what he had personally seen and by calling on those whose lives Enterprise was trying to improve to tell their own stories. These stories had an enormous impact on those who worked for Enterprise.

The vision must be personal for your board of directors as well. We are amazed when we see boards that are not engaged in the organization's vision or that hold onto an outdated vision of where the organization is headed. You need to invest time and energy into working with your board members if you cannot say with certainty that most of them can articulate your current vision. This may not seem to be a huge problem now, but it will likely lead to an erosion of support and directly affect your bottom line in the long run.

In fact, more often than not, board members make even more significant contributions to the organization if they are asked to apply their unique skills to internalizing or moving the organizational vision forward. Rey Ramsey's experience with American Rivers, a Virginia-based national nonprofit river conservation organization, is a good example. For several years, he was a member of the American Rivers board of directors. Its President, Rebecca Wodder, was building a vision for the organization that integrated technology into its service delivery model. Knowing Rey's interest in this topic, she sought his advice on developing a digital strategy and instilling it in the organization. By engaging Rey in his areas of interest, Rebecca was able to receive some of his time, energy, and best thinking. She engaged other board members in a similar fashion, reaped the benefits of greater board support, and ultimately, launched an impressive online presence and built a digital culture internally.

Personal to Customers and Funders

The forces of change facing the industry make it all the more critical for a dynamic organization to make its vision personal to its customers as well. An inspired customer is a loyal customer. Although this has not been done historically, many organizations are now aggressively sharing their vision with their customers and having them shape future visions. Local neighborhood organizations like the Development Corporation of Columbia Heights, a nonprofit housing and community development organization in Washington, D.C., now holds community visioning summits every year. Regional organizations like ONE/Northwest, highlighted in Chapter 5, uses a monthly brain trust meeting of customers and other interested stakeholders to engage them in their visioning. At Enterprise, as a national organization, we created an advisory committee of 25 neighborhood-based nonprofit organizations from around the country and convened them twice a year for this purpose. Senior staff would set out their vision for their program area or the organization as a whole. Our customers would comment, criticize, and commit to helping make the vision a reality. Customers and the need for building customer loyalty are discussed in much greater detail in Chapter 5.

Unlike customers, funders may not need to help create the vision. They do, however, need to understand your vision and, typically, be inspired by it. For obvious reasons, funders have always received a great deal of attention from nonprofits. Most nonprofits have put a lot of time, energy, and resources into educating and reeducating their funders about their vision because they have seen the results—more money. Our experience has been that funders or donors respond best when you present them with a compelling vision and engage them so they understand your business model.

Personal to You

Perhaps the most obvious (and often overlooked) beneficiary of an inspiring vision is you. So much of your energy goes into promoting the vision to others that you could easily neglect yourself. Take time regularly, even if only an hour or two, to reflect on the vision of your organization and how you feel about it. Ask yourself if the vision remains compelling to you; if you can find a sense of yourself in it. If the answer is no, take action. If the vision is not working for you, you can be pretty sure that it is not working for many of those to whom you have been promoting it over the years.

Vision at Multiple Levels

The organization-wide vision is the broader, or macro, vision that informs all others. But we all know that local, or micro, visions exist at different levels within an organization. For example, the communications department's vision might call for a role as "news central"—the first place reporters call for expert commentary on a breaking story. The development department's vision might be for every person on the mailing list to make an annual contribution. Like the broader vision, these micro visions inspire. In contrast, however, they tend to be developed for internal use only by a limited number of staff and are even more personal than the broader vision because of their narrower focus on people's day-to-day work.

Micro visions are good for an organization if they are compatible with the broader vision. Sometimes the vision of one department or unit can catalyze the entire organization into updating or changing its vision altogether. The Dynamic Manager, from time to time, might even need to germinate the seeds of a new vision in some part of the organization and consciously work to create synergy and alignment with the other departments to move the organization forward.

We saw some extraordinary results from this approach at Enterprise. In 1994, we created a new department called Research, Evaluation, and Documentation (RED), with the bold but simply stated vision of capturing our own corporate knowledge and information and disseminating it to the field of nonprofit community development organizations through the rapidly developing delivery mechanisms offered by technology. At a department retreat in 1995, Rey said that "the work of your department is the future of Enterprise, and our aim is to be on the desk of every nonprofit in every city." People within the department felt that they were part of something special. Quickly, the bold vision of this small department began catching on in other parts of the organization. In fact, four years later, in 1998, we dissolved RED because its vision had become an integral part of everyone's vision. Virtually everyone became responsible for evaluating and disseminating information. The dream of being on every desk was not fully realized, but the vision of capturing our own knowledge catapulted the organization's culture into the digital age.

Macro and micro visions within the organization can be productive; however, multiple and incompatible visions at the macro level are almost always counterproductive. Multiple macro visions usually mean that different power centers are clashing and the organization's resources are being diluted to support two visions. Some organizations with more than one strong senior manager wrestle with this problem. Here's a typical comment: "When I talk with Ann, our vision is to grow to be the market leader, but when I talk with Mike, the vision is to shrink and be a high-performing boutique leader." You must ensure that your organization has only one broad vision for itself. It should be developed through a process that allows both peoples' ideas to be expressed, debated, and molded into a vision that can be adopted, in word and deed, by internal and external users. The vision should not be adopted by default (Mike simply talking about his vision more than Ann and wearing people down) or by maintaining the status quo.

Digital Spotlight—The Kaboom! Story

Kaboom! is a national nonprofit that was founded in 1996 to create networks and partnerships to build safe, accessible playgrounds in distressed neighborhoods. Typically, Kaboom! links corporations and communities together to raise the resources and labor to build playgrounds. It functions both as an intermediary, bringing parties together, and as a direct service provider, getting the playgrounds built. To date, Kaboom! has built approximately 250 playgrounds throughout the United States and provides technical assistance to others who want to build playgrounds.

Its leader and founder is Darrell Hammond. Hammond did not set out to start an organization. He simply wanted to make his vision of using playgrounds to improve the lives of children and to build better communities a reality. He took his vision to more established organizations but, perhaps because he was only 23 years old at the time, he was unable to spark sufficient interest. He thus became, as he puts it, CEO by default.

Early on, Hammond made the mistake of being too directive with his staff and, as a result, experienced high turnover. Vision alone was not enough to build the culture that he wanted to build. His vision, however, did help to guide Kaboom! through those tough times. He repositioned himself and his management style. He learned to follow the lead of the early adapters of technology on his staff, the young people, and helped the organization to embrace technology as a tool for advancing the corporate vision. Now Kaboom!'s Web site enables it to have a reach that Hammond never could have dreamed of four years ago. People anywhere in the country can manage their entire "build" online, from assessing the right location and designing the equipment to inviting people to the build and putting the pieces together in the right way. "What we're trying to do for people is meet them where they are at, structure it, provide them with access to resources and confidence, and let them get at it."

Kaboom!'s vision has inspired extraordinary partnerships as well. In the past year, Kaboom! has entered into a partnership with Ben and Jerry's in which the premium ice cream maker and retailer features Kaboom! prominently online and on-the-ground. In fact, this relationship has resulted in the first-ever ice cream "branded" specifically for a nonprofit—"KaBerry KaBoom." Kaboom! is being featured on the Ben and Jerry's home page for a full year and receives a percentage of the proceeds from sales to support its operations. This partnership has also helped secure an agreement with Yahoo! where coupons for KaBerry KaBoom ice cream are offered online on the world's most popular portal.

The vision is spreading. The organization is growing and so, too, is the founder. His vision has built a dynamic organization that is positioned to flourish in these digital times.

REPOSITIONING YOUR VISION: VISION AND THE ROLE OF LEADERS

Kevin Cashman refers to leadership as "authentic self-expression that adds value."[2] We define it simply as the capacity to move an agenda. Either way, leadership and vision are inexorably linked. There can be no inspiring vision without leadership. We believe that Dynamic Managers must play two critical roles if they are going to reposition their organization's vision for the digital age: Leader as Inventor of Vision and Leader as Communicator of Vision.

Leader as Inventor. We expect leaders to invent or reinvent the vision. "Visionary leaders" anticipate change and create a vision that provides a mental portrait of the organization in the future. Where would Microsoft be if Bill Gates had not decided to repeatedly reinvent the vision of his company and even step aside as CEO so he could lead Microsoft's new Internet business model? An effective leader is an inventor of vision.

The digital age demands that you invent or reinvent the vision of your organization as the forces of change and the strategic inflection point takes your part of the industry by storm. The people who you rely on to support the organization and to make it work are looking for a vision for how these changes will be harnessed by the organization and put to good use.

Do you have the power to invent vision? Remember that the inventor process should not be a solo endeavor. It's been a long time since Moses came down from the Mount with tablets. The inventor process should be a participatory activity involving others inside and outside an organization. It should come from the board, the Information Technology (IT) department, and the customers. A group of employees can invent vision if you give them the platform to do it. The best way to make a vision personal is to have people be part of the process.

Following are a few examples of Dynamic Managers in action:

- Fred Krupp led Environmental Defense into the environmental movement's "third stage" but did not invent Environmental Defense's vision for technology on his own (see Chapter 2). He listened to his staff, brought in a technology advisory team of the best and brightest from the outside, gave his staff and board the latitude to be innovative, and helped the organization "demonstrate, not just preach the power of technology."

- Beatriz (BB) Otero founded Calvary Bilingual Multicultural Learning Center in a church 15 years ago, but the organization's current vision (Chapter 8) was "invented" from the bottom up. It began in the computer lab with one teacher and some students, spread virally through the young people and families who were using the center, and was harnessed by BB, who has worked tirelessly to make the vision personal to staff, customers, and even funders. The vision, together with a new building that physically represented all the potential that the vision holds, created a tipping point for Calvary and has transformed the organization.

- John Ball knew he had to make radical changes when he took over Worksystems, Inc. (Chapter 7) during a time of crisis. He invented the organization's new vision by talking to his customers, both community-based job training and placement organizations and corporations who hire people, about what they needed. He then instilled the vision into the organization through staff changes and physically opening up the office workspace.

One important lesson that each of these leaders has learned is that complacency is the enemy of invention. The notion that "we are doing just fine the way we are" or the complaint that "we don't have the time or energy right now" are unacceptable reasons for failing to invent vision.

Leader as Communicator. We cannot overstate the importance of communicating vision. No one plays a more important role in it, than you, the leader. We rely on leaders to articulate the vision and to bring it to life. This is a responsibility, a necessity, and an opportunity. Leaders often become synonymous with the vision of the organization and, under the best circumstances, are seen as embodiments of the organization's values.

Jim Rouse was the most effective communicator of the vision of Enterprise not only because he invented the vision with his wife Patty, but also because he lived it through word and deed—valuing people and place, with the belief that either could change for the better. Jim was the ultimate communicator; he never stopped pitching. Everyone who met him was touched by his vision and associated it with the organization.

Like Jim Rouse, leaders must communicate the vision not just through great speeches but also through gestures, symbols, and actions. Environmental Defense's Fred Krupp doesn't just talk about technology with staff who will listen; he has made the entire organization stop and focus on its growing technology content by showcasing this topic at two of his last three national staff meetings. Calvary's BB Otero doesn't just engage people she meets in a discussion about the role that technology can play in youth development; she literally lines the walls of her building with the extraordinary art developed by the center's young customers. Jim Ball of Worksystems, Inc. doesn't just extol the virtues of technology as a tool for reinventing workforce development for low-income people; he raises the money and brings the technology to his partners so they can make it happen. Vision through words and acts— a powerful combination.

In today's digital age, the Dynamic Manager must use the Internet to communicate the organization's vision. Your vision is your most significant export, and the Web gives you an inexpensive yet powerful delivery vehicle. As described more fully in Chapters 6 and 7, your Web site can expand the reach and possibilities of your organization, starting with a simple brochure online and ideally evolving. Don't allow all communication to be one-way; seize the Web's potential and create energy around your vision. The Internet will not replace people as the inventors and communicators of vision, but it will enhance your ability to reach more people efficiently and economically. In these times when customers, funders, and employees have more choices and get information from more sources, leaders must extend themselves to communicate their vision in every way, lest the vision be drowned out by ever-increasing background noise.

Be careful. Your vision can also be communicated by those you choose as partners. An unsavory partner can undo much goodwill by recasting the vision of your organization in unwanted ways. Nonprofits seeking companies for partnerships and cause-related marketing opportunities (see Chapter 7) must review any proposal through their vision filter. Ask yourself the following questions: Does the vision of the potential partner align with our vision? Are our values compatible? Short-term financial gain cannot offset the losses of a bad partnership.

Digital Spotlight for Vision—Jim Rouse

Jim Rouse was a true visionary. In the 1950s, Rouse invented the term *shopping mall*, built them in strategic locations, and changed retailing forever. In the 1960s, he secretly acquired more than 14,000 acres of land between Baltimore and Washington and built what is arguably the past century's most successful new city, Columbia, Maryland. In 1963, he warned about urban sprawl and called for smart growth, issues only now becoming part of our dialogue and lexicon. In the 1970s, against all odds and the best advice of others, he pioneered the inner-city festival marketplaces—Faneuil Hall in Boston, Harborplace in Baltimore, and South Street Seaport in New York—and led the rebirth of America's cities. At age 65, he retired from the Rouse Company and devoted himself, through The Enterprise Foundation, to helping people at the bottom of society work their way up and out of poverty. He founded Enterprise with a bold mission: "To see that all very low income people have the opportunity for fit and affordable housing and to work their way up and out of poverty into the mainstream of American life."

His inspiration for Enterprise was a community-based non-profit organization in Washington, D.C. that had, against all odds, bought and renovated two dilapidated buildings in a gentrifying part of the city. Jim saw what this organization was able to do with a little bit of help and believed two things: (1) there had to be other organizations like it all over the country, and (2) there should be a national organization available to give these groups technical assistance, access to capital to make it happen, and a forum for sharing ideas and experiences. He built Enterprise to be that organization. Under Jim's leadership, Enterprise started with a handful of people and a network of five groups that wanted help. By the time of his death in 1996, Enterprise and its subsidiaries had more than 200 employees. It worked with more than 750 groups in 40 states and helped bring more than $200 million to distressed communities in the United States.

Jim's extraordinary mix of optimism and vision set Enterprise apart from organizations with similarly broad missions. He believed, "What ought to be, can be, if we have the will to make it so!"; that people just needed to see the possible and then they would do the right thing. He always held up a big vision, a big tent, for all to come under: "We need a commitment to boldness in contemplating the future of this country . . . images of a society that works for all its people." He saw Enterprise as "a light to show the way . . . to invest our time, our energy, and our money—government, corporate, institutional, and personal—in a national campaign to overcome the devastating challenge [abject poverty and homelessness] to our society that rages among us." One of our favorite quotes of his was, "We need to understand the action-generating power of large, bold, rational solutions." When you were around him, you simply wanted to work harder. You believed that the impossible was possible. You bought into the vision personally.

In the last years of his life, Jim worked tirelessly to transform an entire neighborhood in Baltimore. Sandtown-Winchester is a 72-square-block neighborhood that was devastated by drugs, blight, and chronic unemployment. The effort was to be lead by community residents and would address housing, schools, jobs, health care, and civic engagement simultaneously. Jim wanted to build a model of the possible, a guide for government and philanthropy to follow for fixing all of a community's dysfunctional systems at once. Jim's vision, energy, and boldness galvanized the community and brought attention and resources to this effort. Ten years later (five years after

Jim's death), tangible improvements can be seen in the schools, community health, and the state of the neighborhood's housing. His dream of a neighborhood transformed remains elusive, but Sandtown-Winchester has spawned other comprehensive community efforts throughout the country.

Jim was not always right. His visions did not always become reality. But that is not the work of a visionary. A visionary should inspire, bring out the best in people, and move people to take action. Jim Rouse did all that, and more.

VALUES

If vision brings inspiration to an organization's culture, then values give it meaning. James Champy defines values as "the link between emotion and behavior. The connection between what we feel and what we do."[3] The Oxford Dictionary defines values as "one's principles or standards, one's judgment of what is valuable in life." Our favorite treatment of values, however, is found in *Built to Last*. Collins and Porras define values as "the organization's essential and enduring tenets—a small set of general guiding principles; not to be confused with specific cultural or operating practices; not to be compromised for financial gain or short-term expediency."[4] Values are the backbone of the corporate soul.

Values play an important role in grounding an organization. We experienced this first-hand at Enterprise when Jim Rouse passed away in 1996. Many speculated that the organization would decline or lose its focus. Neither outcome happened because our organizational values of caring, innovation, and commitment to boldness guided us. People would say: "Jim would want us to do this." Jim did what true leaders do. He lived the values he spoke of and built a corporate soul that outlived his own life. Values aligned with your vision and your people are critical to a strong corporate culture and a dynamic organization. The challenge for a Dynamic Manager is to articulate or rearticulate your values, if you have not recently done so, and to continuously work to ensure that the organization's words, actions, and relationships with customers, employees, funders, and other stakeholders are aligned with these values.

Articulating Organizational Values

Collins and Porras provide guidance on how to create your own corporate values or evaluate or reposition your existing ones so they reflect your core beliefs. Ask yourself the following questions:

- What values would you strive to uphold for a hundred years regardless of changes in the external environment—whether or not the environment rewarded or you?

- Conversely, which values would you be willing to change or discard if the environment no longer favored them?[5]

In this digital age, we urge any nonprofit striving to become a dynamic organization to add the following third line of values questions to move you toward a digital culture:

- Do you embrace digital solutions, worship the power of ideas, create an ethos of learning, put people first, and center on the customer? These concepts were introduced earlier in this chapter and are discussed throughout this book.

With careful reflection, most organizations can identify their core values; however, we have found that you have to be honest with yourself during this exercise if you really want it to be useful. For example, if you list "diversity" as a core value but consistently maintain a homogeneous workforce, you do not really value diversity. Diversity may not be a core value to your organization, but only a goal. Or, it may be a value but you have not aligned the rest of your organization in order to live up to it. In this case, for example, you may need to invest more effort into recruiting for diversity or into mechanisms that maintain diversity. Either way, the process helps you decide what matters the most. Once you have done this, share your values with all who will listen, over and over again.

Creating or Reinvigorating the Corporate Soul

As we see it, setting and resetting values is important because it is the first step toward creating or reinvigorating the "corporate soul." The corporate soul is the embodiment of the values of an organization and exists only when a critical mass of the organization knows what these values are, accepts them, and acts on them. This goal is achieved when the people, units, and divisions within an organization, even those with their own subcultures, share a common set of beliefs. This connection creates the soul of an organization. A leader who wants to enjoy the full potential of what corporate culture has to offer must achieve this goal. Like the concept described by Malcolm Gladwell,[6] one must reach a "tipping point"—the moment when things just take off like spontaneous combustion or an epidemic.

Environmental Defense long advocated the value of creating bipartisan, efficient, and fair solutions to environmental problems; however, it wasn't until some staff members at Environmental Defense persuaded McDonald's Corporation to replace foam-plastic hamburger boxes with less-bulky wraps and to increase the use of recycled materials that this approach hit the tipping point inside Environmental Defense. The momentum within the organization spread outside as well. In subsequent years, many of McDonald's competitors also changed their practices. Ultimately, this type of effort became a critical part of both Environmental Defense's work and the purpose of a whole new organization, the Alliance for Environmental Innovation, which was formed to help companies improve their environmental performance (see Chapter 2). Once in place, a corporate soul can be a powerful force for change.

We had a similar experience at Enterprise but, unlike Environmental Defense, never reached a full tipping point. For years, we attempted to instill a value that our work on the ground with community-based organizations needed to be integrated into our work with them in cyberspace. We talked about this value whenever we could—at staff meetings of the parent organization and its subsidiaries, together and separately; at annual conferences of all our customers; and at forums with funders of all types. We made great strides toward this end; however, we failed at getting all the parts of the organization to adopt this value. This value was able to permeate significant parts of the organization, including our business model, our customers, and our content, but it never entered Enterprise's corporate soul.

Leaders and Values

Values achieve their fullest potential when they are written down, talked about and lived out, day to day, in plain view for all to see. Leaders have a unique role in making this happen. They must articulate or rearticulate values and bring them to life. They also must avoid expounding on a set of values that they don't really live by or face being dismissed by people inside and outside the organization as inauthentic. At their best, leaders build the corporate soul by mobilizing people around the core beliefs they all share.

PEOPLE

If vision brings inspiration and values bring meaning to culture, then people bring humanity. Your people and their actions ultimately shape your culture more than any other factor. We have found that the strongest organizations are those that are viewed by their employees as putting people first. This means valuing their ideas, providing them with avenues to express these ideas, paying them fairly, supporting them when they succeed or fail, honoring their commitments to family, and having colleagues as diverse as the people being served. There is something about organizations that put people first—they win. They seem to do most things better than their competitors, whether it is raising money, feeding the homeless, teaching the arts, or protecting the land. They outperform organizations driven more by money, stature, systems, or bureaucracy. Somewhere in the haste to "get the job done" or "meet projections," some organizations have lost their sense of what matters most—people.

It often takes a crisis, such as a mass exodus of staff, for organizations to admit that they need to do more to put their people first. Even then, such crises are often followed by public relations gimmicks, employee suggestion boxes, or by blaming the people who just left. As a Dynamic Manager, you need to reflect on your organization and determine if it is indeed a People First place to work. You must take action to reposition the organization if it is not what you want it to be.

What Goes into Putting People First?

Creating a People First culture is not about charts, graphs, or formulas. It is a commitment to creating a place where people are valued and encouraged to grow. It takes time, energy, resources, and thought. We have spoken to dozens of nonprofits of all sizes to characterize a People First organization. We actually define a People First organization, in part with the help of McKinsey & Company. A 2000 McKinsey & Company report, titled *The War for Talent,* described the type of environment that they believe companies must offer employees to get them to join and stay with the organization. McKinsey calls this the "extreme employee value proposition" (EVP) and we adapt it, respectfully, to meet our needs.

The EVP is the compelling reason why a talented person would want to join (or stay with) your company. You will know that the five elements of the EVP are right when the following goals are met:

- The company genuinely cares about its people and the people care about the company. There is pride in being associated with the company's success and each person's role in it. (Caring)
- People have flexibility in where and when they work. Telecommuting, job sharing, and other mechanisms are used that provide advantage to both the company and its people. (Flexibility)
- Great leaders treat people with trust and respect and honor the intelligence of all who contribute to the company. They balance guidance and guidelines with allowing for independence to accomplish great things. Great leaders build capacity in their people, help them unleash their talents, and continually work to challenge them professionally. (Mobility and Freedom)
- The composition of the workforce is as diverse as its community and its customers. The employees have substantially the same racial and ethnic composition as the community where the organization is located and the customers who the organization serves. (Diversity)
- People like what they do and the people they do it with. A great job can be demanding so long as a person finds it interesting and important. People feel good when they are valued. They expect their contributions to be acknowledged and their compensation to reflect their impact on the company. (Valued and Fair Pay)[7]

Caring

Caring is shown through empathy and investment. Empathy, or the power of identifying oneself mentally with a person, is one of the most valued human emotions. You send a clear message that you care about your people when you show them that you understand their circumstances. Empathetic leaders take the time to listen, to fashion solutions to problems facing their people, and to express their empathy through words and actions. The adage "Wear it on your sleeve" really does work. It is okay to tell your staff that you care about them and their needs.

Organizations also should show they care by investing in their people. This may sound like a slogan, but think for a moment about the companies you know that invest in their people. How do the people in those organizations feel about their company? How do you feel when your board of directors spends resources on you and your needs? These are the feelings that you want in your workplace. The inevitable nonprofit mantra is raised: "We do not have the funds to invest in our people!" Although we do not mean to downplay the issue of resources, there is always a way to invest. Not all investments require large sums of money. For instance, some of your new employees may have joined you primarily because of your social mission, with salary playing only a partial role. Invest in these new employees by assigning them a mentor, listening to their needs, and helping them plan their career paths. Consider creating online chat rooms that take advantage of the skills of your workforce. One organization we have worked with is in the process of creating a virtual training campus where the staff maintains the content with minimal guidance from the human resources department. Take the time to understand the needs and potential of your workforce, then tailor the appropriate investments.

The Fannie Mae Foundation is moving in an exciting new direction. The foundation considers its employees to be its most valued assets. Consistent with that perspective, the foundation offers its employees a wide variety of opportunities to increase their productivity and further their careers, including a career development program that provides tools to help employees enhance their current skills and prepare for future opportunities.

The program helps employees map out where they want their careers to be over time. This includes 100 percent financial assistance to employees seeking to enhance their careers through an undergraduate or graduate degree program, as well as numerous career-related leadership, managerial, or technical training courses.

Kevin Smith, Fannie Mae Foundation Senior Vice President, believes that this effort is essential to attracting and retaining the best and brightest talent and to differentiate the foundation from other employment opportunities. "As a relatively small organization, with approximately 100 employees, we realize how unlikely it is that we will have employment opportunities consistent with the long-term career aspirations of every employee. But we're committed to preparing each employee for future career opportunities, even if it may not be here."

This approach, combined with the foundation's employee assisted housing program (providing five-year forgiveable homeownership loans for downpayment and closing costs) and its job rotation program (providing opportunities for employees to spend time in different parts of the organization), makes a profound statement to staff that they work for a caring organization.

Flexibility

A People First culture must be flexible, by necessity and design. A flexible workplace not only allows workers to juggle competing demands at work and at home, but it also facilitates the organization's compliance with laws such as the Family and Medical Leave Act that permit individuals time off to attend to such matters.

Embrace flexibility in your workplace and turn it into an opportunity for your organization. Market the heck out of it. In fact, the leaders of successful "People First" organizations continually tell us that they use their flexible workplace as a competitive advantage when working to recruit and retain staff. We have seen this firsthand. During the span of one week, we interviewed two individuals, and the subject at the top of their list was flexibility. While embracing the workload, they each emphasized their preference for a "quality of life" that would permit them the time to "have dinner with my son" or "watch my daughter play soccer."

Dynamic Managers must work to make flexibility a cultural norm in their organizations. Simply put, it must become "who you are" and "how you operate." It cannot be the slogan du jour mouthed by senior management or viewed as a weakness used by the needy and the lazy. One nonprofit CEO told us that he did not believe in "all of this" and would keep tabs on who was "abusing the system." Consequently, when he mouthed the words "People First" and "flexibility," staff would wait for a safe moment to snicker. Flexibility had not become a cultural norm in his organization.

The real challenge of course is not only declaring your organization "flexible" but also having real policies and programs that back up this declaration. Flexibility in the workplace can mean many things, such as flexible work hours so one parent can be home after school. It can mean flexible work weeks so a week's work can be done in four business days. Several organizations profiled in this book, such as Fannie Mae Foundation and Worksystems, Inc., highlighted in Chapter 7, effectively used job sharing as a means to accommodate individual worker circumstances and to retain two quality employees they did not want to lose. Many organizations also view telecommuting or working from home one or more days a week a viable option. They have found that this option not only makes for a happy employee but can also help alleviate the need for additional expensive office space.

Mobility and Freedom

People First cultures promote mobility and freedom. That means employees have the opportunity to advance themselves professionally through a new job, a promotion, new responsibilities, geographic relocation, or similar things. Obviously, people feel better about themselves and consequently their work when they believe they are moving in a forward direction. At Enterprise, we worked hard to create organization-wide and individual-specific opportunities for high-performing employees. As shown in Chapter 8, we created a new organizational chart, in part to reflect the alignment that we believed was necessary for the organization at the time, but also to create new management opportunities for talented staff who were eager and ready to advance. Wherever possible, we looked for chances to promote from within. Our favorite example is a public policy staff person who had been a Washington, D.C. lobbyist for a decade. He was an outstanding performer who had just secured a $10 million earmark for the organization on Capitol Hill but who did not want to reach his 40th birthday as a lobbyist. We committed to exposing him more to the program side of the business and to looking for opportunities to migrate him out of his policy work. For a year or so, we included him in many program discussions and had him visit with key program managers. When funding was secured for an expanded West coast program, we offered him a chance to start a new career without ever leaving our organization. We kept a talented employee who felt valued and rejuvenated.

Although traditional opportunities for advancement are important, we have found this factor to be less vital in the nonprofit world than the opportunity to have the freedom to dream and to take chances. People want to work in an organization that seems to be fueled by the power of ideas, where the organization is never satisfied, where new programs and ideas can come from anyplace, not just senior management, and where no idea is bad, it's an opportunity to learn. In an organization powered by ideas, employees feel mobile, not because they can get a more prestigious job, but because they can have an impact in ways they never thought possible.

A subset of the power of ideas is another key concept for us—supporting the insurgents. Insurgents are often younger employees, although this is certainly not a requirement, but they are typically people who have little formal power in the official organizational chart. They have great ideas, energy, and the potential to ignite change and spur creativity. As we describe in the *horizonMag.com* story later in this chapter, the actions of these insurgents, while often short-term in nature, can positively advance the purpose and cause of your nonprofit and confirm to all that you are powered by ideas, not just position and power.

Depending on your culture, these insurgents gain notice on their own accord or by a leader's effort to spark change. Insurgents need the Dynamic Manager to actively assist them by clearing a path for their work or by simply getting out of the way. As in the case with *horizonMag.com*, a successful insurgent effort can actually become part of the mainstream—turning the insurgents into managers of a whole new business line or product within the organization. One executive director told us that, "I recruit some people to throw bombs just so that we can shake this place up." Supporting the insurgents just might shake things up for the better.

Digital Spotlight—Support the Insurgents: The *horizonMag.com* Story

During our years at Enterprise, we tried a wide variety of activities and strategies to expand our traditional culture into a digital culture. We constantly sought out ways to create enthusiasm for the use of technology and opportunities for people, at all levels of the organization, to innovate and dream. As it turned out, creation of an online magazine, *horizonMag.com,* became an important vehicle for moving our culture and for creating a perfect platform for insurgents to combine their comfort with technology and their hunger for innovation.

Rey Ramsey actually birthed the idea of *horizonMag.com* on a long airplane ride. It was a byproduct of several factors: the launch of *George* magazine, John F. Kennedy, Jr.'s flashy, popular publication; the success of SLATE, an online publication; our ongoing organizational push toward technology; and our commitment to expanding our customer base. The idea was simple. *George* meets community development: an online magazine about the works of community development from a fresh, youthful perspective. The editorial goal would be to highlight people, celebrities, and everyday folks, and the enormous possibilities that are unleashed by their work in communities. The aim was threefold: (1) attract a new, younger audience to the work of revitalizing neighborhoods; (2) give them opportunities to become engaged in their communities; and (3) excite our internal audience (staff) to get turned on by technology. The trick would be how to get it done.

The first person recruited for this task was David Saunier, the 26-year-old head of online services. David jumped at the opportunity to design a prototype. In fact, David's first prototype was an amazing array of innovative design features and interactive possibilities. Alec Ross, then Rey's 25-year-old special assistant, was then added to the mix. Alec is a natural insurgent—talented, creative, and impatient. He immediately set out to connect other young people inside the organization like Chris Willey, the techno-star of the organization, and other Generation Xers to the effort. This group was now unleashed. They adopted "Project X" as their own and became determined to use it to create positive change. Our role was to just give them room to experiment and the resources and authority to proceed. We kept "Project X" quiet until it advanced further because we didn't want to get the project caught up in internal politics about where it "was to be housed" or in the naysaying that can often accompany new ideas.

Their efforts resulted in a product that was almost ready for prime time. We now needed to integrate their work into the organizational mainstream and to excite other staff members about its potential. We met with our communications department, headed by Sandra Gregg, and our publication director, Catherine Hyde. Catherine was tasked with taking the concept of Project X and turning it into a publication. Neither Sandra nor Catherine had ever produced an online publication and at various times expressed their unease; however, they gave it everything they had. They brought much-needed savvy and discipline to the project, while David, Alec, Chris, and later Gary Mendez brought youthful vision and creativity. We held an organizationwide contest to name the publication and selected *horizonMag.com* (People and Possibilities). The name *horizon* said it all. It represented exactly the message we were trying to send about technology—boundless optimism and hope for the future.

With the name in place, David completed the final design. The communications department produced a short video and CD-ROM to promote *horizon* and planned to unveil the magazine at our annual conference. In front of 1,500 unsuspecting community development practitioners, we darkened the room and delighted the audience with a mix of music from pop group REM and a montage of images and text depicting the inaugural edition of *horizon*. The insurgents and the communications department had pulled it off. The reviews were in. With no marketing budget, the magazine debuted to more than 100,000 hits in its first month. It soon was a bigger draw than our much-used technical Web site. People who had never before heard of us or our work were now contacting us. And our other goal—attracting and exciting an internal audience to the possibilities of technology—was soon realized. Internally, staff were volunteering to work on their own time for the magazine, and suddenly technology and its uses became a mainstream topic throughout the organization.

These young insurgents played a key role in this culture shift, but the value of this effort to the organization didn't stop there. As a result of Project X, Alec, David, and Chris sparked a

> new generation of leadership for the organization. We set out
> to change culture for the better and along the way we showed
> how the power of ideas and freedom to innovate can change
> individuals for the better as well. We supported the insurgents
> and got a huge return on our investment.

Diversity

No organization can claim to value people without embracing
diversity and the corresponding issue of tolerance in the workplace.
The term *diversity* historically brings to mind issues of race and gender. Today, however, it includes other issues such as age, national
origin, sexual orientation, and physical ability. Although federal
laws prohibit discrimination, diversity should not be viewed as a
compliance issue. It should be considered an asset that increases
your corporate IQ by expanding your collective understanding of a
wider range of issues and potential markets. As your knowledge
base and perspective expands, so too does your ability to innovate,
serve an ever-changing customer base, and thrive in the digital age.

What do we mean by diversity? We mean that people who work
in the organization should reflect the population that the organization serves and the community where the organization is located.
One of the most heartening things that we have heard over the past
two years, from for-profit and nonprofit organizations alike, is that
they believe their business suffers when they don't have the breadth
of ideas and views that come from a diverse staff. One high-tech
CEO who runs an online job placement agency put it well, "I now
regret locating in the suburbs where I don't really have access to a
diverse workforce. If our customer base is racially and ethnically
diverse, how am I going to serve them appropriately if I don't have
a workforce that understands them?" This concept is true for nonprofits as well. How can a homogeneous group of managers make
all the decisions for a diverse customer base and an ever-changing
community? Diversity is not just an issue of fairness and justice; it's
really about competition and business.

In our experience, diversity is pursued only after it has been
specifically articulated as a major business goal of the organization.
Once articulated, the organization is much more likely to invest the

resources necessary to make further diversification a reality and to measure progress toward this goal. People First cultures must commit to building a diverse workplace and take actions, large and small, to hire, promote, and retain staff who reflect the population that the organization serves and the community where the organization is located.

Valued and Fair Pay

People First cultures show people that they are valued by recognizing their contributions and paying them fairly. In fact, recognition often is as important to a nonprofit staff person as compensation. Staff work long hours for relatively low pay because they want to make a difference. Take the time to showcase staff members who are performing at high levels and making a high impact. The showcase can be modest as long as it is authentic and sincere. At Enterprise, the communications department created the Spirit of Enterprise Awards to acknowledge the special efforts of certain staff members on a quarterly basis. We sent out memos when targeted program goals were met or grants awarded that applauded the people who made those things happen. We did our best to publicly give credit where credit was due and share credit when it should be shared. We included people in meetings, inside and outside of the organization, as a way to show them that we valued their work, ideas, and efforts. Other organizations do similar things: cash awards for identifying a new funder; vacation days for recommending a new staff person; a parking space in front of the office for the Employee of the Month.

Although recognition is important, it is no substitute for fair pay. A March 2000 study of nonprofit organizations found what we all would expect: Nonprofits pay lower wages and their life insurance and pension benefits are less than the for-profit sector. The disparity between the two sectors has shrunk over the past decade, but it continues to exist and always will. So what does that mean for the People First culture? It means that nonprofit salaries must be competitive with similar organizations, and they should compensate their highest-performing staff based on that year's performance and contribution. They need to have compensation systems that have integrity and are transparent and fair.

One of the most logical changes in this area is the movement toward performance-based compensation (PBC), where every employee receives an annual salary that falls within a range. The range reflects the salaries paid by your competitors to people in similar positions. Every year, each employee sets performance goals with the manager. The organization designates a pool of money to compensate people based on that year's performance. Annually, all employees are reviewed at the same time by their managers. Employees who met their goals receive a merit raise, typically up to 7 percent for the year. Those who exceeded their goals are eligible for the bonus pool. Managers meet to discuss the highest-performing employees to see who should participate in the bonus pool. Those who contributed the most to the organization and whose contribution can be clearly articulated receive bonuses. Charlie Quatt and Judy Stein, from Quatt & Associates, a nonprofit human resource consulting firm, worked with nonprofits around the country to implement the PBC system, with great results. They have worked with organizations as diverse as the National Rural Defense Council and the Public Broadcasting Service (PBS) to the Enterprise and Fannie Mae foundations.

The Fannie Mae Foundation just finished its first full year of Performance Based Compensation (PBC) and was pleased. Employees are focused on performance, striving to exceed their managers' expectations on all major performance goals and objectives. There are no cost of living adjustments here—all salary increases are tied directly to an employee's performance. Some employee salaries remain unchanged due to performance results that fell below manager expectations, while other salaries increase significantly.

The bonus recognition system effectively awarded those employees who did the most for the organization. Less than a third of the staff who were eligible for cash bonuses actually received them. During "calibration meetings," as Kevin Smith calls them, the names of staff who were eligible for bonuses were put on the table and the foundation's senior management team had a robust discussion about their respective contributions to the organization. Each person's actual performance rating (e.g., "exceeds expectations") was set aside to account for possible grade inflation by different managers—the focus was exclusively on performance—the outputs and outcomes that resulted from each employee's contribution. "People just focused on performance," Smith says. "The process had an incredible amount of integrity."

Digital Spotlight—Recruiting Talent, Building Your Team

Organizations that can't hire and retain talent are at risk in the digital age. Although this has always been true, the forces of change at work in our industry magnify the importance of this issue. No one would really disagree with this statement, yet not nearly enough energy and time is spent on this part of the business. Dynamic organizations know that they are only as good as their people. They spend the time and energy necessary to ensure that they recruit and hire the talent they need.

The search for talent today must transcend traditional approaches. You must worry less about the length of the résumé and more about the person. Do they have the capacity to learn and grow? Can they handle change? Are they innovative? Think about adjectives like creative, flexible, team-oriented, mission-driven, and smart. Finding talent is more of an art than a science, so we share what we have learned about building a team in the following sections:

Recruit to Recruit

Adding talent is so important that it must not be left up to one individual or department. Do not expect the human resources department to find the people you need. Everyone at all levels should see themselves as the organization's recruiters. Dynamic Managers take an active interest in recruiting and spend time enlisting others in the process. Recruiting has to become part of your culture.

Create a Talent Pipeline

The most successful organizations look for talent even when there are no job openings. We have found that we lose out on the best candidates if we wait until we have an opening to start identifying them. Meetings, conferences, and other interactions can be fertile recruiting grounds. Look for talent in those settings and begin building a talent pipeline. Once you have met promising people, find a way to stay in touch with them and build an ongoing relationship. Simple gestures like e-mail, invitations to organizational events, newsletters, lunch dates, and so forth can be subtle and effective. If you and your staff do this all year long, you will soon have your pipeline.

Culture is *the* Asset in Recruiting

The vision, values, and people of your organization will contribute more to your recruiting success than anything else. Today, more people want to work in flexible work environments where people are valued, compensation is fair, and the opportunities to grow are abundant. Let the applicants see your culture.

Treat Applicants like Customers

Dynamic organizations treat applicants like customers. A good experience during the interview process has the potential to turn that applicant into a loyal employee, if hired, or a good-will ambassador for the organization, even if they are not hired. You can be sure that applicants will share their experience with others in the field. Make the interaction a marketing opportunity for the organization.

Use Technology to Augment Your Recruiting

Technology should enhance your recruiting efforts; it will never replace face-to-face interaction. Use technology to stay in touch with your talent pipeline, to convey a positive corporate image, and to post job openings; however, we have learned time and time again that most people take a job only after they have been able to establish a personal bond with the people with whom they will be working.

REFLECT AND REPOSITION

- What is the culture of your organization?
- Does your culture help you address the forces of change facing your organization?
- How are you working to sustain your culture?
- Does your vision provide inspiration to you and others?
- Do your values provide meaning to you and the organization?

- Will your values outlive any single person or group of people?
- Are you instilling the values of a digital culture in your organization?
- Do you really put people first in your organization?

GUIDING PRINCIPLES

- Vision inspires and establishes a north star; values define your core beliefs; and people, attracted by the vision and values, put this shared vision and values into action.
- A digital culture embraces digital solutions, worships the power of ideas, creates an ethos of learning, puts people first, and centers on the customer.
- Vision is a mental portrait of what success is that captures the heart (compelling enough to inspire) and the mind (credible enough to be attained). Vision is not a mission statement.
- Leaders must invent and communicate visions that are compelling, simple, clear, inclusive, and personal.
- Values must give meaning and guidance while helping to create a corporate soul.
- A People First culture is caring, flexible, diverse, shows people they are valued, and provides them with freedom, mobility, and fair pay.

NOTES

[1] Kevin Cashman, *Leadership from the Inside Out* (Utah: Executive Excellence Publishing, 1998), 169.

[2] Cashman, 31.

[3] James Champy, *Re-engineering Management: The Mandate for New Leadership* (New York: Harper Business, 1995), 77.

[4] James C. Collins and Jerry I. Porras, *Built to Last: Successful Habits of Visionary Companies* (New York: Harper Business, 1994), 73.

[5] Collins and Porras, 74.

[6] Malcolm Gladwell, *The Tipping Point* (Boston: Little Brown & Company, 2000).

[7]McKinsey & Company, *War for Talent* (2000). The McKinsey report actually listed the following four things: (1) The company genuinely cares about its people and the people care about the company. There is pride in being associated with the company's success and each person's role in it. (2) Great leaders treat people with trust and respect and honor the intelligence of all who contribute to the company. They balance guidance and guidelines with allowing for independence to accomplish great things. Great leaders build capacity in their people and help them unleash their talents. (3) People have to like what they do and the people they do it with. A great job can be demanding so long as a person finds it interesting and important. People feel good when they are valued. (4) Compensation ought to be attractive. Today money buys the house but it equally represents recognition and fairness. Talented people expect their contributions to be acknowledged and their compensation to reflect their impact on the company.

CHAPTER FIVE

The Business Model and the Customer

The culture establishes the tone and character of the organization, but the business model provides the organization's rationale for doing what it is doing in the manner that it is doing it. In the digital age, you must continuously reflect on the assumptions underlying your organization's business model. This means asking "Do we have the right customers and do we know what they want?" and "Are we providing the right products and services (what we call "content") so we can attract and retain these customers and the financial support that we need to continue to thrive?" If your focus on the customer or your content doesn't sing, then the business model is flawed even if your corporate culture is where you want it to be. This chapter helps you reflect on the first half of the business model, the customer. In addition to providing you with new ways to think about customer relationships, we also include strategies for repositioning your organization in order to build customer loyalty and expand your customer base.

DEFINING "BUSINESS MODEL"

We found our favorite definition of *business model* on the Internet: A business model provides "an architecture for product, service, and information flows, including a description of the various business actors and their roles; a description of the potential benefits for the various business actors; and a description of the sources of revenue."[1] For a nonprofit organization in the digital age, we believe that this means being able to articulate: (1) who you want your customers to be and how you expect to attract them and earn their loyalty (Chapter 5); (2) what your content is, how it distinguishes you from your competition and how you are going to deliver it, including taking advantage of all available technology to add value (Chapter 6); and (3) how your customers and content will result in the diversity and magnitude of financial support that you need (Chapter 7).

THE CUSTOMER

Reflecting on Your Customer

The backbone of every business model is the customer. Yet many organizations think of the people they serve as users, not customers. "Customer" seems to imply choice, payment, and expectations of service—concepts not commonly applied to our industry. Maybe, treating the people you serve as customers was not always necessary, but it is now. Why? The following forces of change are likely bringing your part of the nonprofit industry to its strategic inflection point.

Webification of the User. As the users of nonprofit organizations gain greater access to the Internet and the Internet culture becomes ingrained in American society (see Chapter 1), users are expecting nonprofits to work like the Web works. That means users increasingly will want to get relevant information in order to make informed choices about products and services that they want when and where they want them. They will want to be able to ask questions and get an immediate or almost immediate response. And they will want to be able to choose a more responsive service provider if their current provider is not meeting their needs. In short, the Web is making customers out of traditional users of nonprofit services and forcing nonprofits to build customer loyalty.

Consolidation and Competition in the Field. Not only is the user demanding to be treated like a customer, but today's organization must also retain loyal customers in order to survive in a changing nonprofit world. Nonprofits without a strong customer base, from hospitals and food banks to community-based organizations, are being lost to consolidation and/or competition. Consolidation is the process of reducing the number of nonprofit organizations performing the same or substantially similar service in a community, usually initiated by funders. Competition is the act of reducing the number of nonprofit organizations performing the same or substantially similar service in a community, usually initiated by users who vote with their feet and go to a competing organization for their services. Either way it means change.

Increasingly, nonprofits are also seeing competition coming from the for-profit sector. This for-profit "encroachment" has almost always been true in the cultural arts but is ever more prevalent in health care, social services, housing, and community development. John Ball, President of Worksystems, Inc. in Portland, Oregon, puts it best, "The private, for-profit sector is our standard of competition." In either case, the nonprofit that has failed to create a lot of loyal customers is at serious risk in the digital age.

This phenomena is happening throughout America. Nonprofit hospitals have already been through their strategic inflection point. Some hospitals consolidated. Some hospitals competed and survived. Some hospitals disappeared. As noted in Chapter 3, in New York, two organizations serving the needs of young people through technology, MOUSE (Making Opportunities for Upgrading Schools and Education) and HEAVEN (Helping Educate, Activate, Volunteer and Empower via the Net), recently merged to better serve their market. In Portland, Oregon, five nonprofit housing development organizations in the city's northeast sector have been working for three years to consolidate into one or two groups. The local government has finally decided that it is wasting limited public funds paying for overhead in multiple organizations serving the same population. As highlighted later in this chapter, the country's two largest nonprofit antihunger organizations, Second Harvest and Foodchain, announced a merger to achieve scale and create a more efficient system for both collecting and distributing nonperishable foods, such as boxes of cereal and cans of soup and prepared food, such as ready-to-eat surplus from banquets, cafeterias, and restaurants, to the tables of hungry Americans.

Repositioning to Retain, Attract, and Expand Customer Base

Dynamic organizations are constantly repositioning themselves to ensure that they stay customer-focused. They aggressively work to make themselves "sticky" or to keep loyal customers by communicating with them regularly and providing them with an ever-increasing number of choices. But sticky customers may not be enough in the digital age; you may need to constantly seek to expand your customer base as well.

Making Oneself "Sticky": Building Customer Loyalty. In the Internet culture, customer loyalty is often referred to as "stickiness." The stickier a site, the more often customers come back and the longer they stay. Stickiness matters a lot in the digital age. We have found that it is often achieved through robust communications and expanded customer choices.

Robust Communications with Customers

A sticky communications strategy is multifaceted. The nonprofit regularly directs communications to the customer, creates ways for the customer to directly communicate with the organization, and helps customers talk to each other.

Regularly Direct Communications to Your Customers. Organizations should regularly direct communications to their customers for the following reasons:

- *To tell them what's new.* Customers need to know what new products and services are being offered by the organization so they can use them. The more they use your services, the more loyal they become.

- *To tell them about services they have not yet used but should consider using.* This is classic Internet behavior. When you are considering buying a book on amazon.com, you are often told that other people who bought that book also have been interested in specific other books. This also can be referred to as the "accessory" approach to sales. A good salesperson always tries to sell you an accompanying accessory whenever you buy a suit or dress. Once a customer has decided to do business with you, they are considerably more likely to do more business with you.

- *To show successes and build customer community.* Everybody likes a winner. The more you show people how your products and services have helped other people, the easier it is for them to understand how you could help them.
- *To get new customers.* Organizational anonymity helps no one. The more often people hear about you, the more likely it is that they will think of you when they need your products and services and refer you to others who do.

Regular communications directed to customers can be easy. More important, it should be varied. Successful dynamic organizations use some or all of the following to communicate with their customers:

- *E-mail.* You must ensure that every customer you have has an e-mail address. In today's world, through services such as thebeehive (www.thebeehive.org), hotmail (www.hotmail .com) or Yahoo! (www.yahoo.com), you can help your customer get an e-mail address and password for free in less than two minutes. Ben Hecht's eight-year-old did it himself in four minutes. You then need to make e-mail communications an essential part of your customer relationship and your delivery of products and services. Whether people access e-mail at home, at work, in a computer learning center, or at a kiosk in the mall, this simple effort on your part will go a long way toward helping your customer become more comfortable with technology and the Internet culture.
- *Written materials.* Although the Internet is hot, newsletters, magazines, brochures, and newspapers that tell people about you and your work are still important. Although the *Washington Post* is online every day, we still buy a paper and read it with breakfast each morning. Most people still like to sit down with a hard copy of something to read it.
- *Web site.* Your corporate Web site can and should be a hub for communicating with your customer. It should be a place where key information, products, and services that you want to provide to customers are always available; where customers can tell you what is important to them and what they think of

you; and where customers can interact and get what they believe they need from their fellow customers. We talk more about Web sites in Chapters 6 and 7.

Create Ways for Customers to Communicate Directly with You. Sticky organizations also create a variety of ways for their customers to communicate directly to them to achieve the following goals:

- *To find out what is on their minds.* You cannot know what your customers are thinking about or what is currently important to them unless you actually ask them. This may seem obvious, but unfortunately it is seldom done because the organization either has no vehicle for asking these questions or it doesn't know what to do with the information once it gets it.

- *To determine how they think the organization is performing.* Nonprofit organizations seldom ask their customers if they are satisfied with their performance. This means that the organization continually misses chances to better serve its customers and to improve itself. It is a simple fact of human nature that people and organizations assume that everything is going well and don't change unless they are directly told something to the contrary.

- *To gauge what new products and services they want.* This might be considered a more particular subset to the previous issue of finding out what is on their mind. There simply is no better way to determine which new products and services to develop and provide than to ask your customers what they want and need.

- *To understand your competition.* The trends of consolidation and competition, as discussed earlier in this chapter, make it critically important for organizations to understand their competition. There is no better way to know what your competitor is doing than to ask your customers and see what they know and if they in fact have used other nonprofits to secure substantially similar products and services from another organization. This data collection also can help you determine what other products and services your customers want and influence your new product development work.

Customers can communicate directly with you in several ways:

- *Focus groups.* Focus groups are simply small numbers of customers brought together to answer questions and tell you what is on their minds. Depending on available resources, customers can be selected and the group meetings facilitated by professionals or by staff. The easiest way to conduct a focus group is often as an add-on to an already scheduled event where you know that a good cross-section of customers will be in attendance.

- *E-mail surveys.* Once your customers are on e-mail and regularly using it, you can ask them to answer brief e-mail surveys to capture their current state of mind and opinion about your organization and its work.

- *Random reaching out by the CEO.* Every chief executive needs to randomly, but regularly and in a structured way, reach out to customers and talk to them. This can and should be as simple as e-mailing and calling a handful of customers each month and asking them about the organization, its staff, its products and services, and the customer's hopes and concerns for themselves and the organization.

Create Ways for Customers to Talk with Each Other. The digital age is single-handedly responsible for this new and fast-growing approach to building customer loyalty. Unlike the previous two categories that require your nonprofit to be either the sender or the receiver of information, your role here is simply one of convenor or facilitator. Dynamic organizations that successfully bring customers together build customer loyalty not by continually proving what they know but by their willingness (and self-confidence) to be quiet and let customers talk to each other, even if it is about you. In the parlance of the Internet, you are building a community online.

This approach can set your organization apart from the competition by creating a value-added community for your customers. America is a country of joiners. People like to be a part of a larger group working toward a common goal. In many nonprofit fields, customers have few opportunities to join such a community. Organizations that can create a platform where customers feel comfortable coming, staying, and talking with each other position themselves as a trusted convenor, without the appearance of self-promotion or advocating a philosophical agenda. Moreover, this approach provides the organization with a much-needed vehicle for getting communications directly from customers.

There are many ways to bring your customers together to communicate with each other. The best place to do it is often on your Web site. You can make it easier for people to talk to each other and share information, such as on bulletin boards (people post stuff that others can look at and respond to), in chat rooms (where people can ask questions, have others answer them, and have all the questions and answers stored for use by other customers—these can be live or in real-time or ongoing), through e-mail listservs (a self-selected list of e-mail addresses generated by the participants so when one person on the list has something to say they share it with everyone else on that list), and in moderated discussion forums (super chat rooms where staff or other customers act as moderators and try to stimulate and direct the discussions around particular issues). See our Web site, www.managingnonprofits.org, for the most current and best examples of nonprofits who are using these mechanisms to build community.

Whether you utilize one or more of these interactive mechanisms on your Web site to build your community, people who focus on this work have found that the best online communities have the following characteristics:

- *Interactive and built on the concept of many-to-many communications.* There should always be multiple opportunities for people to communicate with each other and to share their knowledge. Communities are the opposite of one-on-one personal conversations. They involve a lot of discussions going on at the same time with lots of opinions.

- *Designed to attract and retain community members who become more than superficially involved in community events and are able to make new friends through the community.* Online communities get people to act, like signing and e-mailing a petition, hosting a moderated discussion forum, or commenting on a document that is forwarded to everyone on an e-mail listserv.

- *A single defining focus that gives people a reason to return.* The community should have an identity that differentiates it from other sites. This is usually based on a narrow, shared interest such as nonprofit housing developers of HIV/AIDS housing, in-home child care providers in distressed urban areas, or people with family members who have breast cancer.

- *Content that meets the needs of members and puts a premium on member-generated content.* The online community should have information, products, and services specifically relevant and tailored to the interests of the community. An online community built for survivors of homicide victims would likely have a place where people could post their personal stories and pictures; an ongoing discussion forum for people to share their thoughts and feelings; and an advice column from psychologists who have experience helping people through both the event and the loss that they experience in the years that follow. The content hits home and is generated, from the heart, by participants. Nothing could be more sticky.

- *An openness to competitive information and access to the community by anyone who wants in.* This is often difficult for groups that are hosting the online community because they don't want to share their customers with anyone else; however, to paraphrase the great U.S. Supreme Court Justice Felix Frankfurter "as is often said, the solution to bad speech is more speech." You will build a stronger, more loyal community if they can see your willingness to let ideas flow freely—even those ideas that are critical of you or supportive of something you don't like. Never underestimate the power of being a neutral platform for ideas and the goodwill you will build from that.

- *A commercial orientation.* Give your members opportunities to act on their interests on your site. For example, pointing to an online bookstore to find out more about issues that are a part of a heated debate taking place on your site can be helpful and appreciated. The problem is knowing where to draw the line. In our experience, an online community that is obviously designed to promote consumerism and not the shared interest of the community will not be successful. On our One Economy consumer site, described in Chapter 9, we encourage and cajole people into becoming part of the economic mainstream through basic banking and investing services. We show them how much money they are wasting at check cashing stores and how much they could save at a bank—then we connect them directly to one of our banking partners to open an account. The commercialism is fundamental to the type of community we are trying to build.[2]

Wally Bock, an online commentator, states: "Communities are characterized by three things: common interests, frequent interaction, and identification." He posits that all three things must be present for an online space to be a community.[3]

Digital Spotlight—America's Second Harvest: How to Better Center in on the Customer through Mergers and Technology

Every year more than $1 billion in nonperishable and prepared food is rescued from food manufacturers, restaurants, and stores and made available to nonprofit organizations dedicated to feeding the hungry. From 1992 to 2000, this "food rescue" work was done by two different organizations. America's Second Harvest was the larger, more venerable of the two, with a $14 million annual budget and 190 affiliated food banks around the country. Since 1980, it focused its efforts on the collection and distribution of primarily nonperishable foods, such as boxes of cereal and cans of soup. Second Harvest would receive almost $500 million in food donations and distribute one billion pounds of food to 26 million people a year. The other organization was the eight-year-old "upstart" Foodchain. With an operating budget of less than $1 million and 70 affiliated local food programs, Foodchain would receive and distribute about $350 million in donated ready-to-eat surplus food from banquets, cafeterias, and restaurants and worked to distribute the food to its affiliates in time to make it to the tables of hungry Americans.

But all was not well in the food rescue business. Second Harvest and Foodchain both faced serious threats. For Second Harvest, food supplies were steadily dropping, demand for prepared meals was skyrocketing, and it was not equipped to distribute cooked meals. Simply put, Second Harvest's biggest customers, donors such as Pizza Hut and the Marriott hotel chain, were offering more prepared meals and fewer canned goods. Add to that the view in the field by its other customers, local food banks and food rescue organizations, that it was too big a bureaucracy and too slow to adapt to change. In fact, in the age of technology, Second Harvest was still notifying affiliates of available food product by fax. Foodchain had its own issues. It didn't have enough staff or funding to keep up with the increasing availability of prepared foods or the expanding demand by affiliates for this product to meet the needs of working families newly off the welfare roles.

The food rescue industry now had a large organization focusing on a declining part of the market and a small organization attending to the fast-growing segment of the industry. Donors of food and money to both organizations began questioning why the groups couldn't work together. Second Harvest board members, especially those from the corporate side who were donating the food, pushed its management to work toward a merger. Bruce Rohde, chief executive of ConAgra Inc., one of Second Harvest's biggest donors put it well, "Every business person knows consolidation is a natural effect of time and learning. It's true in business and in nonprofits. You don't need two of everything."

In 2000, the two organizations became one, with great expectations about efficiencies and scale. Deborah Leff, Second Harvest's President and CEO, called it the "Time Warner" of nonprofit mergers. "We're the best at what we do," she said. "But there's this new, exciting growth piece that's the wave of the future." She cited several immediate benefits to the industry, including operating more efficiently and effectively, sharing financial, administrative, and human resources; while avoiding redundancy in efforts and better coordinating efforts to reach donors and communicate the urgency of hunger to the media.

The two organizations also believe the merger will strengthen existing partnerships among the food industry, food banks, food rescue efforts, and innovative programs being implemented on a local level. For instance, in Raleigh, the Second Harvest affiliate, Food Bank of North Carolina, has partnered with the Foodchain member, Inter-Faith Food Shuttle, to have the Community Kitchen program provide prepared foods to the local Kids Cafes.

People from the community are able to learn culinary skills and get job training, while preparing nutritious meals for the many children who depend on the Kids Cafes.

While the merger may address many of these redundancies and bring Second Harvest's resources to the new opportunities in prepared food built by Foodchain, it did not address the issues that many local affiliates had with the Second Harvest bureaucracy—enter technology and David Prendergast. Second Harvest recruited Prendergast from Baxter Healthcare, a Fortune 500 medical technology company to help bring the organization into the digital age. At Baxter, Prendergast was part of a large systems group that applied technology in a complicated corporate setting. He learned first-hand about the benefits and burdens of building systems in-house versus outsourcing them. He was attracted to Second Harvest by their mission, the ability to be a prime technology decision maker, and the chance to see direct and immediate impact from his work.

Prendergast came to Second Harvest and saw an exceptional senior management team that was struggling with a lot of things technology-wise. It was having a hard time staying current and attracting talent. More important, it was seeing the world changing around it without any idea what it should be doing to stay competitive. It knew that it could provide significantly more to its customers through technology but didn't know what or how. Prendergast saw his challenge: how to provide technology leadership and improve the effectiveness of the overall network of loosely connected local affiliates that the organization has no command and control over. At Second Harvest, it was not a matter of making a technology choice, articulating it, and then watching everyone follow—lock, stock, and barrel. Prendergast knew that his technology agenda had to provide all of his customers, local affiliates, and corporate donors with a compelling vision of the future and work hard to remove obstacles for customers to make it as easy as possible for them to participate.

Prendergast identified five areas where technology solutions were needed. Three of them were focused on improving the relationship between Chicago headquarters and local affiliates through better communications: e-mail, an Intranet, and a wide area network. A fourth solution focused on a specific product application: a uniform inventory management system. The fifth went to the heart of the mission and the relationship between Second Harvest, its affiliates, and its food donors: a food allocation system that would feed into the other systems and the donor systems. He built his solutions with three key principles in mind: (1) provide flexibility and choice—affiliates want choices so they can integrate headquarters' ideas into the way they do business; (2) Web-enable as many applications as possible; and (3) outsource technology infrastructure and Web hosting to the maximum extent possible.

Prendergast systematically set out to make things happen. Using an outsourced e-mail application service provider and the help of Second Harvest's fundraising department, he was able to make it easier for all network members to communicate with Second Harvest and vice versa through free e-mail accounts with a "@secondharvest.org" address. For the first time, Second Harvest could send out an e-mail to executive directors of all affiliated food bank and food rescue organizations and be sure they received the message. Before this new system was implemented, Second Harvest relied on an outdated "ccmail" system that connected with no more than two-thirds of these local leaders. For those local affiliates that wanted to maintain their own e-mail identity, Prendergast made sure that Second Harvest's "@secondharvest.org" e-mails would be automatically forwarded to an affiliate's existing e-mail address.

Prendergast designed the Intranet to further facilitate information sharing and the ability of local affiliates to talk with each other. Once the Intranet, an internal communication system, was available to everyone in the Second Harvest family, people started to find the best uses for it. One of the first things to migrate to the Intranet was the food bank-to-food bank sharing of surplus food. Historically, food banks would have used the ccmail system for notifying other food banks that they had excess food available. It could take days for an organization's offer to be available to everyone else in the network under the old system. Now, local affiliates post their excess inventory on a real-time bulletin board that people can react to instantly.

Prendergast knew that Second Harvest had to help affiliates get faster Internet access if his vision of moving more than e-mail and the Intranet to the Internet was going to happen. This meant facilitating wide area networks that local affiliates could connect to with relative ease. Through participation at regional meetings held by affiliates with Second Harvest, Prendergast heard about great work that Cisco Systems had been doing with affiliates and wide area networks in California and North Carolina. With very little prodding, Cisco agreed to help expand their support nationwide. By providing deep discounts on routers and firewall equipment, Cisco is helping local affiliates to upgrade their high-speed connections and making them available to a whole network within the affiliate, not just one desktop.

This increased bandwidth will be one of the main reasons that Second Harvest's new food allocation system is going to transform food rescue in America. This new system, ResourceLink, is the perfect example of how technology can radically change old ways of doing business and serve all customers better. ResourceLink is a consortium of diverse companies that have pooled their resources to help Second Harvest. Sponsored by Hewlett-Packard, and managed and developed by Cyber Surplus, Inc., the group includes representatives from food manufacturers, transportation companies, government agencies, and charities.

ResourceLink is like a virtual warehouse. Food companies can go online to post inventory available for donation. No phone calls, faxes, and paperwork are necessary. The system securely stores all donor information, including details of previous donations. This one step alone saves hours of reentering basic information. Once Second Harvest accepts the donation, ResourceLink automatically links to an alliance of shipping companies that often can provide no-cost or low-cost transportation. At the same time, Second Harvest member food banks can instantly see what's available and order the products they need using a few easy steps. By linking givers and receivers quickly and efficiently, ResourceLink helps ensure that donations reach as many people as possible. Also, more efficient distribution mechanisms allow Second Harvest to accept a larger volume of food donations that might otherwise go to waste. With the ResourceLink network in place, Second Harvest can quickly accept and remove surplus products to free up donors' valuable warehouse space; landfill space isn't taken up with tons of discarded products; and transportation is provided to donors on request. The donation process is extremely simplified; more meals are served; and everybody wins. Prendergast believes that ResourceLink will cut donation time from eight days to two days.

Only still in the beta testing stage, ResourceLink has already changed the way some of Second Harvest's main corporate customers do business—to the benefit of Second Harvest. Kraft Foods has now converted its entire national distribution system to the ResourceLink application. Now Kraft warehouse participates on its own without all donations having to be reviewed by headquarters. This has allowed more food to be captured by the food rescue industry. Pillsbury has also made important changes. Because of ResourceLink, as a Pillsbury product ages, it goes from Pillsbury's SAP database to ResourceLink's Oracle database and automatically becomes available for distribution. Food is available as a result of preestablished business rules, without human intervention to slow it down.

Of all of the technology issues, the uniform inventory management system has been the most problematic. In fact, this issue remains incomplete. Prendergast shares the story of Second Harvest licensing a complicated software application for use by local affiliates, which never caught on. He knew this approach was flawed when he was out pitching it to some affiliates and they innocently asked if Second Harvest was using the software to manage its inventory. When he had to answer no to that question, Prendergast realized that if they weren't using it, then it was unlikely they could get affiliates to do so. He learned a great lesson about modeling behavior.

Prendergast cites the organization's capacity and commitment to listening as a key reason for its cultural turnaround. On a formal basis, every two years, Second Harvest staff visit each affiliate to review its food handling and management practices.

This enables Second Harvest not only to see and talk to local affiliates in detail but also to find out what is exciting and rich about what they are doing that Second Harvest can share with the rest of the network. In addition, Second Harvest also attends regional meetings held by affiliates every year to foster communication.

America's Second Harvest is building a customer-centered, dynamic organization one step at a time: achieving new market share and economies of scale through merger activities, increasing communications with customers by providing them with e-mail and meeting them where they work and regionally, strengthening loyalty by facilitating discussions among customers through an Intranet, and using technology to fundamentally transform the way they have historically done business.

EXPANDED CUSTOMER CHOICES

In the digital age, communications may not be enough to build stickiness. Organizations also must aggressively try to provide their customers with more choices. Most often, that means providing more content, delivered in more ways.

More Content. Content is simply what you provide to customers, whether it be products or services. The organizations that can provide more products and services that customers want will and should prevail in the end. Chapter 6 discusses content in much greater detail. In that chapter we highlight the qualities that an organization should have if it wants to develop the best content possible, as well as those elements that consistently make good content better.

More Ways. The stickiest organizations not only look to provide more content, but they also look for new and compelling ways to do so. That often means that they look to create as many "points of contact" or ways to communicate with or deliver content to their customers as possible. Today's dynamic organizations commonly use all of the following points of contact to provide their products and services:

- *Live*—Such as customer walk-ins to office or staff house-visits to customers
- *E-mail*—As discussed earlier in this chapter, to provide updates, check-in with customers, advocacy alerts to promote action, and provide test results
- *Internet*—Including 24-hour access to relevant information, support groups, and discussion forums, as discussed more fully in Chapter 6
- *Intranet*—A closed network available only to select customers and employees
- *Mail/publications*
- *Community forums*
- *Toll-free numbers* with voice mail portals for customers and staff

---

Digital Spotlight—ONE/Northwest: Communicating with Your Customers and Providing More Choices

ONE/Northwest was founded in August 1995, in large part with the support of one of America's leading venture philanthropists, Paul Brainard. ONE/Northwest works to provide the communication tools of the new economy—high-speed Internet access, networking, e-mail listservs—to nonprofits engaged in environmental activism and advocacy. The founders saw the power of the technology to do three things: (1) increase communications and move information between people and organizations; (2) help nonprofits shape information in order to change public and political opinions; and (3) bring new customer voices to the environmental movement.

Programmatically, ONE/Northwest provides an ever-expanding menu of content choices to the more than 1,200 customers they have touched to date. These products and services include the following:

- *Network trainers*—support staff placed around the Northwest region to provide hands-on training and consulting to local organizations

- *Networking projects*—equipment, consulting, and training to local organizations
- *Strategic technology planning*—help to nonprofits to develop a technology plan for their operations
- *Volunteer matching program*—pairing of individuals from the Seattle-area technology community with local conservation groups
- *ONEList*—monthly bulletin updates on technology and environment
- *Web University*—e-mail-based training workshops that teach organizations to design and maintain a Web site
- *Networking projects*—on-site service to build local networks among groups
- *Listserv hosting*—maintenance of local e-mail listserv services for local organizations
- *On-call troubleshooting*

ONE/Northwest's Web site offerings, highlighted often in Chapters 6 and 7, may be the single best site on the Internet for nonprofits who want to do their own technology planning, build a Web site, and use technology to do their work better. ONE/Northwest sees a significant role for itself in expanding the ability of small nonprofits to use emerging technology to increase their programmatic effectiveness. But to them, the first step in that process is always to understand the local issues of the conservation groups and to "meld our communications style, which is very technical, to [our partner's] communications styles," says Denise Jones, the Executive Director. "We start where they are, we don't tell them to come to [us]."

ONE/Northwest has built an ethos of listening that allows them to work in diverse communities, from Native American tribal lands to remote rural landscapes and urban conservation efforts. One way they keep in touch with their partners is through their ONEList service, a monthly e-mail newsletter that provides the latest information on technology tools and techniques in online communication. Another method is through their Technology Trainers, staff positions that they have moved out into the field to work locally with conservation groups by networking them together and providing on-site troubleshooting.

Another way that the organization communicates with its customers is through the convening of its advisory board. ONE/Northwest has asked some of "the brightest minds in our region . . . from the high-tech community in Seattle, to volunteer their brain power in bimonthly "brain trust" meetings to ask them 'OK, what are you doing in your dot.com, for-profit world that we should be looking out and preparing for?'" states Denise Jones.

This listen-first approach combined with their expansive content choices has resulted in small and remote rural organizations now finding a voice in regional and even national discussions. The Southeast Alaska Conservation Council (SEACC) needed the testimony of local residents to help block a timber sale in an already badly fragmented area of Prince of Wales Island in the Tongass National Forest. SEACC was one of ONE/Northwest's first "office technology makeovers" in 1996, and after that, their entire organization became skilled electronic activists. SEACC had planned to fly in to this remote location to conduct in-person interviews, but shortly before the deadline, bad weather moved in and shut down air travel in the region. Even worse, the only fax machine in this tiny community was out of order. Fortunately, one of SEACC's local activists had a computer and a scanner—and through ONE/Northwest's help, he knew how to use it for electronic organizing. In a small boat, he traveled around the community to gather residents' handwritten statements. Then he scanned them into his computer and e-mailed them to SEACC.

SEACC got the comments in on time, won their lawsuit, and blocked the cutting of Lab Bay. "E-mail and ONE/Northwest saved our bacon at the last minute," observed Tim Bristol, SEACC Field Organizer. "E-mail allows for rich, timely communication, which made a critical difference in our ability to protect Lab Bay from the chainsaw." This is one example of how ONE/Northwest's ability to communicate and understand its customers, combined with its programmatic focus of maximizing technology's impact on environmental advocacy, has allowed the people living with the consequences of land policy to participate in the political process that shapes their lives.

EXPANDING YOUR CUSTOMER BASE

Communicating with your customers and providing them with more content choices will create greater customer loyalty. Dynamic nonprofits, however, are also developing ways to not just keep existing customers, but also to expand their base. We have seen this happening in four ways: groups are making new markets, expanding their geographic focus, expanding the demographic makeup of who they are willing to serve, and recruiting new customers.

Making New Markets

Historically, most nonprofits have accepted the fact that their customers are limited to those people who know them and use their content. More and more, however, dynamic organizations are developing content designed to go after new markets—customers that do not traditionally use their products and services. This can range from daily free concerts (compared to average ticket prices of $35–60) at the Kennedy Center for Performing Arts in Washington, D.C. that focus on cultures and music not commonly heard to the weekend and evening executive MBA programs offered by graduate schools to attract busy executives.

Expanding Geographic Focus

Another common approach to expanding your customer base is broadening the geographic area that you serve and/or exporting your knowledge and expertise to other organizations and jurisdictions. Unless your organization is limited geographically by mission, charter, or political realities, you should be able to build on your current customer base by expanding where you are willing to work and using your current customers to vouch for your work to others. Where local geographic expansion is not viable, dynamic nonprofits are considering ways to provide their content and expertise beyond their current boundaries. Organizations like Job Link (www.joblink.org) in Minneapolis, Minnesota and CitySkills in Boston, Massachusetts, have made expanding their geographic focus an essential part of their work. They have looked to export their experience or build dynamic collaboratives with partners in other locations to affect more people. Job Link, a centralized, electronic job listing service that provides thousands of job listings annually to small, community-based workforce development organizations in the Twin Cities, is helping create similar services in other parts of the country. CitySkills (www.

cityskills.org) provides job training and placement services in the areas of Web design, network administration, and help desk staffing to urban youth in Boston. They are using their experience and relationships with the high-tech industry to create a database of best practices in the industry and a network of high-performing nonprofit organizations that are doing similar work nationwide.

Expanding Demographics Served

Similarly, many dynamic organizations are expanding their customer base by recognizing the changing demographics of populations in their own geographic target area and acting accordingly. This often means hiring a more culturally diverse staff, developing bilingual capabilities in-house, and working to change the culture of the organization to make it more tolerant of cultural differences. Calvary Multicultural Bilingual Learning Center (www.cmblc.org) which began 20 years ago as a small church-based child care program for Latino youth and their families in the Columbia Heights neighborhood in Washington, D.C., now has a $6 million facility providing early childhood education, child care, computer training and access, financial literacy, homeownership training, dance and photography classes, and more. To evolve their organization and their facility into a community hub, Calvary had to look beyond their traditional Latino base to African-American and Asian-American staff and families. A closer look at Calvary can be found in Chapter 8.

Recruiting New Customers

The other obvious way to expand your customer base is to recruit new customers. Traditionally, this has been done through marketing efforts such as advertising, public service announcements, and building relationships with other organizations and government agencies that act as conduits for customers; however, the Internet has changed all of that dramatically. Expanding membership online has been an incredibly effective strategy for many organizations. The World Wildlife Fund (www.wwf.org) has added more than 120,000 new members since allowing people to join online in 1996. Environmental Defense, as highlighted in Chapter 2, has used the expansion of its online content to dramatically increase its membership base. Environmental Defense (www.environmentaldefense.org) believes that they have increased their reach by more than 400,000 people a year through their online activities.

SUSTAINABILITY

A business model is not just about customers or even content—it's about sustainability. Your business model must allow you to raise or earn enough money to operate and innovate. All the customers in the world and the hottest content imaginable doesn't really matter if they don't translate into the money that you need to pay the bills. Today, more diverse funding opportunities exist than ever before. We describe them in Chapter 7 and provide guidance for repositioning your fundraising efforts so you can build a sustainable business model.

Digital Spotlight—Exploratorium: Expanding Your Customer Base

The Exploratorium is a museum of "science, art, and human perception" located in San Francisco, California. Online since 1993, the Exploratorium was one of the first science museums to build a site on the Web. Included in the site (www.exploratorium.org) are more than 10,000 Web pages and hundreds of sound and video files, exploring hundreds of different topics. The museum currently serves 7 million visitors a year on the site—nearly seven times the number of visitors who show up in person at the museum in San Francisco. That makes it one of the most visited museum Web sites in the world.

The Exploratorium's Web site is an extension of the experiences on the museum's floor. They have created "real" things for people to explore and interact with, not "virtual exhibits." The medium of the Internet makes it possible for the museum to reach homes and schools all over the world. This access has changed the way formal and informal learning takes place, both in the classroom and in the home. The Exploratorium online, and the resources it provides, are available 24 hours a day, worldwide, to anyone with an Internet connection.

Many of the resources on the Exploratorium's Web site are examples of simple uses of information technology, but they are thoughtfully implemented. For example, the site contains instructions for more than 200 simple experiments, all of which may be viewed on any type of Web browser, with even the slowest connection, and easily printed out.

Other types of content have required more creative use of existing or new technologies. In order to demonstrate certain phenomena, for instance, the museum has created a variety of online exhibits using Shockwave technology, which allows visitors to interact with the activity. Many of these online exhibits are patterned after real exhibits on the museum floor. In a few cases, the online versions have provided a richer experience than their physical counterparts.

The Exploratorium's newest experiments with information technology have revolved around Webcasting, in which the museum broadcasts live video and/or audio directly from the museum floor (or from satellite feeds in the field) onto the Internet. Webcasts provide access to special events, scientists, and other museum resources for audiences on the Web. Using video and audio with text-based articles and features lets a visitor choose among different methods of learning about a particular topic. Video and audio also provide the ability to hear or view interviews with scientists, meet interesting people, or tour unusual locations, from factories to rainforests.

The Web audience has given the Exploratorium positive feedback on the use of new technology. This may be because technology is not used for its own sake; instead, it is used when it's the best or the only way to provide information. The museum is careful when implementing a new technology to be sure that whatever is done or created online is as accessible to visitors as possible.

But more than the use of technology, what makes the Exploratorium's site unique is its approach to developing content. The focus is on investigating science behind the ordinary subjects and experiences of people's lives. The topics themselves provide "hooks" that get people excited about science. Then, when they investigate these topics, "surfer" scientists can also look at the historical and social issues surrounding them, thus providing a context for scientific exploration.

The Exploratorium's Web site, like the museum itself, is a work in progress, continuing to grow and provide visitors with meaningful, revealing experiences.

REFLECT AND REPOSITION

- Can you define your business model?
- Who are your customers and who would you want to be your customers?
- Are you providing the right products and services so you can attract and retain these customers and the financial support that you need to continue to thrive?
- Is your business model sustainable or expandable?
- How do you expect to attract customers and earn their loyalty?
- Do you direct communications to your customers, create ways for your customers to communicate with you, and help your customers talk to each other?
- Can you define what your value-added proposition is for your customers?

GUIDING PRINCIPLES

- Thoroughly understand and be able to articulate your business model.
- Your customer is the backbone of your business model.
- Customer loyalty or stickiness is critical as customers increasingly become "webified" and competition and consolidation in the nonprofit sector grows.
- Communicating with your customers and providing them with more content choices will create greater customer loyalty.
- Technology should be one of your primary vehicles for increasing communications with your customers and facilitating communications among your customers.
- Build your customer base by making new markets, expanding your geographic focus, and recruiting new customers.

NOTES

[1] www.hkkk.fi/~tuunaine/37d070/luennot/l2/tsld006.htm

[2] John Hagel III and Arthur G. Armstrong, *Net Gain: Expanding Markets through Virtual Communities* (Boston: Harvard Business School Press, 1997).

[3] Previously posted at www.bockinfo.com

CHAPTER SIX

Content—Products and Services

The business model of the dynamic organization is built around the customer. The Dynamic Manager knows who the organization's customers are, understands and anticipates their needs, and always looks for ways to deepen the relationship with them. Ultimately, however, the business model will rise or fall, and the customer will stay or go, based on content—the array of products and services that you can provide them and the ease by which they can access your content. In the digital age, content is king.

REFLECTING ON CONTENT

What is Content?

Simply put, content is what you do—what you provide to your customers. It includes products and services. Although there really is no great need to draw a line between what is a product and what is a service; generally, the two can be distinguished as follows:

Products. A nonprofit provides *products* when it intends for its programmatic efforts to result in customers having in their possession something they can see, touch, and feel. These would include such diverse things as affordable housing units, theater/cultural performances, museum exhibits, plasma, food, training manuals, organizational self-assessment tools, and other written information.

Services. A nonprofit provides *services* when it intends for its programmatic efforts to benefit customers directly but not in a way that results in customers having something in their possession they can see, touch, or feel. Examples of services include job training and placement, issue advocacy, fundraising and board training assistance, health care, nutrition advice and counseling, HIV/AIDS testing, volunteer coordination, and maintaining online classrooms and discussion forums.

Common Characteristics of Successful Organizations

We have found that organizations that continually develop excellent content have the following characteristics in common:

They Incubate. Dynamic organizations are always incubating new ideas for products and services. Every organization should have a mechanism for people to safely bring forward new ideas about products and services and a laboratory to try out these new approaches. When we talk about safety, in this regard, we mean a process that encourages experimentation and protects people from ridicule. In fact, the most innovative organizations that we know of are purposeful in the way they reward creativity and provide incentives for risk taking. These are places that tolerate mistakes and view them as a step along the way toward providing better content for their customers.

They Are Paranoid. Today, many companies are finding that new ways to deliver their products/services require them to "cannibalize" or substantially destroy their old ways of doing business. The natural inclination of most organizations is to avoid this situation at all costs. They fear losing what they are familiar with and what has worked for years. This view is foolhardy because if there is a better way to do business and you don't adopt it, someone else will. Inevitably, you will lose your existing customers to the competition nonetheless.

Don't assume that you are fine just because you don't believe that your existing competition could come up with this new approach. If the new way relies on technology and information not previously available, a newcomer can come along and make it happen before you even know what hit you. Intel's Andy Grove talks about always fearing being overtaken, either by a competitor or a "strategic inflection point," as described in Chapter 1. His book, *Only the*

Paranoid Survive, is gospel to many business leaders and should be required reading for nonprofits as well.

Common Characteristics for Successful Content

Similarly, we have found that the most effective organizations have a family of products and services that together have the common characteristics described as follows:

They Center on the Customer. The dynamic organization continually asks itself whether it is providing its products and services in ways that are the most valuable and convenient for the organization or for the customer. This may mean developing new services, such as the Mayo Clinic adding a content-rich Web site to complement the hands-on health care provided in the hospital setting (www.mayo.edu) or The Fund for the City of New York's ways to use technology to dramatically improve the way services are delivered. As described more fully in the Digital Spotlight that follows, the Fund for the City of New York has used technology to help people help themselves through the complex domestic violence and landlord tenant court systems.

Customer-centered content means that products and services were designed and are being delivered with the customer's convenience in mind, not the convenience of the organization. Environmental Defense, as described fully in Chapter 2, was able to increase the size of its customer base by more than 10 times by making its information freely available when its customers wanted it—on the Internet 24 hours a day, seven days a week. Regardless of the type of work that your organization does, if you have been delivering content in the same way for the past five years, you can assume that your products and services are not as customer centered as they could be. Read about the new ways that dynamic organizations are using technology to become more customer focused later in this chapter.

Digital Spotlight—The Fund for the City of New York Using Technology to Center on Your Customers and Give Them What They Need

The Fund for the City of New York (www.fcny.org) is a private operating foundation that was launched by the Ford Foundation in 1968 with the mandate to improve the quality of life for all

New Yorkers. Through centers on youth, government, and technology, as well as core organizational assistance, the Fund introduces and helps implement innovations in policy, programs, practice, and technology in order to advance the functioning of government and nonprofit organizations in New York City and beyond. The Fund is committed to developing technology systems and applications that help nonprofits and government streamline operations, expand services, and improve performance in general.

The Fund's work in the technology area first began in the 1970s with the development of management systems that relied on mainframe computers. From there, as personal computers were developed, the Fund proceeded to pioneer the use of PCs in large government agencies. This work included an award-winning pupil transportation system and a school-building scorecard system, both developed in partnership with the New York City Board of Education. Building on its mainframe and PC systems development, the Fund expanded into developing systems and programs that used the vast information and communication capacity of the Internet. In 1995, the Fund established the Center for Internet Innovation to help government and nonprofits obtain the benefits of the Internet and shape its future.

Victims of domestic violence who want to take the first step of going to court to get protection from their abusers face discouraging obstacles—lawyers are hard to find, court pleadings are hard to decipher and confusing to complete, and courts seem unfriendly and daunting, especially for those not fluent in English. On the other side, officials who handle these cases, from police to lawyers to judges, face delicate challenges in encouraging victims to come forward. As experience shows, any delay in the process means the violence will probably continue. The result is that fewer women file for protection and those who do often file incompletely. One of the center's most innovative products, the Domestic Violence Court System, was designed to help overcome many of these obstacles. The system, built for the Internet, guides a victim through the first phase of the protective order process. When a user of the online system—advocate, victim, or staff worker at a shelter— logs on, the system progresses through a series of questions. Each screen prompts the user to click on checklists and type in simple answers that the system then reconfigures from ordinary wording—in Spanish or English—into data that fits standard legal forms. At the same time, the system locates the appropriate courts for the victim's circumstances and prints out maps with the legal documents. At the end of the process, the victim has a complete protective order ready for a judge's signature. This system is now online in three counties in Georgia and four in New York—Kings, Queens, the Bronx, and Schenectady.

The fund has also built and is in the process of building other products that use the Internet to overcome historical obstacles faced by people in need. OLIVIA (On-line Vocational Rehabilitation Service Application System) is the fund's Internet-based system designed to streamline the application process for state-funded vocational rehabilitation services. Designed in collaboration with the Corporation for Supportive Housing and the New York State Office of Vocational and Educational Services for Individuals with Disabilities (VESID) of the Department of Education, OLIVIA is already reducing the application cycle from eight weeks to two weeks at six test sites across New York City. Together with the New York City Housing Court, the fund is developing the Housing Court Eviction Prevention system. This product will walk tenants through Housing Court law, tell them their rights, provide relevant information, and produce court documents that are helpful to residents in preventing evictions.[1]

They Web-Enable the Relationship.   Web-enabling the customer relationship means bringing it, in whole or part, onto the Internet. This can mean migrating administrative functions onto the Internet, such as requiring online reporting of grants, billing and payment for services provided, and online registration for membership, conferences, and courses as well as the delivery of programmatic content in many of the ways described as follows. The sooner the relationship with the customer becomes Web-enabled, the sooner your organization can begin transforming its impact and expanding its reach.

They Facilitate Interactivity.   Dynamic organizations make information available to customers in ways that allow them to interact with them, each other, and interested parties. As some of the examples described in the following sections reflect, technology now allows customers to access your information 24 hours a day, comment on it, process it, and share it. It also gives you a way to provide customers with a platform so they can interact with other customers who have similar interests so they can share their views, problems, and solutions with each other. In the words of John Ball, Director of Portland, Oregon's Worksystems, Inc., "To serve our customers better, we've learned to give up control of information and to help our customers talk to each other, even when it means they end up talking about us." Organizations that are not taking advantage of this type of technology are not fully serving their customers. Worksystems is highlighted more fully in Chapter 7.

They Reflect the Organization's Competitive Advantages. The best nonprofit organizations understand their competitive advantage within their industry and develop and deliver their content accordingly. On the other hand, these dynamic organizations often review their products and services and are not afraid to stop offering content that no longer reflects their unique place in the industry. We did that effectively at The Enterprise Foundation. In the late 1980s and early 1990s, Enterprise took advantage of its national scope and highly skilled trainers on staff to provide a host of basic, live training programs throughout the country. As more organizations in the 1990s were able to provide this basic curriculum on a local level, we all but eliminated these trainings, had in-house staff develop a comprehensive library of easy-to-use manuals and workbooks that local organizations and trainers could use, and began offering customized, online trainings to an even broader audience.

THE NEW FRONTIER FOR PRODUCTS AND SERVICES: THE INTERNET DOUBLE HELIX

The Internet is fundamentally changing the nonprofit sector forever in two ways. One, as we discussed in Chapter 5, the digital culture is making nonprofit customers more demanding and thereby, increasing competition, consolidation, and the need to build customer loyalty. But the other change will be even more profound. It is the fact that the Internet serves not only as a new, extraordinary source of information for nonprofits to use to develop or reengineer existing products and services but also as an unparalleled distribution system for them to make more and better information available to their customers. We call this the "Internet Double Helix" because like the discovery of DNA changed science forever, so will this new power fundamentally change the way the nonprofit sector operates.

The Internet Double Helix already is making dynamic organizations completely rethink how they work. As Fred Krupp, Executive Director of Environmental Defense, an organization at the vanguard of taking full advantage of the Internet to deliver products and services, says: "We have had to begin looking at the whole world through the Web. This is not about Web sites, it's about using the Internet to power your entire organization. We look at everything we do through these new tools and capabilities." As described earlier in Chapter 2, Environmental Defense has been able to capture previously unavailable data; repackage it in compelling ways; combine it with the distribution power of the Internet; and increase the organization's effectiveness substantially.

Repositioning Content in the Digital Age

The Internet Double Helix has created new ways of thinking about and delivering content today. As you review the list that follows, notice how almost all of these approaches are possible either because that information is now available to nonprofits through the Net; because the Net provides nonprofits with a distribution system previously unavailable to them; or both. Today, more Dynamic Managers reposition the content of their organization using one or more of the following approaches and fundamentally transform their business model in the process. Although not all of these approaches are solely Internet-based or require the use of technology, they all seem to be a product of a digital culture.

Expanding Existing Customer Relationships. Chapter 5 highlighted the importance of the customer. Many organizations have a relationship with their customer and don't consider how that relationship can be any different. Dynamic organizations reposition their content to expand on the historic relationship. They perform the following tasks:

Deepen the Relationship. More and more nonprofit organizations are deepening their existing customer relationships by providing them with more content that they want. At Enterprise, we did this by asking customers what they wanted at an annual conference attended by 1,500 customers that we billed as "the Network Conference." In 1998, the customers told us they wanted more opportunities to network but without taking a week off to go to a conference. We then built and managed a variety of opportunities for them to do that under our moniker. These included live, online classrooms; ongoing, threaded discussion groups; and regional programs that combined on-the-ground workshops with online programs.

A common way to deepen customer relationships is to sponsor an online support group for customers to share their experiences with other people similarly situated, such as adults who are caring for their parents with Alzheimer's (Alzheimer Society of Canada, www.alz.org). Other organizations might simply make it easier for their customers to locate hard-to-find items that are important to them, such as special devices for the disabled (www.makoa.org).

Other organizations, like The National Housing Trust (NHT), now offer more specialized products or services. NHT is a national housing preservation organization that helps other nonprofits navigate complicated federal housing programs and directly owns and manages affordable housing. With millions of affordable housing units at risk of loss from the housing stock, NHT believed it had to do something to make it easier for nonprofits to determine if they could afford to buy a property and to identify the potential sources for financing the acquisition. NHT developed a spreadsheet that nonprofits can complete and e-mail back. Within two to three days of receiving the spreadsheet, NHT provides the nonprofit with a thorough analysis of the targeted property, including all possible financing scenarios.

Aggregate Customers for Their Economic Benefit.   Many nonprofit organizations work with populations that have been isolated from the economic mainstream. Despite this fact, they spend a significant amount of money each month on products and services. In urban areas with dense populations, these dollars can add up to a lot of money in the aggregate and can be the basis for negotiating favorable terms with certain vendors. Lawyers, doctors, and other professionals have been doing this for years through their trade associations. Other large, affinity nonprofits such as labor unions and conservation organizations have been doing it as well with credit cards, car rental companies, and so forth. Now, we are seeing nonprofits serving low-income populations doing this, from large church groups (Revelation Corporation of America, owned by the five largest African-American Christian denominations) to our own efforts at One Economy Corporation (www.one-economy.com). One Economy is helping bring Internet access to affordable rental housing units across the country and negotiating favorable costs for hardware, software, and certain products and services desired by the residents of this housing, such as basic banking services, based on the scale of this effort. More information about One Economy can be found in Chapter 9.

Educate Customers, 24-7. The Internet enables nonprofits to help customers train themselves any time of the day or night. Creating online classrooms and courses is relatively easy, inexpensive, and getting more so every day. In fact, once a course is provided online, it can easily be archived and used repeatedly. Many universities have been at the forefront of this effort (e.g., www.umuc.edu, University of Maryland), but other nonprofits are not far behind. ONE/Northwest offers a series of online courses, delivered via e-mail. Each day, over a period of a week, a lesson is e-mailed to the student with course goals and homework assignments.[2] The Learning Institute for Nonprofit Organizations (www1.uwex.edu) provides courses and degree programs for nonprofits. We have built that capability into our operations at One Economy as well. Low-income users of our Web site are able to access a complete library of training courses provided by Smartforce.com (www.smartforce.com). These courses allow users to learn in the privacy of their homes at any time of day or night about a range of topics from basics of the Internet to Microsoft and Oracle certification programs.

Help Customers Change their Behaviors. The Internet has the potential to even help customers change their behaviors in ways that serve the organization's mission and are consistent with the customer's personal goals and objectives. A simple modem connected to a scale in a low-income person's home can send readings automatically to a community-based health facility, warn a health care practitioner of a customer's unusual fluctuations in weight, and stimulate the appropriate intervention. Environmental Defense sees the day when one of their Web sites will help their customers lead the kind of environmentally friendly lives they want to lead by helping them buy food grown with sustainable technologies and state-of-the art, energy-efficient cars.

Help Customers to Find Their Voice. Customers need not be passive recipients of services. They also can be effective advocates for public policy changes that matter to them and to you. Dynamic organizations keep customers informed through periodic communications (e-mail and otherwise) and create vehicles that allow their customers to have a voice. ONE/Northwest, highlighted in Chapter 5, has been incredibly effective in helping local environmental organizations, especially in isolated, rural areas, to use basic technology such as e-mail and faxes to provide people who were previously silent in public policy discussions with an effective voice.

Defining Customers Differently. Dynamic organizations are repositioning their content in a way to reach out to new customers and to broaden the definition of *customer*. The Mayo Clinic (www.mayo.edu) and a group of university-based health care providers in Ohio (www.netwellness.org) have moved their definition of *customer* beyond the patients who walk in their doors to users of their Web sites who come to them for reliable reference information and answers to basic questions. NetWellness, as discussed in greater detail later in this chapter, actually answers any question put to it by users, wherever they live, in two to three days.

Environmental Defense has used its Web sites (www.scorecard.org and www.takeaction.org) to engage new customers beyond those with an historic connection to the environmental movement by making it easier for people concerned about their own backyard to get the information they need to take action and to join a network of activists committed to change.

Letting Go of Information and Web-Enabling Your Knowledge.
One of the hardest things for nonprofits to do is to stop controlling information. In many cases, organizations fear that the only real power they have is the power to make customers come to them for information. This attitude just will not fly in the digital age because whether we like it or not, most information will be available on the Internet sooner or later. That means that the dynamic organization must anticipate this reality and figure out how it can let go of the information now and use its special, historic relationship to the data and the customer to add value on the Internet. That often means creating specialized databases that take the information and sort it in ways that are especially useful to old and new customers. The organization's experience is reflected in the design and sorting of the data.

This intellectual capital makes the database relevant and compelling to customers. The organization's reputation and franchise in the non-Internet world brings customers to the site in the first place.

By Web-enabling its knowledge, a dynamic organization can have impacts in ways it never before contemplated. Structuring information and making it broadly available on the Internet can accomplish the following tasks:

Allow People to Use the Information to Change Public Policy or to Take Action. The West Virginia Citizen Research Group (WVCRG), a recent winner of the OMB Watch Awards, concerned with the role of special interest group dollars in the state's democratic process, created a database of all campaign contributions received by all candidates running for statewide offices during the 1998 campaign cycle. No organization in the state had previously compiled such a database and made it available to citizens and other organizations for free. The WVCRG therefore obtained hard-copy donation records, which they then hand-coded and typed into a database, amounting to some 20,000 records. The database made it possible for the first time for remote citizen groups with little or no access to the state capitol to follow the money trail and see how special interest group dollars were influencing the efforts of their elected officials. Citizen lobbyists were also provided with information on how to effectively contact their legislators and mobilize other constituency members via a daily listserv and weekly e-mail newsletter that highlighted the legislative progress with respect to campaign finance reform bills. Their efforts resulted in the introduction and passage of a bill that, among other things, limited independent expenditures and prohibited a candidate from accepting loans from anyone other than banks, lending institutions, themselves, or their spouses.[3]

Influence the Behavior of the People Who Have Provided the Information That You Are Making Available. An unexpected benefit of making information more broadly available is that the people who are the subject or source of the information are more likely to change their behaviors if they know more people are watching their actions. Environmental Defense realized this as they introduced their Scorecard Web site. Scorecard simply takes corporate reports periodically filed with environmental regulatory agencies and posts the corporation's filing in an easy-to-use and understandable manner. As companies looked at their own results on the Scorecard, they began making changes in their operations so they looked better to those who are now watching more closely.

Developing Products and Services Possible Only because of Internet Technology. Dynamic organizations not only look to Web-enable their current offerings but also look for new ways to serve customers that are only possible because of the Internet. Zero Population Growth (ZPG) and the Institute for Global Communications (IGC) are two excellent examples of this approach. ZPG, a national grassroots education and advocacy organization that addresses population and sustainability issues, developed Zero 24-7, www.zero24-7.org.—an Internet radio station designed to educate and engage new audiences, particularly young, computer-literate, media-savvy target groups not responsive to direct mail or traditional news media. Using state-of-the-art Web technology, Zero 24-7's DJs produce a live, six-hour daily mix of Indie-Progressive music, interviews, and public service announcements repeated three times a day, with no commercials, play lists, or song edits. The technology used by Zero 24-7 permits an infinite number of people to connect and hear their music and their message. On average, 1,000 people tune in to Zero 24-7 each day, with listeners from all across the United States and more than 50 countries around the world. Zero 24-7 serves as an instructive model of how to merge progressive technology with progressive issues to engage widely dispersed, hard-to-engage target audiences.[4]

IGC, www.igc.org, was built on technology and reengineered around the Internet. Begun initially as PeaceNet in 1986 to formalize a network of peace activists in the United States, IGC has grown to a national membership of more than 15,000, with links to networks and activists worldwide. IGC has expanded its capabilities to bring Internet tools and online services to organizations and activists working on peace, economic and social justice, human rights, environmental protection, labor issues, and conflict resolution. IGC has been changing over the past year to take its community of activists and nonprofit professionals into the Internet's next wave by focusing on content, information sharing, and new, collaborative tools. The shift at IGC Internet came after a year long assessment and planning sessions among staff, board members, and outside advisors. To free up the necessary resources, IGC is providing Internet access services through MindSpring Enterprises, instead of being an ISP itself. In addition, IGC's e-mail list services are now being posted for free by Topica, Inc. but remain tightly integrated into IGC's online community with e-mail discussions and newsletters. IGC now features automated Web tools for publicizing events and calendars, action alerts, and information about volunteers and employment in the progressive nonprofit sector. Progressive organizations will also have online donation capabilities.

Making Technology a Part of Your Products and Services. Some dynamic organizations are actually making technology a product or service in and of itself. This is happening in several ways: providing technology to low-income people and providing technology to nonprofit organizations helping low-income people. Our organization, One Economy Corporation, which is described more fully in Chapter 9, focuses in part on helping owners of affordable housing to bring Internet access and technology into the homes of low-income people. Other organizations have different approaches. ONE/Northwest, highlighted in Chapter 5, helps environmentally focused nonprofits to determine their technology needs and then, where possible, to acquire the appropriate technology. MOUSE (Making Opportunities for Upgrading Schools and Education), discussed in Chapter 3, based in New York, works to bring technology into public schools and then teach educators how best to integrate it into their curricula.

Collaborating Virtually. The Internet allows similarly minded organizations to create synergies and influence government service delivery in ways never before possible by working together virtually. The Bay Area Homeless Alliance (BAHA) and Columbia Heights/Shaw Family Support Collaborative in Washington, D.C. are excellent examples of this virtual collaboration. BAHA is highlighted in the Digital Spotlight later in this chapter. The Columbia Heights/Shaw Family Support Collaborative represents an association of social service providers, community organizations, resident groups, and neighborhood leaders, working together to build a family support network to serve more than 5,000 families and their children. The collaborative has explored how to integrate technology within its community-building efforts since its inception four years ago and has supported the integration of the Internet and related technologies into the work of youth development partners over the last two years. With the help of One Economy, the Collaborative and its members have developed a shared-technology strategy that will help them redesign their business practices to be more customer driven. To the maximum extent possible, partners will use the Internet to digitize their services and create an enhanced service delivery system that is based on the following principles: (1) accurate and timely information about the availability of a broad range of services, including available child care and job placement services, will be coordinated and freely available on the Internet; (2) homes will be electronically connected to the services they need, such as local schools, health care providers, and council members; (3) services will be able to be requested by e-mail and responses provided on a timely basis by e-mail (e.g., requests for health care appointments, housing waiting list status); and (4) staff will become "information brokers"— matching people to services they need, when they need them.

Digital Spotlight—Bay Area Homeless Alliance: Collaborating Virtually

The Bay Area Homeless Alliance (BAHA), www.baha.org, is an innovative project that was established in an effort to create change through the collaboration of community efforts and the use of high technology throughout the nine counties of the San Francisco Bay Area. The Community Technology Alliance of San Jose is the lead agency for the project, which consists of 54 collaborative partner agencies.

BAHA's mission is to improve access to shelter, housing, support services, benefits, and employment for homeless individuals and families and those at risk of homelessness. To accomplish this, BAHA has created a regional information system using Internet technology and state-of-the-art telecommunications. Technology has supported the development of a human infrastructure of service providers and organizations working together to ensure increased health and well-being of homeless and at-risk individuals and families in the nine counties of the San Francisco Bay Area.

BAHA has fundamentally changed the way in which homeless and at-risk individuals and families interact with the community through a voice mail component. Voice mail numbers are given to homeless people by case managers at homeless shelters, employment programs, public schools, and other social service agencies. When a person needs to leave a number for medical caregivers, potential employers, or housing providers, they provide the voice mail number that appears to the caller to be a home answering machine, personalized with the homeless person's own message.

BAHA has also developed a regional shelter bed "hotline." Using a single memorable toll-free number (1-800-7SHELTER), callers are asked to choose a county, then choose from several languages. They are then given information about the shelters available, the people served there (e.g., families, women, men), and entry requirements for each particular shelter. This information is available 24 hours a day. Shelter providers can update their information remotely or with a live case worker.

Finally, BAHA has a Provider Library that offers a fast and accurate way for service providers and homeless people alike to retrieve information on the Internet on up-to-date, desperately needed services at a given geographic site or anywhere within the region. Previously, service providers had to rely on paper directories to assist their clients. These directories were often out of date and specific to one jurisdiction, not the region.[5]

Digital Spotlight—NetWellness: Expanding Content and Customers in Dynamic Ways

The Ohio Valley Community Health Information Network (Network) is a partnership of community groups, telecommunications access providers, public libraries, health clinics, and hospitals, including the University of Cincinnati, Case Western Reserve University, and Ohio State University, that came together in 1994 to provide easy, equitable, and widespread access to health information to citizens of the Ohio Valley, including northern Kentucky and southeastern Indiana. What started as a plan to simply make the guts of the University of Cincinnati Health Science library available to a select number of people in public places has become "NetWellness," one of the world's leading health sites. This transformation happened in large part because of the Network's willingness to expand its existing customer relationships, to let go of information by Web-enabling its knowledge, and to develop products and services possible only because of the Internet. In short, the Network has collectively become a leading dynamic organization.

The Origins of Netwellness

NetWellness began as an attempt to expand the traditional customer bases enjoyed by the partners in the Network to include rural Appalachian and urban minority populations. The idea was to determine what information these customers wanted most and then to make easy access to electronic health information resources available in a controlled setting, such as public workstations in libraries, health clinics, hospital waiting rooms, and pharmacies in the region.

With this in mind, the Network launched the program with the support of the U. S. Department of Commerce Telecommunications and Information Infrastructure Assistance Program (TIIAP) and additional funding from the State of Ohio.

The Network began its research into customer preferences as planned. It found that customer demand fell into the following categories:

- Drug information
- Alternative therapies
- Disease information
- Insurance/health planning
- Physician referral/find the expert
- Health literature
- Wellness/general health

What they had not planned for was the extraordinary force that the Internet would become, almost overnight.

Rollout

Despite all of the Network's best-laid plans to roll out its data only to a targeted population through a close-looped public access system, the growth of the Internet demanded that it rethink its distribution and content strategy. The partners repositioned their effort and built a Web site, which they called "NetWellness," that would be available to the general population. Today, NetWellness's customers span well beyond the Ohio Valley into 50 countries and all 50 states. The site gets feedback from more than 5,000 customers a year, who tell them the type of content they want NetWellness to provide.

The site features a breadth and depth of content that was never contemplated in the project's early stages. The site's products and services provide content that was previously unavailable on the ground or on the Web because they had to be Web-enabled to be accessed. Some products available on the site became possible only because of the Internet.

This content includes the following elements:

Ask an Expert. This is the site's premier service, and it is available only because of the Internet. Users anonymously submit questions online. Because questions asked by one person may address the concerns of others, experts' answers are posted in a bulletin board format so readers can review previous topics. Readers may search the database of all previous questions and answers, review the 10 most recent topics, or choose issues from a list of all previously addressed topics.

HOPEline. Another cutting-edge product is HOPEline. HOPEline is an interactive self-help resource for people with substance abuse and chemical dependency issues. HOPEline consists of four parts: Southwest Ohio Community Resources, General Information on Common Substances of Abuse, Self-Assessment Tests, and the Ohio Department of Alcohol and Drug Addiction Services Directory. Users can work through these modules and connect with community resources in Southwest Ohio to get help. HOPEline is one of the most widely used and acclaimed resources on NetWellness, and future plans call for an expansion of HOPEline to a statewide resource.

Health Topics. NetWellness has information on more than 100 different health subjects. In most cases, each subject includes links to electronic texts, reference works, and professional databases where additional information on the topic may be found. Finally, many subjects contain links to resources outside of NetWellness.

In the News. The site features two Web-based news services, CNN Interactive and USA Today Health. These news services are indexed nightly by NetWellness with permission of the publishers. Users can search the index and link to articles on the latest health news.

Referral/Directories. Users can secure a referral to a practicing faculty physician at the University of Cincinnati or The Ohio State University, or search national, state, and local directories for physicians around the country.

The site also includes online access to medical libraries, information on clinical trials, and resources on specialized topics, such as minority or teen health.

Lessons Learned

Steven Marine, Program Director for NetWellness, and Roger Guard, Associate Senior Vice President of the University of Cincinnati Medical Center Academic Information Technologies and Libraries, have shared some of the lessons they have learned from this project.

Core Principles. The site had to achieve the following goals:

- Consistently model integrity, reliability, and consistency.
- Encourage multiple points of view.
- Stay on the "high road."
- Maintain perspective and build trust.
- Avoid topics that are too politically sensitive, especially in teen health.
- Have guidelines for writing content at a sixth- to eighth-grade level.

Partnerships. Partnerships were recognized as a key ingredient for success and as a means of ensuring community involvement and relevance. NetWellness has forged successful partnerships with more than 40 past or current partners from government, business, and the community. Public and private spheres have contributed products, services, funding, and personnel to the project.

From the outset, NetWellness was inclusive in its organization and management. A topic as vast as consumer health requires a "big tent" approach. By engaging partners openly, honestly, and with mutual trust, NetWellness assembled a partnership base that nearly doubled the Federal TIIAP investment. Furthermore, many partners participated actively through representatives serving on the NetWellness Steering Committee and on working teams developing NetWellness systems. Team building was a key factor in NetWellness's success.

Privacy.   Privacy of the user was an important issue. To ensure privacy, the following tenets were adopted by NetWellness:

- No personal information could ever be shared.
- Only aggregate data could be reported.
- No cookies, no user tracking, or profiling were allowed.
- Privacy policies had to be transparent.

Technology.   Technology is changing so fast that NetWellness had to be technologically nimble. For the most part, the project relied on off-the-shelf technical solutions and minimized customization. There were only a few cases where it was deemed important to deviate from this guideline, including moving CD-ROM data files onto a central server and moving to Web browser technology.

The Future of NetWellness

The Network wants to continue to expand the relevance and value of the NetWellness site. One key issue is to fully integrate the site into the K–12 classroom and to have these classes become producers of content, not just consumers. One of the fastest-growing and most popular features on the site has been the Teens on Health area, where teenagers create content with medical students and faculty and then follow these topics through various classes such as English, Biology, and so on. NetWellness also expects to begin providing content to ohio-helps.org, a powerful directory of state and local services that can help people identify health care providers and other services. This partnership should further expand the reach of NetWellness and bring even more customers to the site.

REFLECT AND REPOSITION

- Does your content center on the customer?
- Do you continually incubate new ideas?
- Are you paranoid about the content your competition is working on?
- Are you using technology to expand the quantity and quality of your content choices?

- Have you Web-enabled your relationship with your customer?
- Have you increased your interactivity with your customer?
- Does your content reflect your organization's competitive advantages?

GUIDING PRINCIPLES

- Your business model will rise or fall, and the customer will stay or go, based on the array of products and services that you provide them and the ease with which they can access them.
- Fear is the enemy of invention: incubate and launch new ideas.
- Maximize the value of the Internet Double Helix in your products and services.
- Technology can enhance your products and services dramatically.
- Use your content to attract new, nontraditional customers and to deepen existing relationships.
- Let go of information and Web-enable your knowledge.
- Develop products and services that are possible only because of Internet technology.
- Make technology a part of your products and services.
- Collaborate virtually.

NOTES

[1]www.fcny.org

[2]www.benton.org/Practice/TA/home.html

[3]Description of WVCRG was provided at the OMB Watch Web site, www.ombwatch.org.

[4]Description of ZPG was provided at the OMB Watch Web site, www.ombwatch.org.

[5]Innovation Network, 1999 Computerworld Smithsonian Awards.

CHAPTER SEVEN

Infrastructure

Organizations, like buildings, can withstand incredible amounts of weight, wear, and tear if they are built on a strong foundation. Unlike real estate, however, the foundation of a nonprofit organization, its *infrastructure*, is not permanent or set in stone. It has to be continually reviewed, refreshed, and restored. That is the job of the Dynamic Manager. You must regularly reflect on the organization's infrastructure and ask: "Does it support our culture and business model?" "If not, why not, and what can we do to fix it?" This chapter helps you reflect on your infrastructure. We also provide promising methods for repositioning your infrastructure so it can withstand the forces of change in the digital age.

WHAT IS THE INFRASTRUCTURE?

To us, the fundamental foundation of an organization is built on three things: (1) the environment created by senior management; (2) the availability of a stable and diverse resource base; and (3) the strategic use of information technology. We all know of examples where an organization's new initiative failed despite great fanfare and promise. This often happens because funding was insufficient; senior managers failed to secure staff buy-in, or efficiencies envisioned through technology were never achieved. Quite simply, the infrastructure failed to support the business model.

SENIOR MANAGEMENT

Senior management may be the single most important element of infrastructure. Strong senior management, whether a single executive director or a large operations team, must create an environment that enables people to perform and makes the organization Net ready.

CREATING THE ENVIRONMENT

Creating the right environment is no simple matter. We have found that it is a combination of things, much of which emanates from senior management. More often than not, senior managers who continually challenge the process, model behavior, share information, equip their people, and get out of their way create an environment conducive to success. Kenneth Lay, CEO of Enron, a for-profit energy company, put it well when he said, "You want your top managers to have strong strategic thinking skills and stamina, but creating the right environment is far and away the most important trait."[1]

Challenging the Process

We borrow this phrase from Kouzes and Posner[2] and put it first because of our belief in its potency. If the status quo is worshiped by senior management, you can be sure that the rest of the organization will follow suit. Senior management must make it clear to staff that they support challenging every aspect of the organization. To us, that means looking for innovative ways to improve the organization, from how business has been done historically to how the physical facility is organized. It also means rewarding those who raise the issues and work to make the changes. In our organization, we use the inverted pyramid concept to constantly challenge our processes. When making important decisions, we move from the macro to the micro—in many cases, challenging our assumptions about our vision, people, customers, and content, until we are comfortable that we are making the right move.

Modeling Behavior

Senior management must model the behavior that they want their staff to emulate. That includes how they manage important relationships and how they treat customers, staff, vendors, and the like. It also includes their willingness to take action. We have seen so many organizations become paralyzed into a state of inaction because of their fear of doing something wrong. Chuck Knight, CEO of Emerson Electric, puts it well. He believes that senior management has the obligation to lead, by acting. He says, "We don't care about structure or form—we worry about getting things done. It is absolutely better to do something, recognizing that it may not be exactly right, than to do nothing."[3]

Senior management must also set an example for how the organization uses and embraces technology. That means publicly and privately learning more about technology and regularly using the tools of the trade. The CEO need not be a techno wiz but should publicly exhibit the standard of interest and intellectual curiosity expected in the rest of staff. Obviously, it is easier to follow a CEO's digital vision when the CEO turns the computer on each day and answers e-mails electronically.

Sharing Information

Technology enables us to access and share information, often at great speeds; however, in many organizations, basic information about the entity's financial condition, health and retirement benefits, travel and appointment schedules, strategic plans, and the like, are closely held, especially by senior management. We have seen this secrecy lead to work environments dominated by the negative energy of rumor and gossip, not the positive energy of fact and shared victories. Bill Gates, who made the term *knowledge management* a household word in his book *Business @ the Speed of Thought*, points out that while most companies have invested in the basic building blocks of technology (PCs and networks), they have only received a fraction of the benefits technology can provide because they fail to see the potential of moving information quickly to everyone in the company.[4] Easy access to information, through a "digital nervous system," as described later in this chapter, combined with a culture of challenging established processes results in the "constant tilling of the cultural soil . . . required to sustain growth."[5]

Equipping Your People

In the digital age, senior management must invest time, energy, and money in building a knowledgeable staff and making sure that they

Information That Should be Shared

- Financial information
- Strategic and operating plans
- Performance benchmarks
- Organizational calendar of events
- Organizational chart
- List of strategic partners
- In-house professional development opportunities
- Description of staff expertise and roles

- Customer data (inputs and outputs)
- Organizational goals and objectives
- Reflections of senior management
- Health care and other human resource information
- Detailed description of products and services

have what they need to do their work. That means hardware, software, modems, Internet connections, and, most important, training. Currently, there is a resource mismatch in many nonprofits. They are investing heavily in technology but not matching these outlays with investing in staff training. Training must go beyond software certifications and focus on communications and team building, necessary skills for the digital age. One easy and inexpensive way to equip your people is through Web-based training. Using the Internet to help train staff is described more fully later in this chapter.

Getting out of the Way

In one of our favorite books, *Leadership is an Art*, Max DePree speaks eloquently about this issue. He says that "effectiveness comes about through enabling others to reach their potential—both their personal potential and their corporate or institutional potential."[6] He talks about the idea of making each person feel capable and powerful. Senior management fails to do this when they "find complexity where simplicity ought to be," and "encumber people, rather than enabling them."

Warren Bennis puts it well:

You're not going to attract or retain a top-quality workforce under those silly and obsolete forms of bureaucratic or command-and-control leadership. You cannot release the brain power of any organi-

zation by using whips and chains. You get the best out of people by empowering them, being supportive, and getting out of their way.[7]

There are still too many senior managers who don't get this concept. For some reason, they believe that their job is to help staff identify obstacles, not to help remove them once they have been identified. One past employee of ours described the problem well: "I know my obstacles well, I just don't know how to solve them. Having my boss reinforce my problems only increases my despair and saps my psyche."

HAVING A VISION FOR THE NET

We need to say one more thing about creating the right environment today. Your work will be incomplete unless you can articulate your vision for the Net. We have spoken with several organizations who have 100 percent of their staff networked and online, but management can rarely articulate a vision for the Net. Put simply, your corporate commitment to the Net will never be bigger than your vision for the Net—no vision, no commitment. Articulate an engaging statement for how and why your organization will use these tools. Call them your "Net benefits" and go from there. Whether you are starting a new or repositioning your existing organization, the key here is that your Web strategy and your business model must fit together. Indeed, the more they look like each other, the better.

STABLE AND DIVERSE RESOURCES

The most durable infrastructures that we have seen in the nonprofit industry have stable and diverse resource bases. They have not only a variety of funding sources to draw from but also an array of value-added partnerships with nonprofit and for-profit organizations.

Financial Resources

Funding obviously is critically important. A couple of years ago, we were part of an enlightening study of nonprofit organizations in Cleveland, Ohio, that, as we later realized, was representative of the sector as a whole. It showed that most organizations received more than 60 percent of their financial support from the government, had net incomes of less than $1,000 a year, and secured financial reserves sufficient to fund operations for less than a month. In short,

Ten Guidelines for Making the Net Work for Organizations

Terry Grunwald of Making the Net Work has done an extraordinary amount of work helping nonprofits to capture the power of the Internet. She prepared the following guidelines for a conference.

1. **Prerequisite: full commitment by decision makers (director and board).**
   - The Director has to provide clear, unambiguous leadership.
   - They, themselves, have to model good, consistent use of the Net.
   - Best: Develop a task-oriented working group consisting of the Director and some "core" Board members and then expand out.
   - The Director needs to be willing to be proactive in changing the culture.
   - The Director and the Board must be willing to invest—not just in hardware and software, but in staff time, strategic planning, and workplan revisions.

2. **Be prepared to look at your organization through fresh eyes. Rethink. Re-envision. Stretch.**
   - Who is your audience? Now you have the opportunity to look "beyond the choir" to a wider network: other sectors, media, funders, general public.
   - Who are your issue collaborators? Local, county, regional, national, international?
   - Who are your resource collaborators? Tech resources, volunteers, consultants?
   - What are your information and communication patterns?
   - What are your communications styles?
   - How efficient are your administrative procedures?

3. **Be clear on the Whys—before you tackle the Hows.**
   - What are the compelling reasons?
   - One organization (even an umbrella group) or one person on staff who assumes the role of techno-evangelist is easily dismissed.

- Need multiple reasons: May need to first experience "opportunities lost."
- Hard to predict just what will be the hook.

4. **You will need protocols. Establish roles and responsibilities.**
   - Goal: A computer and Internet connection on the desk of every staffperson.
   - Need to handle the information flow.
   - Who will handle e-mail—how to manage it, how to archive it so it is available to others?
   - Which Web sites will be reviewed on a regular basis? Which mailing lists will be monitored?
   - Who will contribute—provide a high, visible profile for your organization?
   - How will online activities be integrated into an overall communication strategy?
   - When does it make sense to launch a Web site?
   - Who will manage and maintain it?
   - How can you integrate your Web and print media design strategies?

5. **Require a change in organizational culture.**
   - Most important: director buy-in.
   - Use it for internal communication. No options.
   - Need a nudge . . . and a backup nudge.
   - Make it a permanent agenda item at staff meetings.
   - Create incentives. Make it part of each staff person's workplan.
   - Stay positive. Celebrate successes. Make it fun.

6. **Be aware of the tools. Use them in an integrated way.**
   - The real benefit comes from the synergies of making these things come together.
   - Reinforcing them. Broadcast lists integrated into dynamic Web sites.
   - Balance. Be selective about information. Make it succinct, substantive, and annotate to make it relevant to local needs.
   - Goal: Integrated Web and broadcast list strategy.

7. **Identify low-cost resources.**
   - Online
   - In your local community
   - Within colleagues working on similar issues and the umbrella organization that serves them
   - Within other networks and communities of interest
8. **View technology as an ongoing operational cost, not a capital expenditure.**
   - Will need to be an item in your annual budget—just like phone or printing.
   - Plan to upgrade every 18 to 36 months.
   - Build it into issue-based funding proposals.
9. **Design for evaluation.**
   - Monitor.
   - Identify and problem-solve around barriers.
   - Establish feedback loops.
   - Make Web sites interactive.
10. **Be realistic.**
    - Outcomes are not immediately tangible.
    - Goal: Creating a framework for the future.
    - But, once "over the hump," no one ever turns back.

Source: Terry Grunwald for the Women Connect conference, November 1999 in London, England, www.makingthenetwork.org/toolbox/tools/ten.htm

if government funding disappeared, so would the organizations. Expanding and diversifying one's funder base is the key to financial sustainability in the digital age.

Fortunately, today there are opportunities to expand your funding base. Individuals, corporations, foundations, venture philanthropy, earned-income opportunities, and the Internet should all be viewed as potential sources of financing for your programs and operations. Reflect on the categories described as follows. If you don't currently have a strategy in that category, either make a strong case that you don't need one or build a diversification approach—starting now.

Expanding Your Base

Individuals. Most charitable donations come from individuals, amounting to approximately 80 percent of all charitable giving. Today, that means about $100 billion. If that number doesn't force you to take a second look at individual giving, how about this: economists predict that literally trillions of dollars will pass from one generation to the next over the next 20 years. Cornell economists Robert Avery and Michael Rendall suggest that $4.8 trillion will be transferred in the next 20 years. This huge number is nearly twice the gross national product and more than 50 times the total of U.S. private savings.[8] Even if this amount is overstated by 50 percent, that $2 to $3 trillion will dwarf the $130 billion in assets currently accumulated in foundations.

This intergenerational transfer of wealth is starting now. That's why there is no better time for your organization to start focusing on individual giving. First, find out who is already interested in your work and get to know them better, cultivate them. Go back and look at the list of people who came to your annual dinner, bought tickets to your raffle, gave blood at your blood drive. Set a 100 percent participation goal for board giving. Then ask your board members to introduce you to two people whom they think would be interested in your organization. Take this list of past and future supporters and get to know them better.

From now on, whenever you have any event, neighborhood tour, press conference, or fundraiser, invite these old friends and make sure that you have a sign-in list so you can begin building your list of new friends. Communicate with them regularly through e-mail, newsletters, and an annual giving appeal. Cultivation of individual donors takes time, but successful organizations work to engage individuals. They take the time to understand all of their donors' needs and goals and then fashion a strategy to engage them over the long haul.

Our experience and interviews have shown that efforts to engage individuals are most successful when they appeal to the head and the heart. They tend to produce greater loyalty, and they last longer. Many of the wealthy individuals we have met have told us that they want to be asked for their ideas as well as their money. We have learned a lot about individual giving from Jane Metcalfe, cofounder of *Wired* magazine and a board member of One Economy Corporation. We gradually engaged Jane with the power of our idea, our vision, and our business model, and she shared her ideas, relationships, and financial resources. In fact, she gave us our first check, which is framed on our office wall. Jane is one of a kind, but the idea of expanding your base by reaching out to people, engaging them in your work, and watching the sparks fly can work for any organization. It takes time, but it is an investment that must be made.

Share our Strength (SOS), www.strength.org, has mastered the art of engaging individuals. As an organization dedicated to ending hunger, SOS developed three brilliant individual giving strategies that other organizations can model. Both strategies were born from the same concept: Get professionals in a given industry to donate professional products and services to you with the understanding that you would raise money by reselling their donated matter to other individuals.

In SOS's case, its staff went out to chefs at restaurants across America and asked them to donate a recipe for an SOS cookbook. SOS then sold tens of thousands of copies, raising millions of dollars. Once these chefs were engaged and seeing positive results, SOS asked them to do more. With their help and the participation of local restaurants, SOS began sponsoring citywide food fairs called Taste of the Town. For a fee, city residents could come to the fair and sample food from a variety of residents. Proceeds from the fair went to SOS. With an increased profile with restaurants and patrons, SOS then took this approach to the next level. With the support of American Express, restaurants, and chefs, SOS launched its Charge for Hunger campaign. In this program, during the month of December for three years, restaurant patrons who used their American Express card at a participating restaurant got 1 percent of their dinner bill contributed to SOS. This campaign raised more than $21 million to fight hunger. SOS has taken the power of individual giving to a whole new level.

Digital Spotlight—Share Our Strength: Trailblazing Approach to Cause-Related Marketing

Gary Hart's failed presidential campaign and the related debacle with Donna Rice not only changed the face of American politics but also oddly changed the face of American philanthropy as well. At the time of Gary Hart's demise, Bill Shore was one of Hart's key political advisors. He had worked with Hart since 1978 and was devastated by the campaign's swift demise. Disillusioned by politics, he decided to spend all his time with a small hunger organization called Share our Strength (SOS), which was discussed previously. He saw how most nonprofit organizations raised their money and was committed to doing business differently. In short, he wanted to find a way to raise money for SOS by working with corporations to "expand their piece of the pie" in a given market. His theory was that corporations would be happy to share a piece of their expanding pie with SOS as both a business and philanthropic proposition.

Shore was right. SOS has raised more than $90 million through what has now been termed cause-related marketing and has funded more than 1,000 organizations that fight hunger nationwide through this model. The range of relationships has been extraordinary and includes the following organizations:

American Express's Charge Against Hunger campaign from 1993–96 was one of the nation's most visible and successful cause-related marketing partnerships. It provided the company with a crucial edge in the holiday buying season and increased cardmember usage and loyalty, built merchant relationships, and mobilized employees. The program—in which American Express donated three cents from every transaction during the fourth quarter—raised $21 million to fight hunger. American Express initiated its partnership with SOS in an effort to respond to low card acceptance in fine-dining establishments due to the company's higher fees. As national sponsor of Taste of the Nation since 1991, American Express has strengthened its relationships with restaurants and built customer loyalty and brand image.

Barnes & Noble Booksellers enhanced its corporate image among writers and consumers by hosting SOS's Writers Harvest events in more than 500 of its Superstores from 1995 to 1998. In addition to nationwide in-store promotion and direct mail, Barnes & Noble donated a percentage of sales on Writers Harvest day, generating more than $250,000 to fight hunger.

Calphalon Corporation joined forces with SOS to increase product sales, enhance relationships with retailers and premier chefs, and motivate its sales force. By repackaging poorly selling pans co-branded with the SOS name, logo, and a pledge to contribute $5 from each sale, Calphalon saw sales increases of up to 250 percent on these designated products.

Evian Natural Spring Water meets specific objectives for on-premise sales in fine-dining establishments through national sponsorship of SOS's Taste of the Nation events combined with an adjunct program, Quench Hunger. Designed to increase case sales of 1-liter glass bottles, Quench Hunger provides proceeds of sales during the campaign period to SOS. The program has increased Evian case sales by an average of 20 percent—in some markets four-fold—and has enabled the company to acquire two to three new accounts per market. Supported by advertising and on-premise marketing materials, the program raises more than $30,000 annually for national antihunger efforts.

When Tyson Foods began the search for a national cause-marketing partner to focus its hunger relief activities around its 65th anniversary, SOS stood out as a good choice. In May 2000, Tyson launched a $10 million, three-year commitment to the fight against hunger in partnership with SOS, including national sponsorship of Operation Frontline and the donation of 6.5 million pounds of chicken to community agencies across the country. Tyson team member volunteer programs, integrated advertising, and public relations support are also key to the relationship.

Cutco Cutlery's Cutting Away at Hunger program was established in May 2000. As part of this partnership, Cutco has designated several of its most popular premium cutlery sets as a platform for an SOS cause-related marketing program. Additionally, Cutco Cutlery annually provides knives and kitchen accessories for chefs and participants in Operation Frontline's Side-by-Side family cooking classes and awards cutlery prizes to all graduates. Cutco Cutlery, the largest American manufacturer of high-quality kitchen cutlery and accessories, has gained access to chefs, restaurateurs, and promotional opportunities through its partnership with SOS.

> Bread & Circus/Whole Foods Markets has forged strong relationships with chefs, bolstered its customers' images, and created in-store excitement through a unique cause-related marketing program with SOS. Together with SOS-affiliated chefs, Bread & Circus developed Chefs Up Front, in which chefs create prepared meals that are showcased and sold through in-store cooking demonstrations. A percentage of these sales benefit SOS's nutrition education program, Operation Frontline. In addition, Bread & Circus/Whole Foods Market presents Five Percent Day annually at its Northeast U.S. stores, donating 5 percent of sales to Operation Frontline. (Source: Share our Strength, www.strength.org)

Corporations. Corporations in the United States have a time-honored tradition of giving to charitable causes, and nonprofits have benefited greatly from this support, especially those nonprofits that understand how to tie their causes to the needs of prospective corporate donors. This situation is best described as a match where each side "wins." Some just do it better than others—whether it consists of structured volunteer activities for corporate employees, positive publicity, or help in complying with government regulations like the Community Reinvestment Act (CRA). Listening to corporate needs is the key. At Enterprise, we were able to secure grants and low-interest loans from financial institutions, like Washington Mutual, Citibank, and Chase Manhattan, that we reinvested in distressed neighborhoods because we were able to meet their needs of serving these communities and complying with the CRA.

Some more sophisticated nonprofits have expanded their base by moving beyond solicitations of traditional corporate foundations to fashioning a message that appeals to a corporation's marketing side. SOS has pursued cause-related marketing incredibly well, as described in the Digital Spotlight earlier in the chapter. The Calphalon example is a great one. Calphalon agrees to dedicate proceeds from the sale of an "SOS" pan to hunger relief. The pan quickly becomes the best-selling pan for the company. Calphalon's sales increased, awareness of hunger increased, SOS contributions increased—win, win, win.

Technology companies, albeit too slowly for some, have begun to create their own unique corporate giving traditions. eBay, the online auction company, has been a corporate leader. eBay donated 107,250 shares to charity before its initial public offering (IPO) and another 122,750 after going public. The cumulative value of those shares is approximately $42 million.[9] eBay has also pioneered the use of online charity auctions for nonprofits. Real Networks was another early tech pioneer for corporate giving. Before issuing its IPO, Real Networks committed 5 percent of its profits to charity, and CEO Rob Glaser often cites this commitment as an asset and recommends that others follow suit. SmartForce, one of the nation's leading e-learning companies, has provided One Economy with valuable training scholarships for low-income customers of our Web site. If we have learned anything in our work with One Economy, it is that the technology world will give, but they will do it their way. Take the time to understand the technology companies in your community and engage them so you can understand how to meet their charitable and corporate needs.

Foundations.   Foundations have always been a major source of support for nonprofit organizations. Now they are more so. They have a lot more money than they ever had before, and there are a lot more of them.[10] This means there is more money "on the street" and more places to go look for it. No place is this more true than in community foundations. Not only do they have more money, but they also have changing business practices. In some cases, in order to attract newly wealthy patrons, who want a more active role in their giving, and to respond to increasing competition from donor advised mutual funds managed by giants like Fidelity and Vanguard, they are working hard to understand the real problems facing distressed communities and to support nonprofit innovation. If you have not visited your community foundation recently, go back because you are likely to find some changes to your benefit.

Venture Philanthropy.   Venture philanthropy isn't so much a unique source of funding as it is a philosophy for giving. The idea of venture philanthropy is simple: Apply certain practices to the nonprofit sector that are used by venture capitalists in the for-profit sector both when they are considering investments in new businesses or business ideas and after those investments have been made. Generally, that means putting the nonprofit and its business model through a thorough due diligence process. Funding for promising nonprofits that survive that process should provide them with resources sufficient to enable them to focus primarily on their business, not their fundraising. Actively participating on the board of directors of the organization will help you bring all your business acumen and resources to the table to ensure their success.

The venture philanthropy model of The Peninsula Community Foundation (PCF), a leading player in venture philanthropy, captures the process well: (1) investments in long-term (3- to 6-year) business plans; (2) a managing partner relationship; (3) an accountability-for-results process; (4) provision of cash and expertise; and (5) an exit strategy. Investors make long-term funding commitments, closely monitor performance objectives through predefined measurement tools, and problem-solve jointly with the nonprofit leadership team on a regular basis.[11]

This approach is particularly attractive to the "new wealth," or people who have become wealthy in recent years through businesses that were built and grown through venture capital. Venture philanthropy, to some extent, is the perfect mix of individual, corporate, and foundation giving. It provides the donor with the chance to engage in the nonprofit's business, brings the donor's corporation and corporate partners to bear on the activities, and usually operates in an existing foundation or results in the creation of a new foundation organized for this purpose.

We have had the opportunity to spend time with some of the leaders of the venture philanthropy movement. Understanding them and their approach can help you understand how you can find similar people in your community and make venture philanthropy work for you. Some examples of particularly successful venture philanthropists are as follows:

Gib Myers. Myers was a general partner in the well-known Silicon Valley–based venture capital firm The Mayfield Fund and the founder and chairman of the Entrepreneurs' Foundation, which was launched in 1998 (www.the-ef.org). The fund targets successful social entrepreneurs working in education and youth development with classic venture philanthropy strategies. Gib wants to do nothing less than change the culture of the entrepreneurial sector by engaging for-profit companies to develop community involvement strategies, donating pre- and post-IPO stock to support venture philanthropy investments, and making long-term investments in worthy organizations. To date, the Mayfield Fund has more than one billion dollars under management.

Paul Brainard. This founder of Aldus Software and father of PageMaker launched Social Venture Partners (www.SVPSeattle .org) in 1997 with 30 initial partners who committed $25,000 and one hour a week to work with nonprofits. Today there are 200 partners in Seattle and several copycat SVPs throughout the country. SVPs get individuals to invest time, money, and expertise into helping nonprofits achieve their visions.

Mario Morino. Morino sold his technology company for $225 million in 1985 and has never looked back. He has become the leader of the venture philanthropy movement in Washington, D.C., which became a technology town almost overnight. Through his Morino Institute, he has made venture philanthropy investments in groups like Calvary Multicultural Bilingual Learning Center, which is highlighted in Chapter 8, and published a fantastic compilation of venture philanthropy efforts in the country today.[12] In 2001, he led the formation of the Venture Philanthropy Partners, a $50 million venture philanthropy fund dedicated to Washington-area organizations helping youth.

Jerry Collona, Bob Clarke, and Fred Wilson, Flatiron Partners. We know these guys well because they put us through the venture philanthropy model. The Flatiron Foundation was launched in April 2000 by the Flatiron Partners, an early-stage technology-focused venture capital firm in New York. The Flatiron Foundation and its sister fund, the Flatiron Future Fund, concentrate on applying venture capital strategy, discipline, and financing techniques to organizations and companies that aim to have measurable positive social impact. The funds make early-stage investments and grants, and take an active role to help a select number of organizations and companies achieve their goals. Foundation staff and its board of accomplished investors, grant-makers, and entrepreneurs use the extensive company-building experience of the Flatiron Partners and their networks to support the businesses and nonprofits they fund. Unfortunately recent downturns in the economy have caused them to slow down and suspend much of their activities.

We met Flatiron in July 2000 during our third week in business. They warned us that the process would be time consuming with no guarantee of funding. We made the corporate decision to move forward because we literally wanted to "expand our base" of support, and we believed the process itself would enhance our organization.

Perhaps being a startup, we felt we had nothing to lose. Six months later, we were better for it. One specific added value was the formal development and submission of a business plan that included our business model, with relevant milestones and revenue-building strategies. The process also exposed us to a wealth of other resources by way of consultants and corporate contacts. Flatiron's financial commitment to and board involvement in One Economy has dramatically increased our standing with other funders and the level of business discipline in our organization.

Only time and results will tell if venture philanthropy is the future of charitable giving, a current fad, or a little of both. It is not for every organization. Some venture philanthropists want to help only startups, not new projects of existing organizations, whereas others want to help existing organizations to grow and get to scale. Either way, for dynamic organizations today, venture philanthropy can present an opportunity to enhance your business model and expose your organization to new people and markets.

Earned-Income Opportunities. Another significant trend in the nonprofit world is the growth of nonprofit organizations that run successful revenue-generating businesses, either nonprofit or for-profit. We have seen some incredible success stories in this area. As described in Chapter 1, St. Vincent de Paul of Lane County, Oregon, and Pioneer Human Services in Seattle, Washington, are two of our favorites in the nonprofit arena. Both organizations have figured out how to identify a need in a niche market, develop a product that serves that niche and the organization's public purpose, attract the appropriate talent to manage the business, raise the necessary capital, and create a new source of stable revenue for the organization.

Other organizations have succeeded in what some people call the "mixed motive" world. Here, a nonprofit develops a wholly owned, for-profit subsidiary with the express goal of sending profits back home to the parent. Jim Rouse championed this type of effort in 1985, and Mark Sissman built the Enterprise Social Investment Corporation (ESIC) (www.esic.org), a wholly owned subsidiary of the Enterprise Foundation, into a significant financial intermediary from 1985 to 1998. Utilizing Section 42 of the Internal Revenue Code to syndicate low-income housing tax credits, ESIC sells these tax benefits to for-profit businesses and generates enough fee income to support its operations, contribute equity to housing developments, and make significant annual payments to its sole shareholder.

Although extreme competition and shrinking margins challenge the organization today, ESIC is a cover story for the extraordinary potential of earned-income opportunities in the nonprofit world.

Don't get us wrong, creating earned-income opportunities is difficult. You are creating a business that has to live and die in the unforgiving free-market system. As everyone knows, 7 of 10 new businesses fail every year. That means yours is more likely to fail than to succeed. That said, there are resources out there to help you identify and think through opportunities that might be staring you in the face. John Weiser, of Brody & Weiser (www.brodyweiser .com), is a consultant with vast experience working with nonprofits to do just that. John has helped us on several occasions, when starting an appliance recycling effort, a child care subsidiary, and even One Economy. SOS's subsidiary, Community Wealth Ventures (CWV), works with nonprofit organizations to increase their social impact by building and leveraging their assets. CWV does not provide new ways to ask for money. Instead, they work to strengthen an organization by helping it find new sources of revenue. For example, CWV assisted a health care provider to generate revenue by using the excess capacity of its information technology division to provide technical and training services to other area nonprofits for a fee.

Online resources can also help you evaluate and develop earned-income opportunities. The Roberts Enterprise Development Fund (www.redf.org), which supports nonprofit-led ventures, has an array of case studies and lessons learned from its work. The National Center for Social Entrepreneurs (www.socialentrepreneurs.org) has developed an impressive toolkit that can guide you through the development of revenue-generating strategies. See our Web site, www.managingnonprofits.org, for the most current list of online resources in this area.

Using the Net. One of the most direct benefits of building a digital organization is your ability to use the Internet to greatly enhance your fundraising efforts. We have seen organizations that have created a digital culture use the Internet to augment their other fundraising efforts with relative ease. The Internet offers an inexpensive way to reach millions of individuals of varying demographics whose comfort with online transactions continues to grow. In a lot of ways, the Net may be your organization's most productive way to build out an individual fundraising campaign.

This opportunity is exciting because of its potential scale. Although cyber fundraising is still in early phases, of the $135 billion donated by individuals in 1998, $192 million was donated online.[13] Some older, more established nonprofits have wasted little time integrating cyber-giving strategies. The Red Cross is a standout in this regard. It uses the Internet to alert its audience to topical issues such as emergencies and disasters, and then gives them the chance to act on these causes. During the first six months of 1999, the Red Cross received $1.2 million in online gifts for Balkan relief from more than 9,000 donors. The Red Cross combines traditional fundraising with a cyber touch. Their site, www.redcross.org, walks you through a variety of ways to give. Visitors have four options: (1) make a secure donation online with a credit card; (2) donate stock either directly or through a broker; (3) use a toll-free number to give by phone; and (4) send a contribution by mail. Mailing addresses can be obtained simply by entering a zip code.

Net-ready, dynamic organizations are using the Net to increase individual giving dramatically by selling goods through online charity malls and affiliating with online merchants, enabling online contributions, soliciting new members, and conducting charity auctions.[14]

Selling Goods. As *e-commerce* has become a household word, several companies now court nonprofits to create charity shopping malls. These Web sites intermediate between charities and e-commerce retailers. These sites can generate income for nonprofits by allowing consumers to mix shopping and philanthropy. The money comes from commissions paid by e-retailers for customer referrals and purchases. The number of these sites is growing as e-retailers look for a marketing edge and as nonprofits search for new revenue sources. Some of the better known sites include Greater Good, which contributes 5 to 15 percent of the sale to nonprofit organizations, 4Charity.com, and togive.com. 4Charity.com has separated itself from many other charity malls by not taking a fee from donations it receives. Instead, they make their money by selling technology services to businesses and nonprofits to enable online philanthropy. The 140 vendors in this mall donate 4 to 40 percent of each sale to the buyer's selected nonprofit. Tracey Pettengill, CEO of 4Charity, represents a new breed of executive by combining for-profit busy savvy with a social conscience. Along the way, she has created a vessel for businesses and individuals who want to give and for nonprofits that want to expand their base and further their mission.

Several charity malls have added a new twist to the mall concept by creating "Click and Give" sites. At these Web sites, visitors can generate donations for an organization just by clicking and viewing the Web site. For example, www.EcologyFund.com is owned and operated by CharityMall.com as a way to raise new funds for creature habitat and wilderness preservation. When you "click to donate," a sponsor donates to the project you designated to preserve. You can even have the donation made in your own name.

Similarly, more and more nonprofits are also entering into affiliate relationship with e-retailers. In an affiliate relationship, the nonprofit may receive a fixed payment for every person who clicks through from the nonprofit's site to the e-retailer site and/or a percentage commission on the amount of goods purchased on the e-retailer's site from the person referred by the nonprofit. Affiliate relationships with Amazon.com or barnesandnoble.com can be commonly found on nonprofit Web sites.

Some larger nonprofits with significant brand equity are entering into e-retailer relationships with companies to manage their e-retailing operations. In November 2000, The Smithsonian Institution began selling gifts online through a new Web site developed and managed by a private, for-profit company, the MuseumCompany.com. MuseumCompany.com will promote SmithsonianStore.com to the 30 million people who visit Smithsonian museums each year, to the 2 million subscribers to *Smithsonian* magazine, and to the 3 million monthly visitors to the museum's Web site. The Smithsonian expects this relationship to create a long-term source of revenue and be up to 10 to 20 percent of the institution's total retail revenue.[15]

Accepting Contributions.   One of the simplest but most powerful things about fundraising on the Web is the ability of nonprofits to accept contributions online, especially credit card donations. One of the best examples we have heard of is the little Fremont Public Association (FPA) in Washington state. It went from raising $17,000 online in 1999 to raising $50,000 in a day with a single "Leap Day" event February 29 on its Web site, www.fremontpublic.org.[16] That day the organization generated 350 new donors—triple the amount of new donors found through all means during the previous year.

Picking a Charity Mall

One of the best ways to compare vendors is to contact non-profits already listed on the site and ask if their experience has been positive. You will also want to do a bit of comparison shopping by reviewing the fine print and specifics for each vendor on their Web site before you sign on the electronic line. The following questions will help you compare vendors:

- How many merchants, nonprofits, and consumers participate?
- How does the charity mall promote its site?
- What is the monthly traffic?
- Are there any upfront or hidden costs?
- Does the mall restrict recipients to 501-C organizations?
- What is the retail mix? Are these products of interest to your donors?
- What percentage of each sale is contributed to your organization?
- What are the rules in terms of banner/ad link placement on your Web site and other requirements for promoting the charity mall on your Web site or to your audiences?
- What is the minimum amount that needs to accrue before the mall issues a check?
- How is the check issued (snail mail or electronically)?
- Can you enter into relationships with more than one charity mall?
- What is the privacy policy of the site, and how is it enforced?

Source: Beth Kantor, ArtsWire Education Coordinator, www.artswire.org

Setting up your site to accept donations can be costly and time-consuming; however, payment service providers, or PSPs, can manage the donations and payments. The PSP enables your organization to accept credit card transactions by providing a link on your organization's Web site to a pledge or donation page that resides on the PSP's server.

Picking a PSP

Most PSPs allow you to customize the look of your donation page, thank you message, and reports. Rates range from flat monthly fees to a tiered per-transaction or gift amount fee. PSPs that cater to nonprofits include RemitNet and DonorNet. The following questions will help you evaluate vendors:

- Does the vendor offer secure transactions?
- What is the level of technical support?
- How reliable is the service?
- How much does it cost? What is the per-transaction fee? What are the setup costs?
- What is the length of the contract for services?
- How long does it take to set up an account?
- What does the organization need to provide/do for the setup?
- How much control/customization is available on the donation solicitation page, or is it simply a "submit" link?
- Can the confirmation e-mail/screen be customized?
- What type of customer support is provided to the donor if there is a problem?
- What type of reporting is available to organizations online or via e-mail?
- Can it be customized? Can it be exported in my database?

Charity Auctions. One of the most popular forms of fundraising in the past 10 years has been fundraising auctions. These auctions enable people to donate anything from a weekend in their home on the South of France to a date with a basketball superstar. Led by eBay, the Web's leading auction site, but now copied by many sites on the Internet, companies are making their auction infrastructure available to nonprofits so they can hold these auctions online and increase the universe of those who might give.

These last two examples, online giving and charity auctions, are perfect examples of the idea that we have talked about often in this

Picking a Donation Portal

Although many nonprofits set up a giving capacity on their own sites, they may also participate in donation portals. These sites provide information about many different nonprofit organizations, and visitors can select their favorite charity and make a donation online using their credit card. The financial viability of the portals is in question, but if you are considering participating with one, here is some help.

To evaluate vendors, visit their sites and read their materials. Some good questions to ask are as follows:

- What and how many other nonprofits are included on the site?
- What is the cost of registering?
- Are there any restrictions in terms of participating or working with other online fundraising vendors?
- Can the nonprofit organizations provide a direct link to the organization's information page on the charity engine site?

Source: Beth Kantor, ArtsWire Education Coordinator, www.artswire.org

book—digital integration. Your cyber fundraising effort will work best not as a stand-alone activity or strategy but as part of an overall action plan. Link your Web site with direct mail and advertising campaigns and test your message. In fact, integration is what made the FPA Net Day such a success. FPA posted notice of the day on its Web site about 10 days before the event was to take place; found, among its existing members, a matching donor willing to give $100 for every new donor contributing at least $29 on the date of the event, up to about $5,000; had FPA members e-mail their friends with a message containing a clickable link to the page on the site that had the event information; and held a phone-a-thon to reach out to likely donors. The FPA estimates that these non-Web activities generated about 80 percent of the traffic to the site.

Developing a Plan to Expand Your Base

Organizations often talk about expanding their base but seldom execute this goal. Instead, they mine the same old places for revenue.

Expanding your base requires an assessment of the entire organization, not simply a new marketing pitch or a recycled slogan. The assessment should be a top-to-bottom review during which you challenge your vision, business model, customer base, content, and infrastructure. Identify individuals, corporations, foundations, or earned-income opportunities that you haven't pursued before. If new sources of support cannot be identified, then you need to consider building another business model. If Internet fundraising strategies are not deemed possible, then you have been given a sure sign that you have not built the digital culture that you seek.

This analysis ought to involve as many stakeholders as possible. Don't leave this important task to the fundraising staff alone. Although fundraising should be going in the same direction as your programs, the fundraisers often are the last to know about new programmatic initiatives. Even in the digital age, money drives program, but programs raise money.

Once the assessment is complete, develop a fundraising plan that expands the base, using the sources described previously; integrates the vision, the business model, and the Internet; and views everyone on staff as a potential revenue generator. Establish a timeline, numeric goals, staff assignments, targeted sources for revenue, and take action. Plenty of online resources can help you through the technical aspects of writing a plan. The Council on Foundations, www.COF.org, has a wealth of resources to assist you. Innonet has a quality Web site, www.innonet.org, that can help you navigate through the planning process. An up-to-date list of Internet resources can be found at www.managingnonprofits.org.

Resources from Value-Added Partnerships

Money is obviously an important resource for nonprofit organizations; however, in these times of change, dynamic organizations must look to strategic relationships for support beyond money—for resources that will enable them to scale their operations, better serve their customers, expand their content, and compete. We have highlighted many of them in this book. Environmental Defense partnered with McDonald's to help them reengineer their packaging and use more recycled materials. By influencing McDonald's corporate behavior worldwide, Environmental Defense was able to have a more dramatic impact on the environment than it ever could have had through fundraising or a strict philanthropic relationship with McDonald's. America's Second Harvest's partnership with Hewlett-Packard to build ResourceLink may not have raised new money for the nonprofit, but it will significantly increase the amount of food available to America's hungry people. The coalition of state university hospitals that created NetWellness understood that they could do more for underserved people in Ohio and Kentucky if they worked together. Their synergies have turned a humble public access project into a worldwide health resource.

We have always worked hard to find high-capacity for-profit and nonprofit partners to help us scale our programs. There simply is no way that one organization can have a material impact on the great problems facing the world if it tries to do it alone and outside of the economic mainstream. At Enterprise, we partnered with financial institutions that helped make more than $200 million of low-interest loans available to organizations working in distressed neighborhoods. At One Economy, we have AOL Time Warner, Hewlett Packard, Cisco, Sylvan Learning, and others, who are leveraging their resources, relationships, and worldwide distribution systems to bring Internet access and top-of-market information and services to low-income people in their homes.

Like individual fundraising, cultivation of partners is a time-consuming process. Successful organizations take the time to understand their partners' needs and goals. Then they fashion a strategy to engage their partners over the long haul.

Digital Spotlight—Resources from Value-Added Partnerships: The Cisco Fellows Program

In Spring 2001, Cisco Systems announced that earnings would not meet expectations, that more than 6,000 people would be laid off, and that $2 billion in inventory would be written off at the end of the company's fiscal year. Despite the gloomy economic reality facing Cisco at the time, CEO John Chambers announced that he was going to create a silver lining in this dark cloud. If some of the company's best and brightest talent would agree to take a 70 percent reduction in pay, Cisco would keep them on the payroll and lend them to one of Cisco's nonprofit partners for an entire year as "Cisco Fellows."

At the end of the year, if economic conditions changed, they would be welcomed back to Cisco. If conditions didn't change or if they liked their life and career opportunities better on the outside, the Fellows would be free to do whatever they wanted to do with their lives.

Our company, One Economy Corp., was selected as one of twelve nonprofit organizations in the world to compete for the attention and interest of the prospective Fellows. We were also the only start-up, technology-focused nonprofit in the group. Over a two-month period, Cisco staff built the Fellows program from scratch, interviewing hundreds of candidates and helping to make matches with nonprofit organizations. One Economy considered more than 50 applications and selected thirteen Fellows who began work in July, 2001. Some Fellows are applying their extensive networking skills to help wire and connect thousands of low-income households to the Internet. Others are learning to define "sales" in new ways including bringing other partners and housing owners to our work. They all share one thing: They are having very little trouble transferring their work experiences from the for-profit to the nonprofit world. With Cisco Fellows literally doubling our capacity on the ground, One Economy projects that this one year effort will accelerate our business model by 18–24 months.

Cisco was looking for a nonprofit that could excite its highly valued employees about the nonprofit world. One Economy was looking for help in bringing technology to the housing and community development industry and in raising its own corporate technology IQ and visibility. The Cisco Fellows program has provided value-added resources to both parties.

TECHNOLOGY

As you can see throughout this book, technology is a common thread that is woven into the fabric of a dynamic organization. It impacts on every aspect of the Dynamic Management Map. That is why we see technology—applied in the right environment that is being supported by stable and diverse resources—as the basic, underlying foundation that nonprofits need to succeed in the digital age. It is the infrastructure that supports everything else we do.

This section focuses on some of the core principles that we believe should drive the application of technology today. We also touch on some of the issues surrounding the most common uses of technology: internal systems and Web sites. This section is not a technical guide to equipment purchases or the latest software or hardware. Rather, it explains the reasons for and the uses of digital solutions to help you further your mission.

Core Principles

Technology must have a purpose; plans and expected results must be realistic, costs reasonably forecast, and use supported.

Technology Must Have a Purpose. This point seems so obvious, yet the principle of having a purpose for technology is too often overlooked. The number of organizations that are hard pressed to articulate a purpose for technology even though they are investing in it strikes us. This is "old way" thinking that leads to bad investments and underutilization of capacity. Technology can be a transformative force in your organization when its purpose is clear. It can blaze a new path.

It is never too late to step back and define a purpose for your technology. Purpose cannot be hatched in isolation by technology staff and handed over to management if you are working to truly integrate technology into the way you do business both internally and externally. The purpose should be determined by a cross-section of individuals representing the program, administrative, and information technology part of the organization.

Your purpose should not be so overreaching that it means all things to all people. Statements like "We are going to be a Web-enabled organization" are too broad and do not give clear guidance. People should be able to clearly articulate what the purpose is, such as: "Technology will enable staff to communicate more regularly with each other and with our customers" or "Technology will allow us to distribute our specialized expertise more broadly and to have a greater impact on public policy." The more focused and defined your purpose, the better your prospects are for a successful implementation.

Generally, most nonprofits we know use technology to further two broad purposes: (1) to add value to the organization's business model and processes, and (2) to support an ethos of learning within the organization.

Adding Value to the Business Model and Processes

Most people view adding value to the organization's business model (customers and content) and internal processes as the primary purpose for technology. In addition to giving you new ways to communicate with and learn from your customers (described as follows and in Chapter 4), technology can help support your business model by enhancing your programs and services. As described fully in Chapter 5, almost every nonprofit provides programs and services that can be made better by technology. The Bay Area Homeless Alliance (www.baha.org) gave all their clients an e-mail address and voice mail and fundamentally transformed how the world interacted with and viewed them. The animal shelter in Phoenix, Arizona, (www.aawl.org) put pictures of all its stray animals online and quickly matched pets with old and new owners. Adding technology to your business model can be that simple and powerful.

But to be fully effective, technology must also support the broad sharing of information that enables the organization to run. Technology should make information flow better and give you valuable insight into the inner workings of your organization. For example, more timely data about the status of grant reimbursement requests and monthly cashflow will let you know why and how much money you are bleeding. Data on program usage, from drug counseling to free lunches, provides you with a better understanding about the products and services most valued by customers and where your staff should be applied. There are numerous examples of how knowledge gained through technology can be a tool to help you stay on top of and reorder your business processes.

A system that captures the data you need in order to work better and more productively is what Bill Gates calls the "digital nervous system." Technology put to this use has the potential of turning your support staff—all your staff for that matter—into knowledge workers. Knowledge workers, in Gates terminology, focus on processes, not just tasks. What does that mean? With the proper databases, people can now get the information they need to solve problems more easily and often handle much more satisfying and complex transactions. For example, we built a product when we were at the Enterprise Foundation called The Developer's Support System. It was a Web-based product that anyone who worked in the housing and community development field could access for information on how to develop certain types of affordable housing, from soup to nuts. It answered most, if not all, of the basic questions that people always had about the process: What's a development team? A predevelopment loan? Permanent financing? We painstakingly trained all the support staff in our 15 local offices around the country so they were comfortable navigating the site, pointing customers to the right place on the site for answers, and freeing up more senior staff to provide higher-end advice. It worked. Many support staff felt empowered and more a part of the organization; customers got their questions answered fast and were turned onto an online tool that they could use in their day-to-day work. Our senior staff got to do the rewarding, more complex housing development work they liked to do. Everyone wins. In digital organizations, knowledge is decentralized and flexibility is maximized.

We like the mental picture that we get when Mario Morino, the futurist, talks about this issue of knowledge workers. He dreams of the day that social workers will use portable devices and other tools to function as *information brokers*, redefining their role with poor people and their place in the workforce. The more workers have the right knowledge at their fingertips and the right culture, the more people at all levels of an organization will innovate and implement.

Unfortunately, most nonprofits have developed neither the systems nor the processes to capture and distribute the information they need. We see two reasons for this. One, as noted earlier, some organizations have not built an environment that sees information as a shared resource. Even the best systems won't overcome this problem. The other reason is that many nonprofits have dysfunctional internal systems where simply attaching technology to them won't fix them. The systems need to be fixed first. As one of our prior auditors said: "Fix the process first, then apply technology to make it better." As part of your repositioning, fix the processes so they further your business model. Ask "What information do we need to serve our customers, distribute our content and secure our funding?" Then make the needed technology investments. Technology is merely a tool, albeit an important one, that supports your processes.[17]

Supporting an Ethos of Learning. Dynamic organizations often set themselves apart from other organizations because they have an ethos of learning. That means having a continuous commitment to learning and improving. Technology makes this goal so much easier to achieve because it can help you achieve the following objectives:

- *Learn about your customers.* In Chapter 5, we showed you how dynamic organizations are using technology to learn more about their customers and to build "stickiness," or customer loyalty. We raise this point here again to emphasize that technology is not just about internal systems, but about your relationships outside the organization as well. We talk more about this topic later in our Web site discussion as well.

- *Learn about your organization.* Similarly, we highlighted some approaches that nonprofits are using today to get regular, reliable customer feedback about their work. Online forums, chats, e-mails, and bulletin boards can augment traditional, costly, and time-consuming surveys or focus groups.

- *Facilitate learning in your staff.* Ongoing learning for staff is critical to an organization's success and often the last thing funded. We know we have said it before, but investing in people is more important than your investments in hardware and software. This is too often not the case in organizations that have just expanded their capital budgets or that have a hot new idea. Mario Marino has suggested that schools should not just "wire the schools, wire the teachers." It would be a better investment. We have spent time talking about investing in people throughout this book because it is essential in dynamic organizations. In fact, Techsoup, an online technology resource for nonprofits and others, recommends a 70 to 30 percent split of your organization's technology resources, with 70 percent of your outlays going to training and support.

Fortunately, nonprofits can use affordable, online tools to facilitate this learning, 24 hours a day, seven days a week. Organizations such as Community Intelligence Labs, with its Knowledge Ecology University, have created virtual learning environments designed for decision makers dealing with knowledge management and community development. Others are out there as well, like ArtsWire, a program of the New York Foundation for the Arts, which has a host of practical workshops available online, any time of day and night.[18]

In addition, you might consider training support from volunteers, for-profit and nonprofit partners, or even internal teams that train their colleagues. An ever-increasing array of training resources is available for nonprofits at computer training centers, community colleges, customized training, self-paced training, listservs, and message boards. The key to training is to recognize the diverse ways that people learn. Some people are classroom learners, whereas others seem to learn only while at their desks. Commit to training and continuous learning. Provide diverse avenues to make this real.

Plans and Results Must Be Realistic. Some organizations we have worked with have unrealistic expectations for their technology. They want to go from having one computer with Internet access in a five-person office to having all staff networked together, a computer lab open to the public, and modems for all of the customers. Similarly, they count on technology to enable them to help dramatically more people and to lessen their workload, all at the same time. One of the most important things for the Dynamic Manager to do is to manage expectations. Obviously, planning wise, you want to be slightly out in front of your present capacity because you are anticipating the needs of tomorrow, but you don't want to be too far in front. Remember that costs to maintain your technology can be prohibitive. What you don't need now will cost you less later when you do need it. We provide more help on planning for basic technology for operations later in this chapter.

You also have to help people understand what the new technology will or will not enable you to do. Some things can simply be solved with technology, such as getting all your staff connected through a local area network and providing Internet access on every desktop, but other things need a greater change in the organization's digital culture. Web-enabling products and services is more a function of staff embracing technology and transferring their knowledge and expertise to this new medium, not hardware or software. We once worked with a large nonprofit organization that was making an extraordinary commitment to technology. They had hired a million-dollar consultant and assigned their top communications staff to the project. Their goal was to create a Web site that was to be *the* destination for all people and professionals interested in their area of work. Their technological infrastructure was extraordinary. They equipped their staff and every office. The problem was that they hadn't provided the vision for technology to their people, hadn't integrated technology into their business model, and hadn't built the right environment where technology solutions and technology-based content were valued. You can spend money to have the best equipment and build the best-looking Web site, but if your added value is content and your people aren't providing their content on the Web, you don't have much.

All Costs Must Be Forecast.   Your total costs for building and maintaining technology must be included in your annual budget. Typically, a budget includes funds for hardware and software, Internet access, training, and staffing. Depending on the scope of your business, staffing may include a systems administrator and a database manager. It is important to require every part of your organization to budget for its own technology costs. Don't allow a separate technology budget to be built. Separate technology budgets create a silo effect—"technology is IT's problem, not mine." An integrated budget helps bring a certain discipline to all parts of the organization so that the "technology dreamers" are tempered by the "realists," while not having their innovative spirits crushed.

There is no easy matrix or system for determining how much money you should spend on technology. Just remember to look to your purpose for the technology and develop a budget that moves you toward that purpose in a rational way, to the extent your resources allow.

Technology Must Be Supported.   The last basic principle about technology is that it must be supported. Hardware and software must be maintained and upgraded, and there has to be someone to call if people have questions and problems. This is true whether technology is being used for programs or operations. The key issue for resource-starved nonprofits is "how." Primarily, the options are do it in-house, through consultants, or a mix of both. Nonprofits must balance the current cost with the longer-term needs of the organization. When is the right time to start building your own capacity to manage technology as you grow its use?

Hiring a consultant may seem like the simplest solution, but selecting a consultant is as important as hiring staff. They are part of your team, and as a "people resource" must be integrated into your operations. Moreover, you have to know specifically what you want them to do and monitor their performance. Too often, organizations give consultants sketchy instructions and say, "Just get it done." As one consultant once told us, "Some of my customers are simply bad clients. They don't really know what they want, so I have to substitute my judgment for theirs which seldom results in their getting what they had hoped to get." Consultants are also not a cure for bad business processes. As stated earlier, these must be fixed before hiring a consultant. Technology will only mask these problems.

In addition to more traditional consulting, there are ever-expanding options for nonprofits that might choose to rent technology and expertise on a pay-as-you-go basis through application service providers (ASPs). It fact, this option might be your most inexpensive way to take advantage of new technologies. ASPs are an online outsourcing or hosting service for software applications, typically for large businesses with hundreds of users or more.[19] In essence, ASPs develop, manage, and maintain computer systems and software, so you are almost guaranteed that your software, e-mail, or database will never go down. ASPs can help you do a variety of things, from word processing and creating spreadsheets to developing and managing your Web presence or keeping track of donors and volunteers. Time will tell us the extent that ASPs penetrate the nonprofit world, but their future holds great promise. Your organization might also find varying degrees of support from peer-to-peer extranets that take advantage of networks that share files and collaborate on projects without central servers. This too is an early-stage process and will need time to determine its long-term utility to the nonprofit industry.

Another option is working with a growing array of technology consultants committed to working with the nonprofit industry. First begun as "circuit traders" or one technology-savvy person who would visit a host of nonprofits on a regular basis, organizations such as Npower, CompuMentor, and others have institutionalized and expanded this practice.

When making support decisions: Look inward first. Examine your core competencies and project your future needs. Be realistic about finances—that is, does in-house really save money? Often it does not. Ask what is best for your culture, your business model, your customers, and your content. Then look at your range of external options. Tech Soup (www.techsoup.org) has outstanding resource materials to help you select and manage consultants.

Technology Basics

This last section is intended to give you some guidance on building internal systems and a Web site. Our intent is to provide only enough information to give you the right context—to help you to ask the right questions. An ever-growing number of Web sites provide much more detailed and current information. Wherever possible, we send you to these expansive Internet resources. Look at www.managingnonprofits.org for the most current and useful sites.

Internal Systems. Basic systems consist of hardware (i.e., computers, printers, monitors, modems, network hardware: cables, routers, wires, and hubs) and software (i.e., operating systems like Windows, LINUX, DOS, and applications like databases, accounting, and word processing). Software is what enables your hardware to meet the needs of your organization. The key question that organizations must ask is "What technology is right for us?" A basic technology plan assists you in answering that question in two ways: (1) it helps you define your purpose for technology (e.g. expanding your options for delivering content versus improving financial management), and (2) it helps project the costs, equipment, and training needed to meet that purpose. Some terrific Web sites will help walk you through every element of technology planning. Nonprofit Genie[20] provides the nine most frequently asked questions about IT planning. Other sites, like Npower.org (www.npower.org), have a wide array of technology planning resources. Finally, CompuMentor, a San Francisco–based nonprofit organization that has provided technology resources to nonprofits serving low-income communities since 1987, has an excellent free nonprofit technology Web site that has partnered with CNET to share expert advice (www.techsoup.org).

All of these sites have tools for accomplishing the following tasks:

- Evaluating technology needs at every level of your organization.
- Defining and describing ways to improve internal communications and office networks.
- Completing a technology sustainability study to look at where your overall strategy lies and how it needs to be adjusted to fit your current rates of growth and expenditure.

Your Web Site. Think of your Web site as the virtual front door to your organization. The experience that people have when they walk in the door will leave a lasting impression on them. People are not likely to come back if the experience is difficult or frustrating, but they are likely to return again and again if the experience is satisfying. We have found that the following elements are critical to building successful Web sites:

Content. The more content (products and services) you have on your site, the more interesting it will be for your customers. It's that simple. We provide a lot of extraordinary examples of content delivery through the Web in Chapter 6. Unfortunately, many nonprofits have not evolved beyond the "brochure online" phase of site development, where they essentially put their general organizational brochure up as their Web site. If you are in that phase, consider providing additional content tools such as online forums, online fundraising, and frequently asked questions sections to start moving your users into the digital culture. Keep in mind that the tools you select all require varying degrees of support and maintenance.

Community. We spoke a lot about building an online community for your customers in Chapter 5. Acting as this "neutral platform" where your customers can interact with each other may be the most effective method for creating stickiness for your organization and your Web site. After we started Enterprise Online a few years ago, we created a community forum to facilitate peer-to-peer contact. It quickly grew a loyal following and enabled our customers to assist each other in ways we had never thought of.

Customization. Customization allows your customers to reorient your content to a format or design that most suits their needs. We had built our Enterprise Web site with a dozen or more "channels" from fundraising to news to public policy. Customers entering the site who didn't care much about policy could simply customize the page so they saw only the channels they wanted to see. The Internet facilitates mass customization and allows your Web page to provide for "Markets of One."[21] With the click of a mouse, customers can retrieve their desired information in the format they want.

Convenience. Convenience is about making retrieval of customized information and navigating of the site easy and intuitive. Your Web site needs to be intuitive so that the visitor is clear about how it works, and it should be simple to actually use without running into literacy or accessibility barriers. People should not have to understand what you do and how you do it to use your Web site. It also should be fully functional to all users, regardless of their microprocessor speed, platform, display setup, and browser.

Measuring.   You need to determine what you want out of your Web site and develop ways to measure if you are achieving those results. A couple of years ago, most organizations only wanted to find out the number of "hits" or visits their sites received. This approach told them nothing about what people did at their site, how long they stayed, or if they ever came back again. Dynamic organizations want to know much more today. For example, when people access the Kaboom! Web site, Kaboom! wants them to sign up to volunteer or contribute to building a playground with their time or money. Therefore, Kaboom! regularly measures how many people used their site to become an active part of their work. Organizations commonly want to know how many unique visitors came to their site, how visitors navigated through the site, where visitors came from, which pages they viewed, and how long they stayed on the site. Several inexpensive Web statistics programs capture quality information on Web site use. As we said earlier, you will also want to design customer feedback mechanisms so you can capture more information about how you are doing, not only in terms of their site experience but also their overall satisfaction with your services.

Marketing.   Your Web measuring efforts will assist you in your Web marketing efforts as well. They will help inform you about what people want. A good Web marketing strategy must be integrated into the overall marketing efforts of your organization. Resist the urge to have stand-alone efforts. The Web is merely an additional tool to increase traffic and usage of your products and services, online and off.

Web marketing opportunities are numerous. Search engine registration, promotions through e-mail, links from other sites, and advertising on other relevant or popular sites, on a free or fee-for-service basis, are all effective marketing methods. ONE/Northwest, described in Chapter 5, has developed an excellent summary of nonprofit marketing opportunities on the Web.[22] We have included their summary at the end of this chapter. Search engines are by far the most powerful marketing tool. There are a large number of search engines like About.com, Yahoo!, Google, and Ask Jeeves.

Your organization must understand what it takes to get a good "ranking" on a search engine so your site will come up when people search for issues you are involved in. You can find excellent help in this area at www.searchenginewatch.com.

Online marketing can go as far as your imagination will take you. Some nonprofits have been successful in marketing their sites by promoting a campaign or by launching their organization online. Netaid.org is an extraordinary example of this approach. Netaid.org is an initiative founded by the United Nations Development Programme (UNDP) and Cisco Systems. To launch Netaid.org and to show the potential power of the Internet for social good, the partners sponsored a well-publicized series of three concerts held simultaneously in Geneva, London, and New York in October 1999. More than 100,000 people attended these concerts, 2.4 million logged on for a live Webcast, and thousands of villages and homes around the globe tuned in on television and radio. In the following months, the Netaid.org Web site received more than 40 million hits from 160 countries, signaling a powerful momentum for online action against poverty. A new organization, with a sizable constituency, was born.[23]

Help in Building Your Web Site

Many of the same Web-based resources we have cited earlier in this chapter also have great resources and links on building a Web site. Our favorites, at the time of publication, include ONE/Northwest's Building an Effective Web Site;[24] helping.org's suite of pages on planning, creating, and evaluating your Web site;[25] and Makingthenetwork's Web Site Planning.[26] Please go to our Web site, www.managingnonprofits.org, for the best Web site support resources on the Net.

Digital Spotlight—Seven Characteristics of an Online Organization[27]

The following was developed by ONE/Northwest for conservation organizations but we have found it useful for any nonprofit organization.

E-Mail Addresses and Desktop Internet Access for Every Staff Member. Online organizations have unique e-mail addresses for each staff member, and all staff members have access to e-mail and the Web from their own workstations. Individual e-mail accounts maximize the efficiencies that online communication can bring to an organization, and having e-mail and Web access on all desktops allows individuals to tap into these resources as they need them. Many conservation organizations still have only a single e-mail address for multiple staff members and/or access to e-mail (and the Internet in general) is available only from a single machine. Online organizations make these communication tools available to everyone in their organization. They are as readily available as a telephone or a word processor.

A Local Area Network (LAN).   Online organizations constantly share information electronically and make efficient use of their communication equipment and resources. Connecting two or more computers together to form a local area network (LAN) allows an organization to share printers, modems, phone lines, Internet access, and other resources, and allows for centralized storage of documents, databases, and other important information. Creating a small and simple network within a nonprofit office is within the reach of most organizations, both in terms of cost and technical know-how.

Technical Expertise to Keep the Systems Going. Online organizations identify and invest in the people they need to keep their electronic communication systems functioning properly. Although few organizations need or can afford full-time system administrators, every organization needs to devote human resources to keep its systems operational, up to the level of value this technology has for the organization. This investment must include training, time (the time to do this work!), and the support of the entire organization. An online organization recognizes that electronic networking technology takes focused human effort if these tools are to be an asset to the organization.

Technology as a Component of Organizational Planning.   Online organizations plan for the technology and training they'll need and fully integrate this planning into the development of their organization. At a minimum, this means that the annual budget includes line items for necessary equipment purchases and staff training, and a 12- to 18-month blueprint for infrastructure improvements. Ideally, it also means that the use of online communication flows throughout the programmatic work of the organization, with an online strategy articulated for each major initiative the organization plans to pursue.

E-mail Addresses for Important Online Constituencies. Online organizations recognize the power of e-mail and seek out opportunities to use e-mail when they communicate routinely with the people most important to their work (their membership, colleagues, or the media). To be able to use e-mail in this way, an organization must actively solicit the e-mail addresses of its key constituents at all opportunities and ensure that this information is stored in a contact database along with the address, phone, and fax number of the individual. Most conservation organizations in the Pacific Northwest are not yet pursuing e-mail addresses with the same zeal with which they pursue other contact information.

Virus Protection and Routine Data Backup. Some of the most important assets of conservation organizations are now electronic, represented in documents and databases that are crucial to the work of the organization. In the same way that people lock their doors and monitor access to their physical property, online organizations must protect their electronic information from catastrophic problems that can be caused by equipment failure and destructive software viruses. Developing an effective and routine system for data backup and virus protection is crucial insurance to protect what you have and do online and a sign of a mature online organization.

An Organizational Web Site. A Web site that effectively represents the mission, goals, and activities of an organization and provides visitors with useful information and opportunities to act is within the reach of most online conservation groups. A Web site not only allows a conservation group to effectively provide on-demand access to information, but can also be effectively integrated with all other communication media to create a powerful outreach and activation tool. Donors, colleagues, and (increasingly) the media expect conservation groups to have at least basic organizational Web sites, and this expectation will only increase.

Digital Spotlight—Worksystems, Inc.

Worksystems, Inc. has recently completed a comprehensive repositioning. Once a troubled Private Industry Council (PIC) providing services to unemployed and low-income residents of Portland, Oregon, Worksystems is now a three-county workforce development organization that tackles key policy issues in the local economy; contracts for a variety of workforce services for job-seekers, current workers, and future workers (youth); and works with employers to grow their existing talent. The transformation of Worksystems was no accident. It required an extraordinary effort by senior management to rebuild the organization's infrastructure—the environment, the technology, even its approach to raising funds. As we have seen with many dynamic organizations, Worksystems heavily focused on the uses of technology as a central organizing principle for its internal productivity, as well as the way to reorder the relationship with its partners, funders, and the public.

John Ball, President of Worksystems, recognized that in order for his programs to be relevant in the corporate world he had to expand his definition of customer to the corporations that actually hire people and view "the private sector as our standard of competition." To respond to this customer, Worksystems had to get better at anticipating economic trends ("paying attention to the markets"), understanding the profile of current and future employee skill sets, and building the capacity of Worksystems' nonprofit service provider partners to train and support workers who would be in demand in the marketplace. Worksystems also had to adopt strategies such as flexible learning systems and knowledge management that were quickly becoming part of the corporate culture.

The problem that Ball addressed first was one of the alignment and environment. He led the complete reorganization of Worksystems from a hierarchical organization to a flatter system that allowed staff ideas to rise to the top. New staff members who had skill sets that could be deployed into flexible teams were recruited to solve problems and develop new programs. Now program goals and objectives are developed by teams, with each member bringing a different perspective. A consequence is that as the hierarchy was dismantled, many of the organization's tenured staff moved on to other jobs. Managers in particular needed a different skill set, one of compromise and integration, leading by example and sensitivity to diversity. The right environment was being built by a new senior management team from scratch.

A physical representation of that change was the move from the typical office space—corner offices, cubicles—to an open floor plan. All the furniture, cabinets, and desks are on wheels so that teams can form, break up, and reform, as needed. A consequence of the flatter hierarchy and open office is that the traditional stupefying communication structure has broken down in favor of moving information faster and more effectively. No one can block communication when you can simply get up and walk around them.

Ball's team also realized that they had to give up control over information to their customers and partners. They deeply believed that the typical management information systems (MIS) department had to be disbanded in favor of more independent technology staff that could be deployed as needed. Under the old systems, MIS controlled the reporting systems, and therefore the data and, in a way, the performance. Line staff did not own the outcomes. The restructured system deploys reporting to the team responsible for the program, with MIS staff as a resource to the team to structure the data and reporting necessary to measure outcomes. Technology and program were integrated. One did not drive or follow the other.

Next, Worksystems put all of its program materials, reporting, data, and financial systems online. For the nonprofit service providers, this allowed them to access all parts of the program on the Worksystems Web site, from application to reimbursements to reporting. This required a level of technological sophistication and investment on the part of the service providers, but Worksystems was prepared to help them evolve to a digital culture. It first extended its T1, high-speed data line to all of the service providers and integrated its networked software for financial management and program reporting into all of their operations. The providers not only appreciated the speed of the access, but Worksystem's move to require online program operations also functioned as a training opportunity. This, coupled with a healthy use of Worksystems' MIS staff as circuit riders in their offices moved changes steadily forward.

An intended result of both the open office plan and open architecture of its network was an increase in productivity and a boost in communications among all the necessary stakeholders. The productivity changes have been startling—in 1998, at the start of the transformation, Worksystems's overhead rate was 17 percent, by 2000 the overhead rate was 9.9 percent. A corresponding change was increasing the organization's information systems budget from $300,000 a year to $2,000,000 in 2000. The lesson from this change was, as John Ball put it, "moving IS from a capital expense to an operating expense, just as the world is demanding us to."

Lastly, the open architecture of Worksystems's network has allowed providers to communicate with each other and Worksystems in new ways. Although there has always been a common political awareness among the nonprofit providers, this new system has allowed them to share best practices, policy changes, and funding opportunities more effectively. With the use of e-mail, people have begun to couple communication with action, by attaching support letters or program templates to their messages urging action.

When asked to highlight the key things that he has learned through the repositioning, Ball states the following:

- "Kill the Gurus"—empower and support workers/partners to work together through technology. This allows them the flexibility to find their own systems/solutions.
- MIS is a support, not an information controller. Huge increases in production do not come from experts, but from the folks who know the demands and needs of the market.
- Move IS from capital expense to operating expense.
- Embrace the Law of Unintended Consequences that comes from open systems. You never know what people will do with increased access to information. Don't fight it, go along for the ride.
- The private sector is your standard of competition, the public sector is falling faster behind every week.
- Pay attention to environment, jump at opportunities, and develop a tolerance for experimentation.

Digital Spotlight—Publicizing Your Web Site

Once you've built your organization's Web site, the next task is to make sure you've publicized your site as widely as possible. There are two key audiences to which you need to publicize your site: people you already communicate with and people you don't. Each audience is important, but the methods you'll use to reach them are different.

Publicizing Your Site to People You Already Communicate with

It's relatively easy to publicize your site to people you're already in contact with.

General Communication: Add your Web address (the URL, or uniform resource locator) to every piece of communication that comes from your organization. Your Web address should be listed everywhere that your phone/fax number and mailing address is, including the following:

- Business cards
- Letterhead
- Newsletters
- Brochures
- Press releases
- Fax cover sheets
- Action alerts

E-mail Messages: List your Web address at the bottom of every e-mail message sent by the people in your organization (including board members, volunteers, etc.). E-mail messages are often forwarded widely, and it helps if your Web address travels with your e-mail message.

Tell the Media: Consider sending a formal press release about your site to local newspapers, television stations, and other media sources with whom you have relationships. Your site can become a routine information resource for these media outlets and can provide them with easy access to the information you want them to have.

Tell Your Membership: If you have a database of members or others who take an active interest in your work, be sure to tell your members about your Web site (in your newsletter, in correspondence, at events, etc.). With your membership, position the site as another way they can keep up-to-date with the issues and a way they can interact with your organization. A newsletter article about your site can also be a great opportunity to ask your membership for technical volunteers or for donated equipment.

Tell Your Conservation Friends: Announce your site to other organizations like yours in your locality and in the region. This can be done inexpensively (and appropriately) via e-mail or by fax or postal mailing if your site warrants the attention and you can afford it. You should do this within your local community and with other groups that you routinely work with.

Cross-Link with Friends: Contact other similar organizations and ask that they add a link on their Web site to yours (and do likewise for them). Contact groups that are located in your community and with whom you routinely work or share interests. Cross-linking from one Web site to another is technically easy to do and can be a powerful way to market your site. Be careful about how much time you spend on this task, though. It's easy to get carried away with building "definitive" lists of online resources, only to find that they quickly go out of date and add little value or traffic to your site.

Know Your Web Site: The people familiar with your organization are often the best marketers of your Web site. Everyone associated with your organization must be familiar with the content of your Web site and kept up-to-date with major additions and changes. This is particularly true for the executive director, those who most often answer routine inquiries about the organization, and anyone who has routine contact with the media or the general public.

Publicizing Your Site to People You Don't (Yet) Know Commercial "Search Engines." Because there are now so many Web sites on the Internet, it is getting harder and harder to find the specific information you need. Several companies have developed no-cost Web sites that do nothing but help you find other Web sites, based on search criteria you provide. These Web sites are commonly referred to as search engines, and they have become the principal way that many Web surfers find sites that contain the information in which they are interested.

Search engines (and the companies that produce them) constantly seek out information about new sites that have been launched on the Web; the more comprehensive their listing of Web sites, the more people will use their search engine to find information, and the more these companies can charge for advertising on their site. All search engines therefore have created an easy way for you to add your Web site to their listing; you only need to visit their Web site and follow the instructions.

Exhibit 7.1 lists the principal Web search engines you should visit to register your Web site. Each site has specific instructions for adding your Web site URL to its search engine; be sure to read them.

For more reference information on search engines, we recommend Search Engine Watch at www.searchenginewatch.com.

There is a lot of advice on the Web about how to optimize your listings on various search engines. We strongly recommend that you not become obsessed with this because it's a waste of time. Learn to live with the fact that there are thousands of similar groups and that yours will probably not show at the top of the listing when someone searches for your topic area such as "environment" or "arts."

Do be sure to give your home page a descriptive title that includes your organization's name, and make sure that your mission statement or other keywords describing your work appear near the top of your home page in plain text. These simple steps will help ensure that your site is correctly indexed in most search engines.

REFLECT AND REPOSITION

- Does your infrastructure support your culture and business model?
- Has your senior management created an environment that will help people perform to their fullest?

Search Engine	Address of Submission Page	Notes
Google	http://www.google.com/addurl.html	
AltaVista	http://www.altavista.com/ cgi-bin/query?pg=addurl	
FAST search	http://www.alltheweb.com/ add url.php3	
Yahoo!	http://www.yahoo.com/info/ suggest/	Read the directions carefully, and take some time to identify the most appropriate category for your site.
OpenDirectory	http://dmoz.org/add.html	Also requires you to identify an appropriate category. Data used by a number of sites, including AOL Search, AltaVista, HotBot, Google, Lycos, Netscape Search.
LookSmart	http://submit.looksmart.com/	Powers a number of major search engines, including Excite, MSN, iWon. Charges $79, but waives it for non-profits. See link at bottom of page for more info.

Source: From ONE/Northwest, www.onenw.org/toolkit/webdesign/publicity.html

Exhibit 7.1   Principal Web Search Engines

- Do you have a vision for the Net?
- Do you have a diversified approach to resource development, including use of the Internet and strategic, value-added partnerships?
- Does your business model generate revenue?
- Does your technology add value to your business model and processes and support an ethos of learning?

GUIDING PRINCIPLES

- The fundamental foundation of an organization is built on three things: (1) the environment created by senior management, (2) the availability of a stable and diverse resource base, and (3) the strategic use of information technology.
- Infrastructure is not static; it needs to adapt as your organization changes.
- Senior managers who continually challenge the process, model behavior, share information, equip their people, and get out of their way create an environment conducive to success.
- Your corporate commitment to the Net will never be bigger than your vision for the Net.
- Workers today are knowledge workers, and information ought to be treated as a shared resource.
- Resource development goes hand in hand with relationship building.
- Resource development strategies should include individuals, corporations, foundations, venture philanthropy, earned-income opportunities, and the Internet.
- Technology must have a purpose, plans and expected results must be realistic, costs reasonably forecast, and use, supported.
- Successful Web sites focus on content, community, customization, convenience, measurement, and marketing.

NOTES

[1]Thomas J. Neff and James M. Citrin, *Lessons from The TOP: The Search for America's Best Business Leaders*, (New York: Doubleday, 1999), 219.

[2]James M. Kouzes and Barry Z. Posner, *The Leadership Challenge* (San Francisco: Jossey-Bass, 1987).

[3]Neff and Citrin, 201.

[4]Bill Gates, *Business @ the Speed of Thought* (New York: Warner Books, 1999), 24–25.

[5]David S. Pottruck and Terry Pearce, *Clicks and Mortar* (San Francisco: Jossey-Bass, 2001), 35.

[6]Max Depree, *Leadership Is an Art* (New York: Doubleday, 1989), 19–20.

[7]Warren Bennis, 371.

[8]Robert Avery, "The Ten Trillion Dollar Question: A Philanthropic Game Plan," *Initiatives*, The Family Firm Institute, www.ffi.org/looking/factsfb.html.

[9]Dan Goodin, "Charity Begins in the Garage," *The Standard*, www.thestandard.com/article/0,1902,12852,00.html, March 13, 2000.

[10]From 1995 to 1999, foundation assets doubled from $227 billion to $450 billion. More than 10,000 new foundations were formed in this period.

[11]www.pcf.org

[12]www.morino.org

[13]www.benton.org

[14]Extraordinary resources are available on the Internet to help you. At the time of publication, some of them could be found at www.artswire.org/spiderschool/workshops/kit_buffalo_01/puzzle_quest/puzzle/onlinefundraising.html,www.onenw.org/toolkit/online-donation.html, www.michaelstein.net/online-fundraising-primer.html, and www.helping.org/nonprofit/fundraising.adp. See our Web site, www.managingnonprofits.org, for the latest information.

[15]Neil Irwin, "Smithsonian Gift Shops Going Online," *Washington Post*, November 22, 2000, E5.

[16]Catherine Callagy, *Unleashing Technology's Potential for Nonprofits*, www.changingyourworld.com/callagy1.htm.

[17]When you start to fix your systems, start small. Pick a unit or a department or a group of workers and develop systems to deliver to them the kind of information they need when they

need it. Bill Gates summarized the typical organization's experience when he said that it often takes a series of interactive steps
to understand the problem you are trying to fix, and you are better off tackling smaller processes and building on them: Start—
improve—feedback. Gates.

[18]www.artswire.org

[19]See the glossary at the back of this book.

[20]http://search.genie.org/genie/ans_result.lasso?cat=IT+Planning

[21]Thomas M. Siebel and Pat House, *Cyber Rules: Strategies for Excelling at E-Business* (New York: Currency/Doubleday, 1999), 188.

[22]www.onenw.org/toolkit/webdesign/publicity.html

[23]www.netaid.org

[24]www.onenw.org/toolkit/webdesign/publicity.html

[25]www.helping.org/nonprofit/index.adp

[26]http://www.makingthenetwork.org/toolbox/tools/webguide.htm

[27]www.onenw.org

CHAPTER EIGHT

Alignment

The most challenging part of building a dynamic organization is keeping all the parts working together or aligned toward a shared vision. Alignment is an ongoing balancing act that involves making constant adjustments to who you are (your culture), what you do (your business model), and what you need in order to support who you are and what you do (your infrastructure). Alignment, to paraphrase Collins and Porras in *Built to Last*, helps keep in place pieces that reinforce each other, that when clustered together deliver a power combined punch . . . [It's a constant] search for synergy and linkages.[1] Collins and Porras further define alignment as follows:

If you look around your company right now, you can probably put your finger on at least a dozen specific items misaligned with its core ideology or that impede progress—"inappropriate" practices that have somehow crept through the woodwork. Does your incentive system reward behaviors inconsistent with your core values? Does the organization's structure get in the way of progress? Do goals and strategies drive the company away from its basic purpose? Do corporate policies inhibit change and improvement? Does the office and building layout stifle progress?[2]

Collins and Porras compare misalignments to cancer cells that have to be killed as quickly as possible or they spread like wildfire.[3] The Dynamic Manager has to use the Dynamic Management Map and the tools described in this chapter to identify and kill these cells in order to align the organization. In many ways, alignment goes to the heart of what dynamic management is all about because it

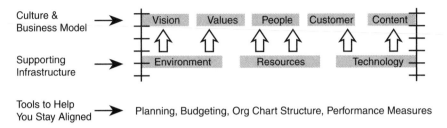

Exhibit 8.1 Organization in Alignment

demands constant reflection and repositioning. The need to align the organization is what makes dynamic management a never-ending, perpetual process.

Exhibit 8.1 shows what we mean by alignment. First and foremost, the Dynamic Manager is responsible for making sure that the culture and the business model are in sync. That means that the vision, values, people, customers, and content all must function seamlessly together as one unbroken, straight line. This "top line" must be secured by a stable infrastructure of funding, technology, and the right environment on the "bottom line." The infrastructure elements not only have to work in unison to make the bottom line, but they also have to be strong enough to support the "top line," the culture and the business model. The organization can get mis-aligned in so many ways. Misalignment can occur all on the same line (see Exhibit 8.2), for example, conflict on the top line between what the customer wants and the content that the organization is prepared to provide, or it can occur between the top and bottom lines, such as insufficient funding to support the new employee compensation system that you told your employees about earlier in the year. The map and the tools provided in this chapter—planning, budgeting, organizational charts, and balanced performance measures—will help the Dynamic Manager keep the top and bottom lines aligned.

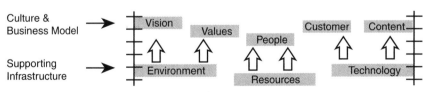

Exhibit 8.2 Organization Not in Alignment

THE ROLE OF THE LEADER IN ALIGNING THE ORGANIZATION

Everyone is responsible for working toward alignment in an organization, but leaders have a unique role. In dynamic organizations, we believe that a CEO is less of a Chief Executive Officer and more of a Chief Alignment Officer, responsible for seeing to it that the parts of an organization fit together for a common purpose. Stephen Covey goes even farther and considers organizational alignment one of the four necessary levels of principle-centered leadership. He defines it for leaders as "the need to organize people, to recruit them, train them, compensate them, build teams, solve problems, and create structure, strategy, and systems [to support them]."[4] Nothing is more important to alignment than the commitment of leadership to make it happen.

TOOLS FOR ALIGNMENT

General Advice: Fix the Big Rocks First

We often refer to macro issues facing our own organization as "The Big Rocks," a reference to Steven Covey's book *First Things First*, in which he uses the story of trying to fill a vase with rocks, sand, and water to illustrate the temptation to take the path of least resistance on a day-by-day basis. To Covey, the big rocks must fill the vase first if they are to fit at all. The sand and the water (being less important) can go later. Aligned organizations, and the Dynamic Managers who run them, have to take care of the big rocks first because they often go to the core of the organization's culture, business model, and infrastructure. Misalignments abound when the macro issues that everyone can see, feel, and touch are ignored or deferred.

Tools

We believe that the Dynamic Management Map, applied liberally and often, is the definitive alignment tool. It requires the Dynamic Manager to reflect on each critical part of the organization, to identify misalignments, and to reposition that part (or other parts as well) of the organization accordingly; however, there are several other concrete tools at your fingertips—planning, budgeting, organizational charts and corporate structures, and performance measurement—that can help you and your staff keep the organization aligned.

Planning.   Planning should be one of the most important tools that a Dynamic Manager uses to further the organization's business model and align the whole organization. As an alignment tool, planning, especially operational plans as described following, facilitates formal organizational reflection. It also provides a structured, regularly scheduled opportunity to reposition activities and resources. Unfortunately, the word *planning* usually evokes a wide array of reactions from people within an organization. These reactions, based on people's prior planning experiences, can range from fear, loathing, and ambivalence to enthusiasm and optimism. The Dynamic Manager has to do everything possible to ensure that planning doesn't become another lost opportunity consisting of needless meetings and board rituals.

Dynamic organizations plan at both the macro level (strategic) and the micro level (operational). They understand that both types of plans serve different purposes and are simply the organization's "best thinking at a moment in time." They accept that blind adherence to a plan once it is adopted is impossible in the fast-paced digital age. Today, even the best-laid plans and inclusive planning processes can become obsolete overnight.

Operational Plans

Operational plans or annual plans are used to set priorities, goals, and objectives for the coming year. Typically, they are developed in conjunction with a proposed operating budget. Although almost every nonprofit does some form of annual planning, many fail to use this process to keep their organization aligned. In fact, the Dynamic Manager should view the annual plan as the most important tool in the toolbox for fine-tuning the alignment of the organization. Why? Because (1) it is done, often even required, every single year; (2) it requires staff to reflect on both current and future operations; and (3) it articulates what the organization should be doing or doing differently in the coming year. You could not ask for a better tool as the Chief Alignment Officer—or for any other manager or leader for that matter.

We are not attempting to provide a guide to annual planning here, only guidance on using planning as an alignment tool. The steps for planning include the following:

1. The plan should include management's analysis of the current issues facing the corporation and its key stakeholders: the organizational context, as we defined it earlier in the book.

2. It should intentionally address markets, customers, and competition. As we have said so many times before, organizations must take a fresh look at their customers to understand who they are serving, who they want to serve, and who else is trying to serve these customers, every year.

3. The plan must focus on content. It should highlight what we call the *signature projects*—the current or future products and services that differentiate the organization from the competition and how resources are going to be deployed to make them real.

4. The plan ought to reflect how technology is being integrated into every part of the organization. Dynamic organizations cannot have a technology plan and technology budget that are separate and distinct from the rest of the organization.

5. The plan must address the learning and growth of the organization's people. Every annual plan should detail the efforts that will be made in the coming year to further the ethos of learning in the organization.

6. The planning process must be inclusive. By including diverse viewpoints and the entire management team in your planning, you will both enrich the end product and achieve the broad-based buy-in that you'll need to implement the plan.

Strategic Plans

Unlike the annual plan, strategic plans are not an instrument used for fine-tuning the organization's alignment. Strategic planning is a process for building or rebuilding the organization's fundamentals. In essence, strategic planning helps define the parts of your organization that the annual plan helps align. Strategic planning is defined as "a disciplined effort to produce fundamental decisions and actions that shape and guide what an organization is, what it does, and why it does it, with a focus on the future."[5] Strategic plans are meant to look much more toward the future. It often requires the organization to look out over a two-, five-, or even 10-year horizon.

Strategic planning entails attention to the big picture and the willingness to adapt to changing circumstances, and consists of the following three elements:

- Formulation of the organization's future mission in light of changing external factors, such as regulation, competition, technology, and customers
- Development of a competitive strategy to achieve the mission
- Creation of an organizational structure that will deploy resources to successfully carry out its competitive strategy[6]

In contrast to annual plans, the strategic planning process should look inward and outward, involving the board, staff, and key customers. In fact, the most common reason for strategic plans to become unused shelf-liners is because the process involved only a select group of people, usually senior management. The process simply failed to achieve the buy-in necessary to formulate and carry out the organization's future mission.

To some extent, the fast-changing nature of the digital age has made traditional strategic planning obsolete. Today, waiting three or five years to take a hard look at the world around you can ruin you. Similarly, in this environment, making projections of any kind that extend beyond a three-year horizon is pure speculation. That's why we believe so strongly in the Dynamic Management Map. Organizations that use the map to regularly reflect on their context, culture, business model, and infrastructure and who are prepared to use the annual planning process to reposition themselves as necessary will use strategic planning sparingly. Strategic planning will be used more often to help organizations manage through strategic inflection points or internal crises in their sectors.[7]

Budgeting.   Annual budgeting should complement your annual planning process. It is a structured way to make sure that the priorities reflected in your annual plan actually have resources allocated to them to make them real. For example, when Environmental Defense's annual plan designated the Scorecard as one of its signature projects, its annual budget that year also reflected this priority by allocating more financial support to it than to other, lower-priority projects. Similarly, when the Fannie Mae Foundation rolled out its performance-based compensation system, as described in Chapter 4, it budgeted more money to personnel that year than in previous years in order to make the new bonus structure work. The budget is undoubtedly a tool of alignment and ought to be treated as such. The budget process gives you an opportunity to take a fresh look at whether you are spending money in ways that are consistent with your annual plan and in support of your business model.

Reflect on your budget process and ask yourself whether it helps you keep your organization aligned. If it doesn't, the good news is that you control this process and can make it meet your needs. How? Start with the Dynamic Management Map, reflect on each element, and identify the areas that need to be repositioned. Develop an annual plan that sets out the actions you want to take this year to support what is working and to begin the necessary repositioning. Develop a budget that clearly reflects the priorities set out in the plan, including allocating dollars to those repositioning activities. If the budget is simply the same budget developed last year with cost-of-living increases, then the budget is not reflecting changes in priorities and any repositioning that must take place. It is not helping you to keep the organization in alignment.

A note about technology: Dynamic organizations include their technology people at the budget table. Avoid the mistake of budgeting in programmatic and functional silos without the advice and, in some cases, consent of the technology people. The days when functional silos were valued and when workers performed only finite functions, in a vacuum, should be long gone. Recognize that technology budgeting must be integrated into both operations (infrastructure) and programs (content). Practically speaking, if you are building a database to track your individual giving for fundraising, a database for collecting data from your Web site, and a database for housing content used in the program, then a budget that serves an alignment tool would reflect funds being allocated to each functional area specifically, not the technology department generally.

Budgeting is both an opportunity to align your resources with your organization's direction as well as a symbol about what is most important. One CEO said it best when he said, "I should see our mission in our financial statements." This is what CEOs of dynamic organizations should say.

CORPORATE STRUCTURE AND ORGANIZATIONAL CHARTS

By design or default, your corporate structure and your organizational chart say something about your organization. Some nonprofits say that structure matters little to them, and they spend little to no time examining its relevance. Others say "we are a flat organization"; yet when you diagram their structure, it looks like a steep pyramid. There is something wrong with both of these pictures. They are opportunities missed. Organizational charts and corporate structures should be used to help you align your organization. They are powerful symbols that should show that you are putting the Big Rocks in their proper place and deploying your most important resource—your people—in a way that is aligned with your culture and your business model.

The real key to corporate structure as an alignment tool is the proposition that its value has a shelf life. Structure, in other words, adds value only when it is dynamic or changes as your needs change. Over time, as your business model needs to be repositioned, so too must your structure. Some might say that this process breeds instability and uncertainty, but we have seen that it fosters vitality in organizations. Dynamic organizations send notice that their structure has purpose and illustrates their willingness to change when necessary. Employees will know that one's position in the organizational chart is more tied to vision, business model, and merit than to tradition or habit. It is yet another way to show that your digital culture puts people first.

Reflect on your corporate structure. Ask yourself: Does our organizational chart really reflect our priorities and what we want people to believe our priorities are? Does it further our vision and business model on its face? If it does not, then you probably need to reposition it.

We were constantly working to keep our corporate structure aligned with our vision and business model when we were at Enterprise. Early on in his tenure as President, Rey Ramsey created a stand-alone Technology and Information Services Department that reported directly to him, moving it from a subsidiary role under the Chief Financial Officer. This change not only sent a strong symbolic message of the importance of technology to the organization but also signaled that structure would be used to reflect organizational realities.

As our customers and the Internet became a more integral part of our programs, we also repositioned the organizational chart in the program area to reflect its expanding importance. As shown in Exhibit 8.3, we made three critical changes. (1) We reduced the number of departments in Program Service from five to three. We

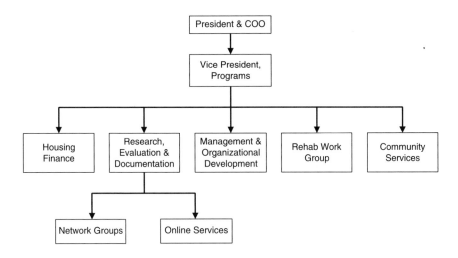

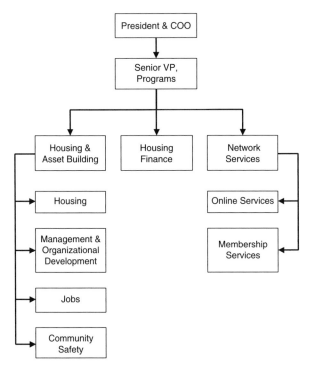

Exhibit 8.3 Redesigned Organizational Chart

made sure that the three departments reflected our operational priorities: on-the-ground technical support (Housing and Asset Building), lending to community-based organizations (Finance), and the building and servicing of our customer base (Network Services). The elevation of Network Services to a department level sent exactly the message we wanted to send about our heightened focus on the customer. (2) We moved our online services out of the Research and Evaluation Department (RED) into the new Network Services department to align our statement that our online presence was not about communications and research but about delivering content that our network wanted. (3) We abolished RED as a separate department and spread its staff into the on-the-ground department (Housing and Asset Building) in order to give staff members working in those divisions the wherewithal to capture what they learned from field work and translate these learnings into new online products like the Developer Support System described in Chapter 6.

Performance Measurement.   We saved one of our favorite alignment tools for last—performance measurement. We strongly believe in the age-old adage, "What gets measured, gets done." That means that dynamic organizations must have an organizational, and related individual, performance measurement system that measures and monitors the issues most critical to maintaining alignment in the organization. Labovitz and Rosansky in *The Power of Alignment* put it well: "What managers decide to measure sends a signal to everyone that that is important. That signal drives behavior of employees and that behavior ultimately creates the business culture that we end up with. Our goal is to create a culture that is naturally self-correcting and self-aligning, therefore we need to be careful about what we measure."[8]

Measurement has always been a challenge for nonprofit organizations because we deal with dual bottom lines, financial and social change. We have to be able to measure and report that we earned or raised enough money to survive and hopefully put some money away in a reserve account—the financial bottom line. Our financial management systems are often so stressed that we can't even produce reliable and timely reports that allow us to measure that. Programmatically, we have to be able to measure and report that we were able to improve the world or the lives of some people who live in it—the programmatic bottom line. Few, if any organizations, have figured out how to do that in any meaningful way. Sometimes that is because of lack of funds, other times it is because of a corporate culture that equally values process and inputs as much as product and outputs.

We would argue, however, that even if we had reliable ways to measure these dual bottom lines, we would still fail to be measuring all that should be measured. Financial and programmatic measures simply report on past performance—where you've been, not where you expect to be going. Nor do they provide any insight into your most important asset: your people. If we believe that we are aligned only when our vision, values, people, customers, and content are in sync and supported appropriately by our infrastructure, then we need ways to measure if that is in fact the case. We believe that this idea of measuring performance by balancing several factors is essential in the nonprofit world given the multidimensional nature of our work.

We are excited about the Balanced Scorecard, or a variation of the Balanced Scorecard, for that very reason. The Balanced Scorecard was developed at the Harvard Business School by Robert S. Kaplan and David P. Norton. In their words, it "complements financial measures of past performance with measures of the drivers of future performance." The objectives and measures of the scorecard are derived from an organization's vision and strategy. They explain the Balanced Scorecard's purpose as follows:

> *Many people think of measurement as a tool to control behavior and to evaluate past performance . . . the measures on a Balanced Scorecard should be used in a different way—to articulate the strategy of the business, to communicate the strategy of the business, and to help align individual, organizational, and cross-departmental initiatives to achieve a common goal. Used in this way, the scorecard does not strive to keep individuals and organizational units in compliance with a pre-established plan.*[9]

They view organizational performance from four perspectives: financial, customer, internal business processes, and learning and growth:[10]

- *Financial perspective*: Managers identify traditional financial measures that summarize past activity.
- *Customer perspective*: Managers identify the customers and markets in which they compete and develop measures of performance in those markets.

- *Internal business processes*: Managers develop measures of performance for innovation (designing and developing future content), operations (delivering existing content), and service (maintaining relationships after delivering content).

- *Learning and growth perspective*: Managers identify the investments that will have to be made in people, information technology, and systems to keep the organization aligned.[11]

Vanessa Kirsch and Kelly Fitzsimmons, founder and co-founder of New Profit, Inc. (NPI), a cutting-edge nonprofit dedicated to bringing venture capital–type resources to later-stage nonprofits with scalable models, have been trailblazing the use of the Balanced Scorecard in the nonprofit arena. The Balanced Scorecard interested NPI because they thought it gave them a chance, in Kelly Fitzsimmons's words: "to understand what it takes to be a good chef—to have the right set of ingredients in the pantry so they could use them to bring out the best virtues in the food they were cooking." They chose to use the Balanced Scorecard as one of their alignment mechanisms for their own operations; one that would speak to NPI's investors, its board, and its staff and would denominate the delivery of social change. They also adopted it as a way to measure the performance of its portfolio companies, the nonprofits that received NPI's "venture capital."

NPI's experience with the scorecard is informative. Instead of the four perspectives set out by Kaplan and Norton, NPI had five areas of focus: financial, investor, performance of portfolio organizations, internal business processes, and learning and growth. As Exhibit 8.4 reflects, each focus had strategic objectives and performance measures tied to it that were uniquely relevant to NPI.

NPI found the scorecard to be a powerful tool for describing to partners and investors how they viewed the world. It helped both to translate the NPI vision and to serve as a snapshot for the organization's critical paths. NPI's board is not holding management accountable, per se, for the scorecard on a regular basis, but they are reviewing it annually together with the proposed budget for the coming year. According to Kelly Fitzsimmons, "It bounds the tops of conversations with board members and sets an outline of what we are reporting on and talking about." Interestingly, the scorecard has been a powerful reporting tool to foundations that have accepted it as the only formal reporting they need.

New Profit, Inc. is a nonprofit venture philanthropy firm. Our goal is to affect large-scale social change by applying venture capital practices to philanthropy.

Focus	Strategic Objectives	Measures
Financial	**Fund Capitalization**—secure $4 million in fund commitments from investors using pyramid strategy	• Raise $4.5 million
	Operating Revenues—secure 500k operating funds from foundations and friends for FY99 & FY00	• Maintain operating cash flow with three months surplus
	Sustainability—manage cash flow to maintain an operating surplus with 3 months cash on hand	
	Efficiency—maintain ratio of 1:4 staff $/pro bono $, optimize pro bono and volunteer resources	
Investor	**Build Investor Community**—close target investors and engage them in key aspects of NPI network through events, formal roles, etc.; develop reports to inform investors of performance	• Close three founding and three lead investors
	Investor Satisfaction—use satisfaction survey and one-on-one interviews to solicit feedback	• Achieve 80% satisfaction
	Focused Investor Strategy—develop investor segmentation, profiles, and marketing strategy to optimize size and scope of funding base	
Performance of Portfolio Organization	**Growth**—set and reach specific growth targets (e.g., increased revenue, expansion to new sites) with portfolio organizations for the life of fund (5 years)	• Create four scorecards with specific targets
	Social Impact—set & reach specific targets for increasing the scope of portfolio organization's social impact (e.g., # of customers/clients served) for the life of fund (5 years)	• Achieve a minimum of 80% performance for portfolio organizations
	Balanced Scorecard Performance—build and implement first scorecards for each portfolio organization	• # shared learning and collaboration events between portfolio organizations
	Satisfaction with Fund Services—solicit satisfaction and feedback from portfolio organizations regarding NPI and Monitor resources; use survey on fund launch; implement feedback	
	Best Practices—share best practices across portfolio organizations	

(continues)

183

Focus	Strategic Objectives	Measures
Internal Business Processes	**Portfolio Management**—Q3: set terms with portfolio organizations, implement performance management system, Q4: deploy Monitor and NPI resources, continue pipeline development, and develop reporting infrastructure	• Finalize terms process with portfolio organizations • Meet targets for press hits and invitations to speak • Secure relationships with 100% of potential intellectual partners
	Define Leadership Position—Q3: establish collaborative relationships with intellectual partners (e.g., secure Fidelity relationship, orient key players and larger Monitor community), establish marketing and external community relations; launch public relations, positioning strategy, market research, and focus groups; Q4: establish best practices for performance based funding, become policy spokesperson on philanthropic issues (e.g., # of conferences invited to attend, # of press hits, invitations to speak)	
	Board & Governance—Q3: define role of Board, Q4: expand and develop national Board, and develop Academic Board	
	Plan NPI Institute—Q4: plan for Institute; determine resources (human and capital) necessary for introduction; formalize leadership position and learning focus	
Learning and Growth	**Fill Strategic Positions**—hire fundraiser, design strategy for attracting and retaining talented staff	• Fill 100% of necessary strategic positions • Finalize HR strategies for attracting and retaining staff
	Technology—Q3: identify technology needs and plan for procurement	
	Knowledge Management—Q4: develop limited but targeted system for improvement and learning related to key processes (due diligence, terms setting, BSC); develop template for process improvement	
	Alignment—ensure that open lines of communication exist between investors NPI and portfolio organizations through culture building, events, reporting, and focus groups	

Exhibit 8.4 New Profit, Inc. Balanced Scorecard: FY99

NPI has also learned a lot about the Balanced Scorecard and the use of a balanced performance measurement system by working with its portfolio companies. As Kelly Fitzsimmons states, it is not a "just add water" solution. The organization has to do a lot of spade work honing its strategies and developing a plan for the future before trying to use a system such as an alignment tool. The backbone of the Balanced Scorecard is the identification of the key strategic objectives in each focus area, and NPI has seen this process alone bring age-old, internal fights over strategy and tactics out of an organization's closet. At times, these fights have literally paralyzed the organization and its ability to move forward.

But those organizations that have defined strategies and a plan for growth have really prospered with the Balanced Scorecard. Citizens Schools is one of those organizations. Citizens Schools' co-founder Ned Rimer has found the Balanced Scorecard to be an invaluable alignment tool. Citizens Schools is a Boston-based non-profit operating at 11 different schools, what it calls campuses. Its mission is to educate children and strengthen community with a vision of building a bigger and better after-school sector. Although the organization only first used the system in 2000, Citizens School has fully integrated the Balanced Scorecard into its entire organization for 2001. It is using the scorecard to focus the entire organization, individuals and departments, on the strategic objectives that further the overall growth strategy. Rimer says the scorecard is helping them to "focus the talent, energy, and human resources so you have the right compass bearing . . . that you are putting energy in the right place at the moment."

How is Citizen Schools doing that? As Exhibit 8.5 shows, Citizens Schools has set out five areas of focus, what it calls *aspects*: social impact, financial, customer, operations, and learning and growth. Each aspect has between one and four objectives. Each objective has one or two measures of performance that define success. In some cases, there are even "stretch" measures, or measures that the organization will not be penalized for failing to meet but that raise the bar for all involved.

Everyone in the organization is spending time learning and understanding each aspect, each objective, and each measure in the scorecard. Staff members are told that everything they do should be furthering one of the scorecard's 14 objectives. Ned Rimer says, "So, now if one of the staff comes back from a long meeting with a principal from one of our school partners and is frustrated that she wasted

Mission: Educating Children and Strengthening Community
Vision: Build a Bigger and Better After-School Sector
Strategic Priorities of Growth Plan: 1) Impact, 2) Scale and Sustainability, 3) National Leverage

Aspect	Objective	Measures
Social Impact	1. Deliver a superior quality program that educates children and strengthens community by building skills (writing, data analysis, and oral presentation), access, leadership, and community connections.	• Student impact rating of 4.0 or higher on a 5-point scale (composite of up to 10 key questions from various stakeholders). • 75% (or more) of students at campuses focusing on writing (currently 9 of 11) will increase by one rubric level their writing skills during the academic year. 75% (or more) of all students will improve their oral presentation skills (data from both rubrics and staff assessments).
Financial	2. Receive $7.5 million in new cash or commitments toward our four-year, $25 million campaign.	• Stretch goal: greater than 80% of above measurement. • Reach the $7.5 million goal by December 31. Stretch goal: greater than $8.5 million of above measurement. Second Stretch Goal: non-foundation funding increases faster than operational expenses between 2000–2001.
Customer	3. Stay within 2001 budget. 4. **Students:** Expand student demand and enrollment.	• Post 5%+ surplus and stay within budget of $4.8 million. • Student enrollment increases from 1248 in 2000 to 1530 (+ or – 5% [1450-1600]) in 2001. Stretch goal: demand grows significantly as evidenced by 2/3 of campuses with a waitlist of 10% or more of enrollment for fall 2001 program.
	5. **Citizen Teachers:** Provide outstanding volunteer experience and thereby increase pool of volunteers.	• 85% or more of CTs surveys indicate they would a) return and teach a future apprenticeship, b) refer a friend to teach an apprenticeship, and c) rate the experience as 4.0 or greater on its positive impact on the volunteer.
Operations	6. **Training Partners:** Deliver high quality, high impact training to first-year CSU partners. 7. Develop more precise evaluation instruments for measuring program impact.	• 4.0 (or better) rating of quality and impact of training by Executive Directors and participating staff from 2+ partners. • Complete the following: hire external evaluator for three-year evaluation, revise constituent surveys and develop strong measurement tools in all key outcome areas.

(continues)

Aspect	Objective	Measures
	8. Set stage for national leverage of CS model.	• Publishing: Document and internally publish Version 1.0 CS Best Practices. • Policy: Four meetings with local officials, four with state/national officials, and favorable coverage in five media outlets.
	9. Deepen school partnerships.	• Eight of twelve Campus Directors, and eight of twelve school principals (or primary school liaisons), rate the following components of the partnership as 4.0 or greater: a) academic alignment, b) enrollment demand, and c) community engagement.
	10. Consistently implement Action Plan.	• Successfully accomplish 75% or more Action Plan goals within one quarter of goal. Stretch goal: 85% or more of Action Plan.
Learning and Growth	11. Maintain high full-time staff retention and increase staff diversity.	• Retention of full time staff at 75% or higher for staff employed as of January 2001. Stretch goal: 85% of above measure. • Develop recruitment strategy to increase hiring and retention of people of color.
	12. Technology serves as a reliable communication and operational tool.	• By the end of the second quarter, each workstation has the following functioning software: database, e-mail, Internet, MS Office. Each full-time staff member has access to e-mail and voicemail.
	13. Further develop full-time staff training program.	• All full-time staff employed throughout 2001 will participate in the following trainings: CS strategic plan, CS Balanced Scorecard, database, office technology, and two other organization-wide topics as determined by leadership. Stretch goal: these trainings receive a participant satisfaction rating of 4 or greater from CS staff.
	14. Improve communication by developing and implementing high quality, human resource procedures and protocols.	• All staff will have by year-end: a) job descriptions, b) performance reviews, c) ongoing benefits training, and CS will develop a new employee checklist, and exit interview process.

Exhibit 8.5 Citizen Schools Balanced Scorecard for FY2001

187

her time, I can ask her if that meeting fit within one of 14 objectives. When she sees it helps number 9, "Deepen school partnerships," she knows her actions, while frustrating, were moving us forward. That makes a difference. What she did was aligned with where we are trying to go." In addition, the scorecard is going to be reviewed throughout the organization every quarter. If measures, such as student improvements on writing skills, are falling behind their stated measures, the organization can potentially retool the program to influence that measure for the remaining part of the year.

The organization also is tying compensation to performance on the scorecard. Anyone in the organization, from the founders to administrative assistants, who has been with the organization for two or more years receives a bonus if the organization meets all of the measures on the scorecard. Everyone gets the same bonus regardless of salary or role in the organization. Fifty percent of the bonus is paid in December and fifty percent in July of the next year. This program not only serves as a retention incentive, but it also sends the message that everyone in the organization is equally important if the scorecard's measures will be met.

Citizen Schools also hopes to tie the scorecard to individual performance evaluations in the coming years. In 2001, each of the 11 campuses has drafted its own Balanced Scorecard that ties into the overall organizational scorecard. Because each campus director has some autonomy over how the individual campus program is run, Citizens Schools is likely to to use the campus's Balanced Scorecard to evaluate individual performance of the campus director.

The aspects and strategic objectives set out in the Citizens Schools Scorecard not only help the organization move beyond the financial bottom line, but they also help the organization build its digital culture, as we defined it in Chapter 2 and talked about so often in the book. The scorecard focuses on impact—the real difference that the organization is having on customers and society—not just process. It focuses on the people who work there, showing them that the organization will measure whether it is maintaining a caring, flexible, and diverse workplace that compensates them fairly. It focuses on customers, in this case, students, teachers, and partners, and measures how well they are building and maintaining those relationships. Finally, it focuses on supporting an ethos of learning within the organization by making the pursuit and sharing of knowledge paramount.

Why does the Balanced Scorecard work for Citizens Schools? Ned Rimer believes that it is largely because of the clarity of the organization's mission and its vision. With this clarity, people are able to focus on overall strategic objectives. NPI's Kelly Fitzsimmons agrees and adds her own perspective: "[The scorecard] has helped Citizens Schools evolve from an organization with 35 employees to one with 60 employees. They have been able to use it to articulate and hold people accountable for a growth plan when you have grown too big to rely solely on close personal relationships." Kelly Fitzsimmons further summarizes their experience and the real value of the scorecard well: "In essence, the Balanced Scorecard approach is a powerful tool for aligning key stakeholders around critical issues facing an organization. It helps the organization to leapfrog over conventional financial measures so it can have a robust discussion around accountability and performance."

Digital Spotlight—Getting and Staying Aligned: Calvary Bilingual Multicultural Learning Center

In 1995, Calvary Bilingual Multicultural Learning Center was a small day care center and after-school program in a local church with 100 children, 40 staff, and an annual budget of $400,000. The program had been operating the same way since its founding in the Columbia Heights neighborhood of Washington, D.C. in 1985 by Executive Director Beatriz (BB) Otero and a small group of Latino mothers who wanted a place for their kids to learn and grow. Two events that year rocked the organization to its core and jump started the Learning Center on its journey toward becoming a dynamic organization. The first was notification by the church pastor that the church needed its space back. The comfort and protection of the church, not to mention the free rent, was about to end. Regardless of the costs to relocate, however, the dearth of space in the densely populated and gentrifying neighborhood threatened the existence of the organization. The second event was the solution to this problem—the donation to the Learning Center of a 75,000 square-foot building previously used by the local telephone company, Bell Atlantic, now Verizon Communications, as a switching station one block from the church.

The Learning Center took its brush with death and rebirth, with more than 10 times the space it had before, as an opportunity to reflect on who it was and what it wanted to become. Like the stories we have heard from so many nonprofit leaders, BB knew in her heart for years that the organization had to get its arms around technology, but she didn't believe she could do it in the old, cramped location. She also knew that she wanted a community center for her community that was just like the one she grew up with—open, warm, parents teaching parents, young people teaching young people, generation after generation. This new space could provide these opportunities.

BB and senior management set out on a strategic planning journey to determine where the Learning Center should go and to identify what it had to do to ensure that all parts of the organization would be fully aligned to make it happen. She started with technology and began to educate herself on how other organizations were applying technology. She met with computer technology centers, local corporate leaders, and others. It quickly became clear that the Learning Center not only had to provide more access to technology to its customers, but it also had to integrate technology into the organization itself. At that point, BB did what every good Dynamic Manager in that situation should do. She looked to insurgents, the young people, for guidance, support, and to start building programs to see what would catch on with customers.

Nick Blachford lived in the neighborhood and was interested in developing his own program to work with young people going into junior high school. BB invited him into the new building to do his work. He recruited 15 junior-high-age young people for his own program and pushed his friend, Marta Uquilla, who was running the Sister-to-Sister program for the same age girls, to join him. With BB's help, they secured three used computers and put them in the back room of the new facility, but Nick wasn't satisfied. He kept pushing BB to do more. She then entered into a joint venture with George

Washington and Howard universities that brought a technology class to the Learning Center together with AmeriCorps members. PJ Uquilla then came in to run these programs and increased the number of computers by trading a bunch of donated laptops for 486s. All of a sudden, a 12-to-15-station computer center helping young people focus on becoming producers for the Internet, not consumers of the Internet, was born. Now, instead of just fighting for space and attention, these technology programs were taking off. The young staff began researching the best practices being used for integrating technology into education and defining for themselves what it meant to be a youth worker in communities.

While program was evolving with a strong technology focus, BB was also continuing her quest for knowledge and for a philosophical foundation on which to build the Learning Center's future. She found it in Mario Morino and his work at the Morino Institute. Morino, highlighted in Chapter 7's discussion of venture philanthropy, was planning to launch his Youth Development Collaborative (YDC) Pilot, a multiyear program dedicated to understanding ways to effectively integrate technology into after-school programs. He and his team believed that integrating technology would work best if it was a part of existing programs and institutions, not as a new stand-alone initiative. BB liked what she saw in Morino. He was walking the walk, hiring experts and young people, and supporting them to provide a wide range of resources to each of the four YDC Pilot core partners. He also was intent on creating an incubator to study the issues and capture the knowledge from the Pilot.

Their relationship blossomed, and so did the Learning Center after it was selected to be one of four YDC Pilot sites. YDC status brought hands-on assistance, including financial and technical resources, management and staff training, and exposure to other organizations struggling with the same issues. The experience convinced BB that the future of the Learning Center should not be that different than the past. It should be a catalyst in the neighborhood; it should provide early childhood, family support, arts, and technology programs, and they should all be deepened and integrated to the maximum extent possible. For example, technology should be part of the early childhood programs, with young people teaching it, and part of the family support program, with a special focus on helping people bring technology home with them. BB wanted to build a place that was the center of the community, not just a community center. She wanted a facility where parents taught parents, young people helped young people, and where other community-based organizations could come to meet, train, and work their magic.

These efforts helped build and define the new business model, but they did not help ensure that the corporate culture was going to be aligned with it. Change had to take place inside the organization as well. Some of this happened naturally. As more young people began coming into the Learning Center, the technology programs began expanding and getting a higher profile. That was important but not enough. Two simple but important actions were taken that had a great impact on the culture. One, the door to the technology center was kept open at all times and made available to the staff. Soon, the child development teacher began using it for child development teacher training. The early childhood center staff began bringing children in. Even the administrative staff started coming into the center to make graphs and print out reports. Then, support from YDC Pilot brought new state-of-the-art computers for the technology center itself, and all the old computers were removed, put on the desktops of all Learning Center staff, and networked. This final step—universal access for all staff—is credited with making the organization's cultural transformation complete.

BB also knew that the organization could not continue to be structured as it always had been. She knew that a fundamental reorganization of the Learning Center's corporate structure was both practically and symbolically important for purposes of alignment. While program and culture changes were occurring, BB began working with a consultant, staff, and the board to realign the corporate structure. Instead of having three senior managers running the whole center, a new eight-person leadership team was put in place. Directors of the key areas—development, administration, early childhood development, family support, arts, and technology—were given broad responsibility and authority. BB's role in day-to-day activities was reduced, and she evolved into more of a Chief Executive Officer. This had the practical effect of providing new leadership opportunities for staff and opening up a lot of BB's time to focus on the $2.5 million capital campaign to complete the build-out of the new building. It also has helped the Learning Center to continue its efforts to diversify its funding base. From a high of 98 percent of funds coming from public sources in 1992, the Learning Center now brings in more than 40 percent of its funds from nongovernmental sources.

What does the future hold? The fully renovated Learning Center officially reopened in March 2001 with many of the same programs that it always had (e.g., early childhood development, family support, school age/youth development, and multidisciplinary arts programs). What was different from the past, however, was not only some new services, such as broadcasting, video production, dance, theater, and a state-of-the-art community technology center, but also a new culture and business model. BB and her leadership team know that this is when the really hard work begins: keeping the old customers satisfied while attracting new and different customers to the new services and facilities. Tracy Gray from the Morino Institute put it best:

The Learning Center must continue to evolve into a dynamic organization that can handle existing and new relationships. Many people over the past 15 years relied on a cradle-to-grave relationship where their children went there at age 2 and kept coming back through high school. They were like family to BB and her staff. With expanded space and services, many new people walking in the door will want only a particular product or limited services from the Learning Center, not a relationship. Building a community center and serving a customer base with such a diversity of expectations for the center will be a challenge.

BB is well on her way to creating a special place in Columbia Heights—a place that truly is the center of the community; however, the increased scope and complexity of content being offered, relationships being managed and developed, and people being served will make alignment job one for BB and her leadership team.

REFLECT AND REPOSITION

- What actions do you take to keep your organization aligned?
- Do you use your annual planning and budgeting process to stay aligned?
- Does your organizational chart further your vision and business model on its face?
- Do you have an organizational and individual performance measurement system that measures and monitors the issues most critical to maintaining alignment in your organization?

GUIDING PRINCIPLES

- Alignment is an ongoing balancing act that involves making constant adjustments to who you are (your culture), what you do (your business model), and what you need in order to support who you are and what you do (your infrastructure).
- The Chief Executive Officer should be more of a Chief Alignment Officer, responsible for seeing that the parts fit together for a common purpose.
- Fix the Big Rocks first.
- The annual plan is the most important tool in the toolbox for fine-tuning the organization's alignment.
- Budgeting is a structured way to make sure that the priorities reflected in your annual plan actually have money allocated to them to make them real.
- The technology people must have a seat at the budget table to avoid budgeting in programmatic and functional silos.
- Organizational charts show that you are deploying your most important resource, your people, in a way that is aligned with your vision and your business model.
- Measure performance by balancing several factors, financial and otherwise.

NOTES

[1]James C. Collins and Jerry I. Porras, *Built to Last: Successful Habits of Visionary Companies* (New York: Harper Business, 1994), 214.

[2]Collins and Porras, 215.

[3]Collins and Porras, 237.

[4]Stephen R. Covey, *Principle-Centered Leadership*, (New York: Summit Books, 1991), 31.

[5]This definition was adapted from *The Internet Nonprofit Center*, www.nonprofits.org/npofaq/03/22.html. The Internet Nonprofit Center is an excellent online resource for nonprofit management.

[6]Ibid. The Internet Nonprofit Center has extensive resources on planning.

[7]See the discussion of strategic inflection points in Chapter 1.

[8]George Labovitz and Victor Rosansky, *Power of Alignment* (New York: John Wiley & Sons, 1997), 139.

[9]Robert S. Kaplan and David P. Norton, *The Balanced Scorecard* (Cambridge, MA: Harvard Business School Press, 1996), 8.

[10]Kaplan and Norton, 17.

[11]A summary of these perspectives can be found in Kaplan and Norton, 25–29.

CHAPTER NINE

Living the Map:
The One Economy Story

In July 2000, we launched a new, national nonprofit organization, One Economy Corporation. One Economy is headquartered in Washington, D.C., with a West Coast office in Portland, Oregon. Our mission is to maximize the potential of technology to help low-income people raise their standard of living and build assets. This mission grows out of our vision of an inclusive economy in which all people have an equal opportunity to meet their full human potential. We believe that there is a greater opportunity for low-income people to have the ability to move up and out of poverty if they have greater access to information and vehicles that enable them to turn that information into assets and wealth.

We were determined to build One Economy as a dynamic organization from the get-go and to apply the Dynamic Management Map as we went along. In this chapter, we invite you to come along with us as we live the principles of our Dynamic Management Map. We do not hold ourselves out as a model, but rather as an example of what can happen when these principles are applied. As we open our doors to you, you will see our lessons, frustrations, and mistakes along with our achievements, hopes, and dreams.

WHO WE ARE AND HOW WE GOT HERE

We have taken different paths to get to One Economy, yet in so many ways our paths are similar. We both lived and grew up in

New Jersey, children of hard-working, middle-class families that value service to others. Like many other lawyers, we found our way to Washington, D.C. Ben Hecht is a CPA who practiced and taught law at Georgetown University Law Center for 10 years. At Georgetown, he also founded the National Center for Tenant Ownership, a national nonprofit that assists community-based organizations with property acquisition and other community development issues. Rey Ramsey's path took him to Oregon, where he practiced law and served two governors as head of that state's Housing and Community Services Department. From these separate backgrounds, little did we know that we would meet to form a strong and ever-growing alliance and friendship.

Jim Rouse, as we mentioned in Chapter 4, was a dynamic leader, and his vision for America was magnetic—so much so that Rey ended his state career to come work for Jim and the Enterprise Foundation. Jim had a way of drawing you in so that you would believe in yourself and other people. We met soon after Rey's arrival to seek ways for our two nonprofits to collaborate. Within a year, Rey convinced Ben to volunteer to help Enterprise shape its "best practices database," the parent of Enterprise Online. Our relationship continued to grow. One day in 1996, after a brief negotiation over bad food in a bad restaurant, Ben joined Rey at Enterprise to build the foundation's programs beyond housing—to use housing as a base or platform to help people get the other skills or services they needed, such as jobs, child care, and savings, to lift themselves up and out of poverty. In helping build and expand our programs, we constantly asked ourselves: Are there other ways to help people build assets and wealth?

As we have discussed in other parts of this book, we also spent a lot of time trying to figure out how to best take advantage of technology. Technology seemed to have so much potential for an organization like ours, with a national reach to more than 1,600 organizations in 48 states. The question would be how to make it work for us. As described in Chapter 6, our first foray into this new world was to establish Enterprise Online, our online database of best practices, model documents, and case studies designed and developed for practitioners in our field. We soon launched our first Web site, which, like that of many other nonprofit organizations, initially resembled an online brochure. With David Saunier's unique talents, however, it soon became the hub for our online activities. When Ben joined

Enterprise, we began launching more online products and services every several months. Soon there was a customized developer support system for practitioners who were building affordable housing, then MoneyNet, a tool to enhance nonprofit fundraising. At our annual conference led by our Chief Technology Officer, Gayle Carney, we introduced the Cyber Café, a technology expo for nonprofit practitioners. The genie was out of the bottle, technology had become an important part of our culture, and our organization and the customers we served were better off because of it.

At Enterprise, our primary customers were other nonprofits. For the most part, these nonprofits included community development corporations (CDCs), public housing authorities, and other community-based organizations that specialized in housing development, child care, neighborhood safety, planning workforce development, and economic development. The work of these organizations has been a well-kept secret from most Americans. In the face of seemingly insurmountable odds, these nonprofits have in some cases turned around whole neighborhoods, built thousands of homes, and improved the lives of many people. These social entrepreneurs have formed alliances with religious institutions, local governments, and businesses with an eye on leveraging the resources necessary to get the job done. The central ward in Newark, New Jersey, now the home to a new performing arts center and other large public works projects, was literally kept afloat by Father Linder and his nonprofit New Communities Corporation in the 1980s and 1990s. Today, Linder's organization owns $500 million of real estate, including a shopping center with a Pathmark grocery store. Go ahead and drive through the South Bronx today. Fifteen years ago, few people would even have proposed such an idea, but nonprofits there provided the leadership and ingenuity to redevelop neighborhoods block by block to make them places where people now want to live. We can point to similar work by other organizations throughout the country, such as Bethel New Life in Chicago, New Economic for Women in Los Angeles, and the Cleveland Housing Network in Cleveland.

The community development movement continued along with steady growth in the 1990s. At the same time, the U.S. economy was experiencing its greatest expansion ever, fueled by the boom in technology. The Dow Jones and NASDAQ were hitting high-water marks that few would have dared predict. Talk about stock portfolios became a regular part of office chitchat. Unemployment was hitting record lows, and the first results of welfare reform were in—the rolls were falling. Companies were searching for employees, and recent graduates were commanding eye-popping salaries. The digital revolution, as some would call it, was upon us.

But as we traveled across this country, we were seeing two Americas: One part was enjoying the fruits of this robust economy and the other was completely unaffected or perhaps hurt by it. We continued to see neighborhoods with populations that were no closer to prosperity than they ever had been. Help wanted ads would stay posted, with no hope of being filled. Far too many people lacked the skills to compete in this digital age and, worse yet, lacked the requisite comfort to even try. In the other America, people were connected. They were searching the Internet and using it as a tool to help their children, a guide to health care, a means to improve their skills, and a tool to find jobs. When the U.S. Department of Commerce used the term *digital divide*, what they were doing was exposing the divide between the haves and the have-nots in our society, where those who have resources were increasingly becoming connected to the tool of our age, but those with less resources were increasingly being isolated from the mainstream. We were both troubled by this reality.

HOLDING THE MIRROR UP TO OURSELVES

We were proud of what we had been a part of at Enterprise, but we had to ask ourselves if there were perhaps even better ways to help people who were being left out of the economy. Our individual inner journeys led us to more reflection and, at times, self-doubt. Independently, we started to hold a mirror up to ourselves, to our own work, and to our own expectations about ourselves. As we look back on it, two key events actually deepened our reflection and ultimately led us to take action together.

In the summer of 1999, we both had the privilege to be part of a festive event, the demolition and rebirth of a public housing development in Washington, D.C. Everyone was there, including the mayor, city councilpeople, neighborhood leaders, and past, present, and future residents. The moment was symbolic of a failed housing policy that encouraged the warehousing of large numbers of low-income people in a densely populated housing site, far from jobs and other services. A unique partnership of nonprofits, resident associations, and a talented public housing administrator, David Gilmore, brought us all to this occasion with the financial support of a successful federal program called HOPE VI. Although we were excited to celebrate this influx of more than $50 million to redevelop the property and to provide better housing for more than 250 families, Ben couldn't help but turn to Rey during the long speeches that were taking place, and ask, "What would happen if these people were given the funds directly and cut out from all of the complex deal making? Do the math. Fifty million dollars divided by 250 families is $200,000 a piece." The intent was not to disparage a good program but to challenge our own thinking about the economic opportunities of the people, not the housing. What type of choices would they have if they had their own financial resources? We had a gnawing sense that something else was needed, but we were just not sure what it should be.

We went back to our regular work and continued to be challenged almost every day with ideas from Rey's special assistant, Alec Ross, about how our work could change through the use of technology. Alec would read every technology magazine, on and off line, and leave clippings wherever we went as food for thought.

Our collective tipping point occurred on November 8, 1999. Today we affectionately refer to it only as "The Russian Tea Room." The Russian Tea Room is a restaurant located one block from Carnegie Hall in Manhattan that is steeped in history. It has long been a place for the rich and influential to mingle and celebrate. Recently restored, it looks like something right off the pages of *Architectural Digest*. That night, we were holding a fundraiser to support the work of our New York City office and to celebrate the success of community development. The rooms with majestic furnishings and ornate fixtures were filled with philanthropists, bankers, businesspeople, government officials, and some of our nonprofit partners. We were treated to a great performance of Broadway tunes by James Naughton. Things went well by any measure: More than $250,000 was raised for a worthy cause, the guests were happy, and discussions were being held about where next year's event would take place. It would be hard to ask for much more than this. The Russian Tea Room with all of its trappings was the right place for this event. What we didn't know was that we were individually asking ourselves a different question: "Was it right for us?"

After the show, we started to walk down 57th Street back to our hotel. What happened next is something we will never forget. On chorus, and almost on cue, we looked at each other and said, "Great event, but it's not for me." Nothing against the Russian Tea Room or James Naughton for that matter. We just realized at that moment that we had to try to get people engaged in the mainstream of the American economy in a different way. We could not keep celebrating our "successes" when we believed that the things we were doing were never really going to get to the many people who continued to be left out. For us, in retrospect, it was a moment when a weight was lifted from us—one of those times when everything becomes clear. We sat in the hotel lobby until 2 a.m. and planned what later became One Economy Corporation. The Russian Tea Room for us will always be the origin of our venture, at least in a symbolic sense. We wrote our plans on a couple of napkins. Boy, did we stretch our imaginations that evening. We discussed funding, time frames, and locations. It was a night of dreaming bold. Each of us harkened back to the people in our lives who encouraged us to think big, take risks, and do the right thing. We knew it would be hard to turn back now.

Later that week, we shared our experience with Alec over dinner. Over the next few months, the three of us would meet after work, on weekends, and often talk late into the evening about our plans. With each meeting, our plans became more real. We established some aggressive benchmarks for ourselves: financial commitments by March, with startup in the summer. Much would have to happen between November and July if this was to become reality, especially given the fact that we were working full-time jobs that we cared a lot about.

BUILDING THE CULTURE: VISION, VALUES, AND PEOPLE

Vision

We knew that we had to articulate a clear vision that inspired people and captured their imagination if we were going to be able to raise enough money to launch our effort and ultimately, to recruit staff. In fact, no area took up as much of our time early on as did the building of our vision; however, we didn't spend a lot of time creating a formal vision statement. Instead, we consciously worked to put words to our collective dream. One day we would spend all of our time talking about digital access solutions and our vision would center around hardware and Internet service providers. Another day we would focus, like a laser beam, on content and the opportunities around content development and content aggregation. And just when we thought we had our vision clear, we said: What about people's comfort and aptitude with technology? Should our vision of our new venture include helping people to change the culture in their family or neighborhood about the role of technology in their lives?

Once we developed more of what we called our macro vision of One Economy, we needed to develop a vision about how we would operate. What kind of organization would we be—local, regional, or national? Should we be an intermediary, a direct service provider, or both?

We were excited about our vision of (1) an inclusive economy where all people have an equal opportunity to meet their full human potential; (2) being the sum of many parts by attracting high-capacity partners to engage in the work of helping people help themselves with technology serving as one important means to this end; and (3) implementing a rational approach to achieving that vision through the following:

- The operation of a consumer Web site, www.TheBeehive.org, to provide low-income individuals with a suite of Web-based products and services focusing on financial services, education, jobs, health care, and homeownership, among other areas that help individuals build assets and raise their standard of living.
- Initiatives and partnerships that enable and encourage Internet access in the home and use of the Beehive site.
- The implementation of "digital communities" in select geographic locations to increase the aptitude and comfort of low-income people with the Internet culture and to demonstrate new applications for the Beehive site.

What we didn't know was how others would receive our vision, especially in the technology and funding community. One of the first people we approached was an extraordinary individual, Jane Metcalfe, co-founder of *Wired* magazine and a respected and successful entrepreneur from the Silicon Valley. Jane asked us hard, probing questions and reviewed our recently drafted concept paper. The special moment came—that point when someone places their belief in you—when Jane e-mailed us and said that the idea was "hot" and said, "How can I help?" We cannot adequately describe our elation over this simple expression of interest. Once we started One Economy, Jane made several financial contributions, including that special "first" check. Today she is an active member of our board. Her kindness, intelligence, and commitment have been invaluable to us.

Similarly, we were fortunate to earn the trust and support of an important opinion leader in the funding community, Melvin Oliver, Senior Vice President for Community and Asset Building at the Ford Foundation. Melvin quickly saw the transformational potential of our approach and assigned us to work with a talented program officer at Ford, Dr. Queen Esther Booker. Queen literally worked around the clock to help us secure the grant that enabled us to pursue our dream of One Economy on a full-time basis. We are forever indebted to Melvin and The Ford Foundation for believing in our vision and hope that we are the next organization to follow Ford's rich history of launching successful nonprofit organizations like The Local Initiatives Support Corporation and SEEDCO.

Early on in our organizational life, our vision kept us going. Our vision gave us comfort when people told us that "what you are attempting to do is impossible" or "needlessly ambitious." Now, as we add staff to our team, we spend a lot of time sharing our vision and explaining it to them. These are the folks we are depending on to enhance the operation. It is important that they understand the vision, embrace it, and make it their own.

Values

We held a weekend retreat in the first few weeks of One Economy's existence in order to bring all of the people who had helped launch us together to lay the foundation for One Economy's future. Joined by interested individuals and partners, we spent half the retreat in one way or another discussing the issue of values. Each participant shared his or her personal journey with the group. One person, a medical doctor, traced his roots from North Carolina to Harvard to now the University of Chicago, where he teaches medicine and spends considerable time in Africa helping low-income individuals.

He was an early believer in us and came to the retreat at his own expense just to help us create something special. Our stories that day were not about how hard we had each worked to get where we were but about what we valued in life. We encouraged people to share what had brought them to help One Economy and what hopes they had for the organization. People spoke from their hearts about the types of values the organization should have and promote. It was both an affirming and humbling moment at the same time.

From that retreat, we have developed our values or core guiding principles:

1. Our customers, the low-income households who use our Web site, should be provided content from top-of-market partners and be able to use that content to make decisions that are in their own self-interest in the privacy and dignity of their own homes.

2. Our for-profit and nonprofit partners should be the best in their business and committed to working with us to make a robust market of low-income households.

3. Our staff should be encouraged and rewarded for being innovative, taking risks, and providing leadership in our organization and in the field.

We do our best to live out these values every day. In fact, it is always fun when new college interns sit in on their first Monday morning "Big Rocks"[1] staff meeting, and they are called on, like the rest of the staff, to contribute to our thinking. We tell them that we expect them to bring their own views about our work with them to the table and to be prepared to share something with us the next week when we get around to them. The next time, without fail, the interns are ready when asked and never look back. They regularly make their contributions and then walk around our office with an extra snap in their step. They feel good and we feel even better.

People

The people part of our culture was probably the easiest element for us at the start because the three of us knew each other really well. In looking for people beyond the three of us, however, we knew that we had some skills gaps. Recruiting would be complicated by the fact that we had limited funds, modest salaries, and loads of uncertainty. The best we could do was offer a lot of vision and some compelling values. The first person to join us was a natural—David Saunier, our former head of Online Services. When he asked to join us, willing to accept the risks, it was a resounding "Yes" on our part. David, at 28 years old, was already a seasoned Web design artist, credentials we certainly lacked. With our new Chief Net Officer on board we could focus elsewhere for talent. Later in the fall, we added David McConnell to head up our West Coast operations. His knowledge of the region, commitment to change, easygoing personality, and fabulous sense of humor made him an easy selection. Others have joined our team, bringing more talent and ideas with them.

In many ways, the early hirings were easy because we knew who we were hiring. This is not to diminish their talents. It simply is always harder to hire who you don't know. We have sought to make a "cultural fit" with every new hire. This does not mean sameness. In fact, we greatly value diversity in every way. Fitting into our culture means sharing our vision, values, and commitment to people. One of our staff members put it this way: "You have to hate poverty and hierarchy and love big ideas and aggressive approaches to bringing about real change." We liked that comment when we heard it.

We talk a lot internally about always keeping your eyes open for talent. Everyone on staff, including the interns, have made helpful staffing recommendations and referrals to us. We know that our best recruiting tool is trying to create and maintain an environment where people want to be. It's not the money. It's about being in a place where people feel valued, safe to try something new, and cared for when good and bad things happen personally and professionally.

We have been fortunate to be surrounded by many other volunteers and consultants who have helped us build our culture. In fact, we are not sure how we would have made it through the earliest days without people like Tom Raffa, whose free office space and tech support allowed us to just do the work and not worry about office operations. All of the people whom we have been able to work with have, broadly speaking, contributed to making this the kind of culture we had hoped for. Our job now is to enrich and expand it. As the McKinsey folks would say, we want to score high on the employee value proposition scales.[2]

We know that creating culture is one thing, but sustaining it and transforming it into a digital culture, as we define it in Chapter 3, is an entirely different matter. We have yet had to do this in One Economy. The promising beginnings will be tested by new hirings, growth as we open more regional offices, and our collective maturation from startup to mature organization. Despite these challenges, we are hopeful and optimistic that culture will continue to be an asset. In those crazy moments, of which there are many, we have reminded ourselves to "value people and ideas," and things have always seemed to work out.

DEVELOPING THE BUSINESS MODEL

We launched One Economy with a concept paper but no real business model or plan—we hadn't had time to build one. Stopping our activities to study and to plan was not an option, given our need to show some quick results to potential funders. We knew that we were going to build a Web site that catered to the needs of low-income individuals who lived in affordable rental housing by providing them with an array of products and services ranging from health care information to financial services. We hoped to limit the amount of original content on our Web site by becoming a content aggregator that would repurpose existing content to meet the needs of our customers. Our primary distribution network would be through our previous working relationships with owners of this housing, particularly nonprofits. We would get owners to take a Digital Access Pledge, which committed them to helping bring Internet access into all of their units and to connect their residents to training opportunities in their neighborhood so they could make full use of the technology. Key to us and other potential supporters was the issue of sustainability. How would One Economy support these business activities? Early on, we projected that our revenue would come from a combination of corporate sponsorships, individual contributions, and traditional philanthropy.

We knew that we needed to bring more discipline to our thinking. As luck would have it—or what some would call providential intervention—a board member of ours, Lisa Sullivan, introduced us to Jason Scott, who was just about to take a job with a prestigious venture capital firm in New York City, Flatiron Partners. Jason had his own impressive background in technology and saw a glimmer of possibility in us. He asked for our concept paper and after redlining it (read: fixing it up), he invited us to come in and meet a few folks in New York. We were eager to talk with anyone who was willing to talk to us, but admittedly we weren't quite sure what we were getting into.

Flatiron has invested millions into high-technology firms and is often credited with creating the "Silicon Alley." They decided that they wanted to expand their charitable giving by formally creating a venture philanthropy program.[3] Their aim was to make investments and use their leverage to help existing organizations "go to scale." In our first of many New York sessions, we met with Jason and Flatiron Foundation President Cathy Clark, who seemed shocked when we told her that we had only been in business for eight weeks. After several weeks of hoping, guessing, and second-guessing, "the call" came from Flatiron. We were being invited to participate in their venture philanthropy program and to undergo a rigorous due diligence process with no guarantee of funding at the other end. In fact, Flatiron needed a formal business plan and wanted to know when we would be prepared to submit it to them. We knew that these were reasonable requests, but we had not even drafted a timetable for writing such a plan. To do this right, we knew it would cost us money that we just didn't have. With the help of Michele Kahane at the Ford Foundation, we were able to quickly secure the funds we needed to write the business plan and to commit to deliver it to Flatiron by Thanksgiving.

We retained a business planning firm and an Internet consultant to assist us in this venture. Our consultants, Jason and Cathy all forced us to challenge our every assumption. Although we met or spoke with housing nonprofits, community technology centers, city council members, property managers, and residents to repeatedly test our hypotheses, we caught ourselves in a "group think" where we would validate each others' ideas without really checking them with the marketplace. Soon our business model became clear.

Customers. Our customers fall into two categories: (1) low-income households that would use our Web site and (2) owners of affordable housing who would take our Digital Access Pledge. We defined our primary market as the 12 million people who live in the 5.5 million units of government-supported, affordable housing in the United States. Roughly 1.3 million of these units are owned by public housing authorities; 3 million are owned by nonprofit and for-profit organizations that receive federal section 8 rental subsidies; and the remaining units are owned by nonprofit and for-profit organizations that maintain affordability through such tools as the Low-Income Housing Tax Credit and other federal incentives.

Content. We would have distinct content for each of these distinct customers. For the low-income households, we would have our consumer Web site, the Beehive. It would be the central point of our vision to maximize the potential of technology to help alleviate poverty, and the home page for many of the people who we have helped connect, and a destination for low- and moderate-income consumers generally. It would be comprehensive—focusing on financial services, education, jobs, health care, homeownership, and government services—and a vehicle for people to learn about and access benefits that they may be eligible for, such as the Earned Income Tax Credit and Child Health Insurance Program. For the owner of housing, we would have our corporate Web site, www.one-economy.com. This site would support both our pledge partners and our affiliates. All the services of One Economy would be Web-enabled there. Pledge partners would be able to take the Digital Access Pledge and identify our other pledge partners. Property owners would be able to determine the menu of technology options that they have to facilitate Internet access in their rental units and to take advantage of the various relationships we have negotiated with hardware, software, and Internet access and bandwidth vendors in our Digital Marketplace. Our Web and economic literacy curricula would be available for downloading and use for training residents. Similarly, our affiliates will be able to download One Economy marketing materials, receive instructions and support for using local content templates, access our fundraising database, and communicate with each other.

Our content would also include two on-the-ground demonstrations. Some call these our *proof-of-concept* efforts. For us, they are simply learning environments. In two very different cities, Washington, D.C., and Portland, Oregon, with others to follow, we are working in selected neighborhoods to create digital communities. We created partnership teams consisting of nonprofits, residents, and business and government members who are working to bring the Internet, hardware, and training to the homes of low-income individuals and to help local social service agencies to enhance their service delivery. We are helping to obtain local content about that neighborhood and the city and to integrate it into One Economy's theBeehive. These local business sites allow us to create stickiness for theBeehive and to learn more about what our customers want and use. This is where we encounter customers face to face. These interactions have taught us more than we can tell. Our cyber strategy is key to our business model, but it does not shape every aspect of what we do.

Competition.   We found that our focus on home access, content that helps low-income people build assets, and a distribution channel built on a national affordable housing infrastructure set us apart from other Internet initiatives. Other efforts either focused exclusively on access, without providing relevant content, or supplied content built around entertainment, lifestyle, and commerce for segmented affinity groups. For example, national and local organizations creating digital divide programs around access primarily focused on schools, libraries, and computer learning centers. PowerUp, Gates Library Foundation, and Computer Technology Centers (CTCs) funded by the Department of Education all raise awareness and bring resources to centers. Similarly, a handful of local programs focus on bringing technology home, such as Technology Goes Home (TGH) in Boston and targeted neighborhood initiatives in New York. These sites have enthusiastically endorsed our effort and are working with us to disseminate their lessons learned.

Affinity portals could have been viewed as potential competitors to the extent that they were targeting some of the same geographic and demographic populations; however, they differed significantly from One Economy because they (1) relied on developing costly original content, not content aggregation; (2) relied solely on customers choosing to go to their sites, not making a market by providing access to those who do not have it; (3) focused on a single issue or demographic, not a holistic site that helps people build assets and improve their lives; and (4) relied solely on generating revenue from their site, not a blend of philanthropy and revenue generation from Web and corporate partners.

Sustainability.   We realized that we would have to develop multiple revenue sources in order to be successful. Although many Web sites at the time were relying predominantly on advertising revenue, we understood that this source would not be sustainable over the long term. Therefore, we built our revenue model based on sponsorships, advertising, e-commerce, and fundraising from local and national private and corporate foundations. In addition, once theBeehive is up and running, we plan on creating an online vehicle, OnlineForGood.com, for contributions by wealthy individuals and e-retailers who want to help resolve the issues of the digital divide and economic inclusion.

We turned our business plan in days before Thanksgiving, just making our deadline. Within weeks, we received Flatiron's grant commitment and interest in adding one of their partners to our Board of Directors. The Flatiron investment transcended money. It was validation of our approach by a respected third party. Their approval would open doors for us and provide us with more resources. Looking back on this experience, it is clear to us that the business planning process was perhaps our most important undertaking. It structured our organizational reflection by literally forcing us to stop, think, and listen. We not only learned more about our market and our concept, but we also learned more about ourselves. The money mattered—as a nonprofit and a startup their unrestricted gift was essential—but the effects of the process will be with us long after their check is cashed.

The difference in our business model today compared to our earliest moments in July 2000 is profound. It is somewhat humbling to know how much we didn't know when we got started. We have no doubt we are going to learn a whole lot more along the way. Our vision has endured. The business model is just our means to that end.

BUILDING THE INFRASTRUCTURE

Infrastructure issues in a startup are unique. You don't have an environment, business development approaches, or technology systems that you can lean on when you are exhausted. On the other hand, you are not bogged down by entrenched customs or practices. We have felt from the start that "we can try almost anything and make it work." As senior management of a new company, we have the opportunity and the responsibility to ensure that our infrastructure fits our culture and our business model and not the other way around. In our first months of operation, we focused our collective energies on resource development and technology.

Resource Development

In terms of resource development, our aim was two-fold: to increase our revenue and to begin building relationships that would enhance our content. We made sure that everyone in our organization understood that we needed them to play a role in resource development. Our Internet maven, Alec Ross, fashioned our strategy for corporate relationships and fundraising, and we structured our foundation efforts. We had some early and quick successes with entities like the Ford Foundation, the Annie E. Casey Foundation, and the Fannie Mae Foundation, which actually allowed us to get through our first year. Invariably, and fairly so, we had to convince program officers that we had a rational, staged approach to our work and defined goals and objectives in mind. Other foundations simply told us that our vision was too ambitious or to "come back when things are real." We will go back to them in year 2 and 3 once they can see some tangible successes.

Similarly, on the corporate side, we had some early successes with companies like America Online (AOL), which was interested in working with us around content and fundraising but in many cases, we had a difficult time getting the attention of corporations as soon as they heard we were a nonprofit organization. It was critical for us to get these corporations to hear our business pitch before assuming that we were only a philanthropic play. We were proposing a business relationship, with earned income to us through sponsorships, click-through relationships, and targeted advertising, as well as a philanthropic relationship, with donations from their corporate foundation. Nowhere was this more important in our business model than with our Digital Marketplace. The Digital Marketplace, on our one-economy Web site, is where nonprofit businesses will take advantage of our corporate relationships and we can earn revenue as a reseller, by purchasing merchandise such as hardware and software or securing an application service provider in order to bring technology to their housing units.

We became more successful as more people took the time to listen to what we had to say, but it was not easy getting to that point. Some corporations got it quickly. SmartForce, the world's leading e-learning company, which was referred to several times earlier in the book, appreciated that we were making a market of low-income households and wanted to get its workforce training classes to this population. They quickly committed 5,000 scholarships to our efforts. Discovery Communications, a publicly spirited company with some of the best brand-name cable stations in the world, offered their 40,000 hours of television programming, retail outlets, and stature in the industry to us. Sylvan Learning Systems committed to work with us to bring its high-end programs for young people from K–12 to low-income people through One Economy.

We have aligned our human resources with our resource development needs by having everyone participate in these efforts. We also have not been afraid to continually seek guidance from others who have used innovative methods for building their businesses. These have been uncharted waters for us, but there are plenty of people out there who we can and have learned from, like Bill Shore, Vin Cippolla, Mario Morino, Doug Becker, and others. Our challenge will be to judiciously provide more support to this function while also dramatically increasing our productivity in other areas. As a startup, it makes sense to put most of your efforts into resource development. As we mature, we know that we have to find more of a balance.

Technology

Technology is a part of almost everything we do at One Economy. It is on everyone's desktop. We seem to live and die on e-mail. Our Web sites, www.thebeehive.org and www.one-economy.com, are the primary mechanisms we use to deliver content to both of our key customer groups. Despite the importance of technology to our operations, we decided early on that we would not support and manage all of our technology needs in-house. Our Web site development work is managed by a tech team led by our Chief Net Officer, David Saunier, and several other consultants, volunteers, and college interns. Initially, our Web sites are hosted by AOL Time Warner in northern Virginia. Our internal, local area network (LAN) and e-mail system is managed by Raffa and Associates, who provides us office space and the technical support we need when we have problems. This structure has been cost effective. Most important, it has allowed us to stay nimble and innovative on a limited budget.

We have ambitious plans for maximizing the capabilities of broadband technologies in our work. Once broader bandwidth is more common in households, we will be able to serve our low-income customers with content that is more easily accessible at all literacy levels. Streaming video, for example, is less reliant on the written word and capable of using pictures to tell the stories we want to tell. We are committed to pushing the technology envelope to ensure that thebeehive.org is the premier gateway for people to enter the social and economic mainstream.

ALIGNMENT

Obviously, as a new and small organization, we don't have all that much to align; however, we do some basic things to make sure that we are keeping all of our parts working together. We hold Big Rocks staff meetings every Monday morning at 10:30 a.m. These meetings take place no matter who is in the office at that time. Our staff members call in from wherever they are in the country, and everyone walks through the main issues they are working on. We run through the most pressing issues concerning customers, content, business development, and technology. If we have a particularly important meeting, presentation, or visit coming up that week, it would receive special attention at the Big Rocks meeting. Every week, we also take time to look forward to the issues that we see on the horizon. We think we have created a "safe place" at these meetings where people can raise any issues they think we should be talking about. To date, they have been the glue that has kept our hectic operation together.

We have also used the annual planning and budgeting process to align ourselves and to stay aligned. As we developed our budget and workplans for our second year of operations, we spent a lot of time making sure that we actually were putting our money and our people where they needed to be put. Although we had a lot of aspirations for One Economy, we had to take the time to prioritize things that we actually could get done in the coming year, not things that we hoped would get done. This may sound easy, but it is actually quite difficult when you have a whole plate of exciting ideas and possibilities in front of you. We used the annual planning and budgeting process to bring that type of discipline to our work.

Finally, we are building a more formal balanced performance measurement system to keep us aligned so we can meet our aggressive growth plans. From the outset, we have set goals, objectives, and measures of success for ourselves in five areas: (1) home access to the Internet, (2) regular monthly use of theBeehive, (3) strategic partnerships, (4) civic engagement, and (5) fundraising. We are using the Balanced Scorecard model to refine our thinking and integrating those goals, objectives, and measures into our individual performance evaluations.

WHAT THE FUTURE HOLDS

We could not be more excited about what the future may hold for us. Programmatically, we have an ever-increasing array of for-profit and nonprofit partnerships that have great promise. Partners like Oracle, which is working with states on making government services and benefits available on a self-service basis, are a perfect product for the Beehive. We are pursuing opportunities to help people turn their consumption into savings through negotiated rewards programs with companies like Wal-Mart that puts money into people's mutual funds every time they shop.

We also see more and more low-income people getting access to technology in their homes. Statistics show that families earning less than $25,000 a year have been the fastest-growing segment of the population that is using the Internet in the past year and a half. The growth of wireless technologies and broadband will only make this happen faster. The faster people get access, the more quickly our content gets to our targeted market.

Organizationally, we are building affiliate relationships with nonprofits in cities across America that look to the Beehive to deliver content to their low-income constituencies. These potential affiliations range from community technology center collaboratives in Seattle to a network of housing development and single-family homeowner weatherization programs serving 60,000 families in metropolitan Cleveland. We are building our own corporate rituals, like a holiday staff dinner party, and our corporate photo album, which we are using to document milestones in our history, like our first week of work, our first board of directors meeting, early meetings in our Digital Communities, and so on. Finally, on a more personal level, we are committed to supporting our growing staff as they venture on their own journeys. Even on our limited budget, we are encouraging staff to go to conferences, meet with people who they view as important to their professional growth, and to read everything they can get their hands on to stay ahead of our competition. In our first week of work, we subscribed to the four leading technology magazines so they would be ever-present in our offices.

We are doing everything we can to live the map. We are continually taking the pulse of the world around us and encouraging our staff to do so. We are building a digital culture by showing our people that they come first, by valuing the power of ideas, by centering in on our customers, by embracing digital solutions, and by instilling an ethos of learning. We are pursuing a rational business model based on multiple sources of revenue and supportable by an infrastructure that we can sustain. We are doing what we can to keep this all aligned on a weekly basis. Most important, however, we are making reflection and repositioning part of our corporate vernacular.

SHARE YOUR EXPERIENCES LIVING THE MAP

We hope that our story has helped to bring the Dynamic Management Map to life. We know many of you have experienced or are experiencing many of the same issues that we have talked about in this chapter. As you travel the path to building a dynamic organization, we invite you to share your own thoughts, stories, and experiences with us and others at our Web site, www.managingnonprofits.org. We have learned two important lessons over the years: (1) there is no better way to learn than from your peers, and (2) there is no better way to return the favor than to share your knowledge with others. We hope to see you there.

NOTES

[1]See our discussion of Big Rocks in Chapter 8.

[2]See our People First discussion in Chapter 4.

[3]See our discussion of Flatiron in Chapter 7.

CHAPTER TEN

What's in Store for the Dynamic Manager: Looking at the Future of Nonprofit Management

We believe so strongly in Dynamic Management because it positions you to deal with whatever the future brings. The organization that continually reflects and repositions wins. The organization that puts its head in the sand and imposes a "moratorium on creativity," loses. This dichotomy will only get more severe in the coming years because, as we've said so many times before, much of the nonprofit industry is only in the beginning of its strategic inflection point. While we have no crystal ball, we see trends on the horizon that have the potential to overwhelm nonprofit organizations that are unprepared or unwilling to adapt to change. We describe these trends in this chapter and feature the comments of other important voices in our field who feel strongly about what the future holds for nonprofit organizations.

THE HORN & HARDART-IZATION OF CUSTOMERS

We have talked throughout this book about the need to spend more time communicating with, wooing, and servicing customers. We have provided many examples of nonprofits that are going out of their way to talk with their customers, to enable their customers to talk with each other, and to attract new customers through new products, services, and distribution channels. The driving force behind our urging in this area and the actions of the organizations highlighted in earlier chapters is consumer choice. Never before have consumers of nonprofit services had so many choices for where they can go to get information and services. Those organizations that build customer loyalty keep those customers coming back, one way or another, even when other choices are available.

In the coming years, consumer demand for choices will increase dramatically. More and more people, in fact, will demand both the opportunity to get information and services where and when it is convenient to them as well as the ability to act on it themselves—without the help traditionally provided by nonprofits. We call this the 'Horn and Hardart-ization of the customer.' When we were growing up, it seemed that there were Horn & Hardart cafeterias on almost every block in New York City and Philadelphia. You would walk in and there would be a wall of little doors with different sandwiches, vegetables, and desserts behind every door. You would walk down the aisle and pick and choose what you wanted from this almost overwhelming array of choices. This is what consumers of nonprofit services will increasingly demand.

Why do we think this is coming our way? Because it is already here. Customers are no longer waiting to walk into the neighborhood health clinic to figure out what may be wrong with them. They are going to NetWellness, asking a doctor for advice, and taking the appropriate action. Alternatively, they are going onto the Internet, researching the symptoms, and coming in the clinic door with a preconceived notion of how they should be treated. In either case, the traditional nonprofit–customer relationship has been obliterated and a new one created in its place. Our work with Oracle has also convinced us of this impending tsunami. Oracle is well on its way in Utah, and soon in other states, toward integrating government databases that track a plethora of government programs that low-income households historically participate in, such as welfare-to-work, child care, and food stamps. Once Oracle's work is complete, families will be able to apply for eligibility and then actually help themselves to the government services that are available to them. Government services and subsidies are coming to a Horn & Hardart near you. If you are a nonprofit that is currently serving as a link in that chain, either by helping people determine their eligibility or by serving as an expeditor to connect people to the right services, you may soon be out of business.

Will this trend affect you? You need to reflect on your existing work. If you attract many of your customers because you hold the information they want, then you are probably vulnerable. One way or another, they are likely to get that information from another source soon. You need to let go of the information and Web-enable your knowledge so people will see your value-added benefit. Your organization's experience will be reflected in the design and sorting of the data. Your intellectual capital will make the database relevant and compelling to customers. Yes, you may be cannibalizing your traditional walk-in business by making your information more broadly available, but you will be repositioning your organization for the future, not simply holding on to the past.

Another interesting thing about your future customers: They may very well be other nonprofits, not just low-income individuals. More and more, we are seeing business-to-business relationships taking off in the nonprofit arena. For example, organizations that have figured out how to run their own internal technology systems (e.g., e-mail, local area networks) are actually outsourcing their excess capacity to other nonprofits. Other organizations, like Share our Strength, which have mastered the art of one element of Dynamic Management, such as cause-related marketing, are building consulting arms to help other organizations do the same. As your traditional customer relationships change, don't be afraid to look for untraditional, new customers.

THE MELTING POT IN THE LUNCH ROOM

The great American melting pot is rapidly changing the face of the nonprofit and is likely to continue to change at an accelerated pace in the coming years. This is true at both the staff and the chief executive or senior management level. Staff members are increasingly reflecting the racial, ethnic, and gender composition of the customers and the communities that are being served, for several reasons. One reason is the growing recognition by those of us who run nonprofit organizations that this is necessary and the growing intolerance of customers to accept anything else. The other factor is the changing demographics of the American worker today. Population projections based on preliminary results from the 2000 U.S. census show that most of America will be non-White in the not-too-distant future. Organizations that continue to fail to build a diverse workforce and a corporate culture that celebrates and honors diversity will not be able to compete. As we have said so many times before in these pages, nobody is fooled by words and if they are, they are not fooled for long. An organization's commitment to diversity must be worn on its sleeve, transparent to people inside and outside the organization, and supported by recruitment and retention policies. Those organizations that live these principles will flourish; those that talk a lot about it but don't act, will not.

The face of nonprofit leaders will also be changing dramatically but not necessarily for all the same reasons. Demographics and wealth will be driving change at the top. Put simply, every year that passes brings more and more non-White leaders, African-Americans, Latinos, Asian-Americans, and others to top positions in the nonprofit industry. This change can be explained in several ways. One is the sheer numbers. We are finally getting to the point when most Baby Boomers are of the age and experience to run our own organizations. Two is the educational and experiential opportunities that we have been able to accumulate because of the trail blazed 40 years ago by the civil rights movement. Now, in the early years of the 21st century, we are seeing the ever-increasing pool of talented, non-White senior managers and executives who have had the chance to go to college, graduate school, and on to important positions in the past four decades.

Wealth is another factor impacting on the faces we see in non-profit leadership. As we write this, the United States is coming out of the longest sustained period of economic growth in its history. That has resulted in an extraordinary number of young people becoming rich at very young ages. We are already seeing some of these people retire from the business that made them rich and look to putting their energies into giving back, into managing a nonprofit organization. Sometimes these organizations are ones they start up themselves (like OneNorthwest highlighted in Chapter 5), but other times they look for existing nonprofits that they can take to the next level. Some say that an economic turndown will put an end to this trend. That is not what we have seen. In many cases, the degree of wealth built over the past 10 years for many of these individuals makes them immune from changes in market conditions.

What will the changing face of leadership mean to you? It will likely mean more and better competition. In fact, a competitor with a minority CEO who made enough money to retire early may have two distinct competitive advantages over you: (1) its leader at the top is someone who looks like the customers that the organization serves; and (2) the retired CEO will be darn sure that the business has the systems and the discipline that he or she was used to in the for-profit sector. These advantages can both mean disaster to your organization.

GOOD-BYE TONTO, OR THE END OF THE LONE RANGER

The future will be a lonely place for nonprofits that try to make it on their own. Call it what you will—strategic alliances, collaborations, joint ventures, even intermediation—few nonprofits will be able to continue playing the role of the Lone Ranger, out to save the world on their own. We see this happening everywhere, in every facet of the nonprofit world, from sharing staff to developing programs, and providing the necessary infrastructure. Why? We believe it is largely because the traditional roles of nonprofit, for-profit, and government are being increasingly blurred. eNature.com, a for-profit Web site offering users free access to reams of pictures and data on localized nature, nature literally in people's backyards, had a service that the National Wildlife Foundation (NWF) wanted to offer to its 4.5 million members. Instead of building its own inventory to compete with eNature, the NWF simply bought the company. The NWF now focuses on what it does best and eNature focuses on what it does best, all working in the best interest of NWF's customers. The Smithsonian hired MuseumCompany.com to manage its 30-million-person customer base and its online retail sales that it projects will raise more than $10 million a year for the Institution. One Economy is partnering with groups like Power Up and America Connects—nationwide, nonprofit, community technology center (CTCs) support organizations—to bring technology home to people who go to CTCs and to connect people who have technology at home to training and programs at CTCs. The City of Dallas hired Lockheed Martin to manage its welfare-to-work program, not because it had expertise in dealing with people in need but because it knew how to build and manage a complex database.

A dynamic nonprofit organization in Dallas should have won that contract by bidding on it with a Lockheed Martin competitor so its bid would have brought both business and humanity to the table.

Who you define as a competitor or collaborator is likely to be more fluid in the future. America's Second Harvest and Foodchain were vigorous competitors serving distinct markets in the donated food sector until funders and board members brought them together to increase the fight against hunger. The University of Cincinnati, Case Western Reserve University, and Ohio State University never saw a reason to work together before they created NetWellness and almost overnight their collaboration improved health care information delivery for citizens of the Ohio Valley, including northern Kentucky, southeastern Indiana, and people in more than 50 countries.

To some extent, this trend is driven by the need for nonprofit organizations to show their impact. Clearly, your work will have a greater impact if you are also able to take credit for the work of your partner. As Mark Weinheimer, a long-time consultant and evaluator of nonprofit community development corporations, states, "there is increasing pressure on nonprofits to both address multifaceted and comprehensive issues facing their communities as well as to show measurable results from their work." Strategic alliances or collaborations enable you to do that.

Collaborative work is not easy. It requires compromise, negotiation, and flexibility. Even more important, it requires an honest understanding of the value-added benefit your organization brings to the relationship and the impact the relationship will have on your corporate culture. But the risks of not aggressively seeking the right partners are enormous and not worth taking.

THE CORPORATE FACELIFT

Many nonprofits today look and function in ways that are different from the way nonprofits functioned for the past 40 years. They may sound like they are still doing the same things they always did, but they actually have had a facelift, and maybe even more invasive surgery, when you look at them more closely. What's changed? They are structured in new ways; they are funded in new ways; and they use business practices rarely seen before in the nonprofit sector. Those organizations that have already made these changes will continue to evolve. More important, many of the organizations that haven't yet made these changes will be doing so in the coming years. Those that don't may perish, merge, or become marginalized.

These new corporate structures more closely mimic those of for-profit organizations. They are run by chief executive officers and often have chief operating, technology, and even information officers to manage the key parts of the organization. They commonly act as a parent to other related subsidiaries, if they have for-profit offspring, or to supporting organizations, if the offspring have a nonprofit mission. In fact, this structure has made nonprofits much more willing and able to establish single-purpose offspring corporations in order to take advantage of opportunities or strategic alliances that further some part of the organization's mission. It also makes recruiting a lot easier. The corporate structure is much more understandable to people who want to figure out where they would fit in the organizational chart or what they would be taking on if they were being recruited to run the place.

Funding comes from diverse sources. They work aggressively to reduce the amount of public subsidy or support that comes in from government agencies, as a percentage of total organizational revenue. More revenue than ever is being generated on a fee-for-service basis from for-profit, nonprofit, and foundation customers. The fees earned are often enhanced or incentivized when the organization's performance meets certain milestones. More and more often, venture philanthropists are working with them to provide stable multiyear financial support that is tied to performance and organizational measures of success.

Their business practices and applications of technology mirror those of the for-profit sector. Carol Berde, Executive Vice President of the McKnight Foundation, puts it well: "Now and into the future, high-performing nonprofits must have up-to-date technology and business practices. Those that fail to strengthen the business side of their operations impede their ability to fulfill their mission." That means implementing financial management systems that work and that are used to keep the organization in alignment. Organizational and individual performance measurement systems must measure and reward performance based on achievement of the things the organization wants to see changed, not what the organization did to try to change it.

In many cases, it means that technology is being used in ways that (1) allow an organization to scale—to use its information assets, often as the first-mover in the industry, to get to a lot of customers, both old and new, fast; (2) enable the organization to deliver a high-tech/high-touch approach, combining physical and information/digital assets, that gives it a distinct competitive advantage and the ability to play a broker role with traditional and new customers; (3) compel strategic alliances or networks of alliances with collaborative partners and the building of mechanisms to share information and knowledge with strategic partners to enhance collective competitive advantages; and (4) force a realignment of players in the organization's industry so some organizations get forced out as a result of new technologies and others emerge as new infomediaries that are able to gain enormous power by mining customer data and making mass customization possible.[1]

HOW DO I RESPOND TO THESE TRENDS?

Begin acting now. As Rey Ramsey likes to say, the beginning of tomorrow starts today. If the first nine chapters didn't convince you to try Dynamic Management in your organization, maybe this chapter did. Start taking your organization's pulse today. Move your way through the Dynamic Management Map and reflect on your culture, your business model, and your infrastructure and ask yourself if all the parts of your organization are aligned, working toward a common purpose. If you aren't so sure that you like what you see, start repositioning those parts that matter the most to you. Maybe your culture is the problem because your staff has been turning over more than usual. Maybe your content isn't working because you see your competitor actually picking off some of your old customers. Maybe your funding model is flawed because you are too reliant on government funds and have never even thought about e-commerce. Whatever it is, do something. Your action will set off reactions and new energy that you can't even begin to imagine. It will send you on your way toward building a dynamic organization, an organization increasingly ready to change and thrive in this digital age. You'll never look back.

Digital Spotlight—Nonprofit Trends According to Jed Emerson

The nonprofit manager of the future will find him- or herself operating in a changed context unlike anything we know today.

He or she will have ridden the crest of the following four major trends just now beginning to move through the sector.

The Morphing of Corporate Structure

Traditionally, one worked in government, nonprofits, or the private, for-profit sector. Future organizations will evolve to become integrated entities, encompassing parts of each sector and pursuing a blended value proposition. Nonprofit development corporations will provide an array of services to their communities, as government departments complete the move toward total privatization of services. For-profit companies entering domestic and global emerging markets lacking traditional infrastructure will continue to advance business models pursuing economic goals, yet executing social and environmental strategies as well. The result will be the evolution of fully hybrid corporations, with for-profits sponsoring nonprofit affiliates and nonprofits owning for-profit subsidiaries. The line between the two will be strictly a function of whether the social and economic equity generated by the corporation is distributed to outside shareholders or held in trust by collective stakeholder groups.

The Bouncing Boomers

As Baby Boomers live into their nineties and hundreds, they will not settle for either traditional retirement or passive volunteerism. Leadership of future organizations will find themselves confronting a new type of player—the part-time employee/ volunteer who simultaneously holds both salaried and non-salaried positions and is actively engaged in operations, not passively acting as a "nice community service volunteer." Having run the major corporations of the world, having driven the digital revolution, having actively lived life, these individuals will enter a period of years with nothing to lose and plenty to gain by being fully engaged on their own terms. They will demand meaningful roles and expect to be adequately valued for their contributions. They will require a new level of engagement from both the organizations with which they affiliate and those purporting to address their needs.

The Transparent Organization

With 990s on the Web and wireless communication bringing every corporation (whether nonprofit or for-profit) under the public microscope, the nonprofit manager of the future will have to get used to immediate accountability and real-time public access to information regarding hires, resource allocation, program effectiveness, and virtually every area of organizational performance. The days of closed-door board meetings and vaguely written minutes will end as social investors increasingly demand documentation of effective execution of stated strategies. Transparency will not be an option, but rather a requirement of the nonprofit capital market.

21st Century Managers

To succeed and thrive in the digital age, nonprofit managers of the future will find themselves drawing on a variety of management tools. They will need to be well versed in understanding options for capital-structured finance as they move from fundraising for social change to investing in the creation of social value. They will command the skills of entrepreneurial management, continually responding to shifts in not simply local or regional politics and circumstance, but also international capital, information, and demographic flows. They will be multilingual as the United States continues to reflect the power shifts of the world and our own population becomes driven by Hispanic and Asian influences, demanding that leaders be able to move smoothly among audiences of stakeholders that are both homogenous and heterogeneous. The nonprofit manager of the future will hold degrees in business, social work, and cultural arts—and require the skills of each!

(Jed Emerson is a Senior Fellow with the William and Flora Hewlett Foundation and holds the position of Lecturer with the Graduate School of Business at Stanford University. The Nonprofit Times has twice selected him as one of its "50 Most Influential People in the Sector," individuals whose thoughts and work are believed to have an effect on the future of nonprofit organizations.)

Digital Spotlight—Nonprofit Trends According to Joan Fanning

We have seen nonprofits grapple with the challenge of using technology as a tool for furthering their missions. That is why we focus on helping these organizations to make the most out of technology through strategic planning, assessment, hands-on consulting, and support services. Despite all the rhetoric, technology is fundamentally about organizational change. We believe that nonprofits will go through three stages of change—each building on each other like a wedding cake—as they work toward mastering technology as a tool for achieving their missions:

Stage 1.   In stage 1, technology is used to enhance the organization's operations and make them more efficient. In this stage, the focus is on making staff more productive and technology reliable, stable, and transparent. Stage 1 builds the foundation that needs to exist before you can move up and use technology in the direct delivery of service. Today, 80 percent of the nonprofits are in this stage.

Stage 2.   Stage 2 is the natural evolution from internal operations to the substantive work of the nonprofit—direct service delivery. In stage 2, technology is used to expand the organization's programmatic reach and deepen the impact of direct services. For example, once staff are comfortable using technology, they will use it to enhance their core work whether it be online advocacy or literacy classes. About 15 percent of nonprofit organizations currently function in stage 2.

Stage 3.   Stage 3 is achieved when nonprofits actually begin creating their own technologies and technological applications. In stage 3, you get enough critical mass and corporate self-confidence that one or more significant players in a sector of the nonprofit industry believe that they can and should develop new applications that would change or "cannibalize" the way work has been done historically. Stage 3 organizations and their leaders provide entirely new ways to deliver content to people and communities by harnessing technology and informing it with goals, values, and a lucid understanding of who it is they want to help. Stage 3 organizations have the skills to inform the creation of new technologies and applications and to put them into their toolbox. The work of the Fund for the City of New York is a great example (see Chapter 5). Taking a cue from the for-profit industry that has created document assembly packages for years for real-estate transactions, wills, etc., the Fund created the same type of package for victims of domestic violence. This is a great example of people who care passionately about an issue and who understand technology making the most out of what's available to them. Fewer than 5 percent of nonprofits today function at stage 3 but they will within the next five years.

Joan Fanning is the Executive Director of Npower, based in Seattle, Washington. Npower is one of the nation's leading nonprofits dedicated to helping the nonprofit industry to make information technology a powerful ally for advancing their work.

Digital Spotlight—Technology and Nonprofits According to Mario Morino

Technology Will Define and Differentiate

Technology is rapidly helping redefine entire markets and industries. It has been the fundamental enabler of globalization. It has changed and will continue to change the way organizations and people communicate, transact, and gather the resources they need. Worse, the rate of technology change continues to increase, only widening the gap between the application of technology in the private and nonprofit sector.

In time, the deployment of technology may well be the key differentiation for certain nonprofits, versus others in their category or class, whereas others run the risk of being ostracized from the resource networks that will be available to those who are empowered to use technology effectively.

Technology Must Be Used to Solve a Nonprofit's Most Pressing Needs

Although technology has the potential to differentiate your organization from others, it can only achieve that if applied right. Technology is a tool, a capability, that when effectively applied to solutions helps organizations do things more effectively, less expensively, and sometimes do things they would not be able to do otherwise. But like most other things, if there is not a clear purpose for its deployment, its value can, at best, be questionable—even counterproductive. The application of technology stands to yield the greatest return to an organization when it is focused on helping solve the organization's most pressing needs. For instance, what good does a technology center focused on teaching technical skills have when the problem is one of basic literacy, helping children and adults learn to read and write?

Technology Training, not Technology, Is Paramount

Technology training in management and staff is critical. We go so far as to recommend that for every $1 directed to technology, 70 cents of it should be applied to helping the organization and staff develop an understanding and expertise in using it and for developing the processes to support its use, with the remaining 30 cents used to purchase the hardware and software itself. Technology will never have its full impact if people don't know how to get the most out of it.

Mario Morino, a former software entrepreneur, is Chairman of the Morino Institute, Chairman of Venture Philanthropy Partners, and a Special Partner at the private equity investment firm General Atlantic Partners. Through the nonprofit Morino Institute, which seeks to harness the power of the Internet and New Economy to advance social change, Mario has launched various path breaking ventures: the Potomac Knowledge Way, an organization that helped to build the National Capital region's potential as a technology power in the global economy; the Netpreneur program, which has helped to catalyze entrepreneurship in the region; the Youth Development Collaborative Pilot, which helped create networked learning centers in low-income neighborhoods of the District of Columbia; the Youth Learn initiative, which provides resources and tools for integrating technology into out-of-school programs; and Venture Philanthropy Partners, an ambitious effort to increase the level and effectiveness of philanthropic giving nationwide.

Mario is a trustee of Case Western University and a director of the Community Foundation for the National Capital Region, the Brookings Institute, the Internet Policy Institute, the National Commission on Entrepreneurship, and the Mid-Atlantic Venture Association.

Prior to establishing the Morino Institute, Mario enjoyed a 30-year career in the information technology industry during its developing years. In 1973, he co-founded Morino Associates, a software firm that merged with another firm in 1989 to become LEGENT Corporation. LEGENT was acquired in 1995 in what was then the largest transaction in the computer software and services industry.

Mario is a graduate of Case Western Reserve University, a native of Cleveland, OH, and is married with three children.

NOTES

[1]Sendil Ethiraj, Isin Guler, and Harbir Singh, www.knowledge@ wharton.edu. See our discussion of this topic in Chapter 1.

Resources for Online Fundraising

<u>Note:</u> Please see www.managingnonprofits.org for up-to-the-minute resources for online fundraising.

2du.com   www.2du.com

This site lists sales, specials, and events in local communities. Businesses or organizations can make a listing online for free or can purchase fancy ads ($30). A fundraiser can sell fancy ad tickets or can merely promote the site in their community so donors visit and purchase ads online. Up to 45 percent of any money made from your assigned city is shared.

3rdSector.Net   www.3rdsector.net

Offers a broad range of applications designed for nonprofits over its Web site—accounting, payroll, donations, event registrations, membership processing, and intranets. (Ad in *The Nonprofit Times*, 2/15/00.) "3rdSector.Net's fee for online donations, event registration, and membership renewal is $29.95 per month. This fee includes 100 transactions per month. The cost per transaction, after the first 100 transactions per month, is $.40 (40 cents) per transaction. The one-time setup fee is $185." (E-mail 3/29/00)

4charity.com   www.4charity.com

4charity.com develops Web-based products and services for companies, nonprofits, and individuals with the goal of making charitable giving quick, easy, and a part of daily life. 4charity.com offers workplace giving solutions and nonprofit donation tools, hosts a large online charity mall, and offers direct donations. In addition, 4charity.com will soon provide a searchable database of information about every nonprofit in the U.S. All funds contributed are distributed to the designated organizations.

Acteva   www.acteva.com

A Web-based marketing, registration, and payment service for all types of activities and events. Offers control over the special-event management process. (Adapted from the Web site 5/8/00)

Active Computer   www.activecomputer.com

Active has an outstanding reputation for providing high-quality support and software to the association/nonprofit industry for more than eight years.

Affinity Resources   www.affinityresources.com

This is a for-profit organization—fundraising counsel—with particular emphasis on online fundraising. It helps design and construct Web sites for nonprofits.

All Charities   www.allcharities.com

Changed its name to *CoreMatter* in September 2000. Scheduled to launch in October 1999: "The mission of AllCharities.com is to be the premier provider of applications and services to the collective marketplace of nonprofit organizations and philanthropic-minded individuals. AllCharities.com will leverage the efficiency and power of the Internet and emerging technologies to empower nonprofit organizations and to educate and inspire individuals." (From the Web site)

Animal Funds of America   www.animalfunds.org

Provides a portal site where donors can find national animal welfare charities they wish to support. Donations can be made online to any charity via check, credit card, or gift of stock. AFA is a membership organization that reviews and certifies its members annually. In addition to its web site, AFA places its members into workplace employee fund drives, the largest being the Combined Federal Campaign for federal employees.

Authorize.net   www.authorizenet.com

"We use Authorize.net [for donation processing]. So far, we've been pleased with them. They sometimes give a special rate to nonprofit organizations, so worth looking into. . . . " (E-mail to orgwebmaster, 5/2/00)

Barnes & Noble   www.bn.com

The Affiliate Program allows Web sites to sell Barnes & Noble items online and receive royalties from the sale. MyBNLink provides links for people to put in their e-mail. Whenever someone uses the link, the sender receives 5 percent; they can donate the money to charity (one of five) or keep it for themselves. In addition, 1 percent of such sales is donated to First Book, a group in Washington, D.C., that gives books to poor children.

BayBuilder.com   www.baybuiider.com

Provides customized auction sites as plug-ins for commerce or charity Web sites. (E-mail from BayBuilder.com, 2/22/00)

BeamUs   www.beamus.com

BeamAge Shopping Portal: 100 percent affiliate and merchant revenue donated to nonprofit members. Free Web sites and Web exposure with direct donation pages, nonprofit forums and chat, Web ring and links. (E-mail 8/15/00)

BenefitEvents. com   www.benefitevents.com

Offers online auctions for charities and consulting and other services in support of charity-auction fundraising. (Web site 5/11/00)

buy2share   www.buy2share.com

Buy2share.com offers your supporters the ability to shop for name-brand products while providing the organization with continuous royalties. Buy2share.com is 100 percent revenue accountability, monthly checks with no minimums, product updates, and promotions to build and maintain site traffic. (Advertisement 3/27/00)

Canadian Government   www.communitystorefronts.com

Community Storefronts has been created by the Canadian federal government to encourage use of the Internet for electronic transactions of all kinds, commercial as well as charitable. Currently has 25 non-profit organizations accepting donations.

Care4Free   www.care4free.net

Care4Free is a UK-based organization, "a free Internet Service Provider (ISP) for people who care. Our mission is to provide a wide array of free benefits to charities and organizations in the caring and nonprofit-making sector. We aim to achieve this by allowing good causes of all sizes to harness the power of the Internet for communications and fundraising. We are unique in that a proportion of 75 percent of profits go directly to registered charities. And, since any individual can choose Care4free as their free Internet provider, funds are raised every time that person goes online." (From "about" on the care4free Web site, 12/9/99)

causeLINK   www.causelink.com

"Online network that provides new fundraising solutions to nonprofit organizations through online charity auctions and e-commerce solutions. A new way to raise funds and generate revenue for any nonprofit organization using the Internet." (E-mail 8/8/00)

CelebrityAuctions.com   www.celebrityauctions.com

Interactive celebrity Internet auctions for charities. A service of TEN97 (q.v.).

Changing Our World   www.changingourworld.com

Mike Hoffman & Associates offer iCampaigns, "a new way of fundraising that combines professional campaign management and web technology." (From the Web site, 12/15/99)

CharitableGift   www300.charitablegift.org

Fidelity Investments allows owners of assets held in Fidelity accounts to make transfers into the Charitable Gift Fund (a Fidelity service) and direct disbursements to charitable organizations using a World Wide Web interface.

Charities Today   www.charitiestoday.com

Provides comprehensive and analytical information about charities to potential donors and other supporters.

Charity.ca   www.charity.ca

"I wanted to post a brief informational message to let you know that Canada's first donor-driven charity portal will be launching at the end of the month. We're doing a cross-country tour starting tomorrow to introduce ourselves to charities. Please visit our site at www.charity.ca or contact us at (416) 593-4240 if you would like more information." (E-mail on NONPROFIT from susan@charity.ca 4/3/00)

CharityAmerica   www.charityamerica.com

Unites donors, volunteers, businesses, and qualified charities, building a powerful nonprofit network.

CharityBall   www.charityball.org

A Kentucky-based organization.

CharityFundraiser   www.charityfundraiser.com

A free auction service designed to help raise money for charity (per the Web site, 5/4/00). Buyers are charged a premium on every purchase; 50 percent of this premium is given to the seller's designated charity.

CharityGifts   www.charitygifts.com

Invites purchases that will result in contributions to a short list of well-known charities in Britain.

CharityMall   www.charitymall.com

"Shop at over 200 top e-retailers [here] and every order you place will send money to your chosen charity." (From the Web site, 7/16/01)

CharityUSA   www.charityusa.org

CharityUSA is building a user-submitted search engine/directory of nonprofits online and resources for nonprofits online. It offers free classifieds, a free auction feature for nonprofits, numerous message boards, chat rooms, and so on. It also offers nonprofits a free Web page, free e-mail@charityusa.net, and our own brand of free ISP is coming soon. The goal is to Web-enable as many nonprofits as possible and empower them to take full advantage of the opportunities online.

CharityWave   www.charitywave.com

"CharityWave.com is a free, charity-support service that makes sure 100 percent of every dollar you donate goes directly to the cause or organization that you want to help. All transaction costs are paid by Wave Systems Corp., so the charities benefit from every single dollar of your contribution. CharityWave guarantees that your personal information is kept secure and confidential, and it protects the privacy of your charitable donation." (From the Web site, 12/9/99)

CharityWeb   www.charityweb.net [or .com]

"CharityWeb is an e-commerce ASP for charities. Charities using our service can accept donations, sell their own items, and offer event registration from their Web site without having to install, maintain, and customize all the software on their own servers." (E-mail from company, 6/8/00)

Children's Charities of America
www.childrenscharities.org

Provides a portal site where donors can find national children's charities they wish to support. Donations can be made online to any charity via check, credit card, or gift of stock. The CCA is a membership organization that reviews and certifies its members annually. In addition to its Web site, the CCA places its members into workplace employee fund drives, the largest being the Combined Federal Campaign for federal employees.

ClickRewards

See Netcentives.

Communitybids.com   www.communitybids.com

Community Bids allows organizations to hold online auction fundraisers and is a great way to raise money and have fun! Fast and simple to set up, this full-service site will walk you through the whole process of holding an online auction.

Conservation and Preservation Charities of America
www.conservenow.org

Provides a portal site where donors can find national environmental charities they wish to support. Donations can be made online to any charity via check, credit card, or gift of stock. The CPCA is a membership organization that reviews and certifies its members annually. In addition to its Web site, the CPCA places its members into workplace employee fund drives, the largest being the Combined Federal Campaign for federal employees.

Consumer Saints   www.consumersaints.com

An online shopping mall that allows users to raise money for the charity of their choice. Just for stopping by, users automatically receive $3. Users can shop at more than 200 stores, including Amazon.com. Real-time statistics and payment monitors allow users to see exactly how their money is being sent. (E-mail from Consumer Saints staff, 1/6/00)

Contribute.com   www.contribute.com

"Contribute.com works quietly and invisibly behind the scenes to enable your donors to make contributions from your Web site. We custom build an online payment form to match the look and feel of your existing Web site. It looks just like you had created it yourself." A processing fee is charged. (From the Web site, 12/15/99)

CoreMatter   www.corematter.com

Provides e-giving solutions for workplace campaigns in Fortune 1000 companies. Formerly known as All Charities. (Rick Christ newsletter story, 9/21/00)

CreateHope.com   www.createhope.org

Nonprofit organizations can present a profile of their organization and cause; and donors will be able to come online, research the charities, and make an online donation. CreateHope also provides e-commerce capabilities to nonprofits for their own Web sites. (From e-mail, 12/17/99)

CyberGold   www.cybergold.com

Allows donations to selected charities.

CyberGrants   www.cybergrants.com

A philanthropy Web site that streamlines the grant application and grantmaking process for not-for-profit organizations and corporate and private foundations. Foundations can now establish an immediate, free Web presence that lists their grant guidelines, mission statement, and other pertinent background information, and obtain a free 30-day trial of the system's robust Web-based grants management software. Nonprofits can access CyberGrants free of charge to research grant guidelines and to create, maintain and submit online proposals directly to member foundations. (Adapted from a press release dated 12/16/99)

The Data Bank

See thedatabank.com

Denari Online   www.denarionline.com

An online version of desktop donor management software. (Advertisement in 5/15/00 *Nonprofit Times)*

Do Unto Others   www.duo.org

Provides a portal site where donors can find national and international relief and development charities they wish to support. Donations can be made online to any charity via check, credit card, or gift of stock. DUO is a membership organization that reviews and certifies its members annually. In addition to its Web site, DUO places its members into workplace employee fund drives, the largest being the Combined Federal Campaign for federal employees.

Dollar-A-Day Campaign   http://users.mis.net/~sphere

Sphere Publishing invites nonprofit organizations to list themselves (by state) on a Web site that invites visitors to send coded checks to any organization they want to support. In return, the recipient is expected to send 10 percent of any funds received back to the sponsor of the Web site. (E-mail announcement and Web site, 6/8/00)

donate.net   www.donate.net

An application service provider of online e-commerce donation software. Formerly known as Conscious Change. (E-mail, 7/27/00)

DonationDepot   www.donationdepot.com

"DonationDepot.com is a complete online giving community. Our main focus is to educate consumers on the financial and tax benefits of charitable giving. In addition, we offer online services that make researching charities, finding volunteer opportunities, and donating to charity easy, safe, and fun." (From the Web site, 5/4/00)

DonorDigital   www.donordigital.com

An Internet consulting and Web development company specializing in helping nonprofit organizations use the Internet for fundraising, marketing, and advocacy. Donordigital.com works with large and medium-size nonprofits to help them use e-mail and the Web. (From "About" on the Web site, 12/18/99)

DonorNet   www.donornet.com

DonorNet offers a wide range of services for nonprofits wishing to use the Internet for fundraising and event registration.

DonorLink IT   www.socialecology.com/dl/index.html

A high-end relationship management tool built and priced for nonprofits. (Announcement, 6/8/00)

Donortrust.com   www.donortrust.com

Donortrust.com is a full-service e-donation solution developed by Merkle Direct Marketing, Inc. to benefit nonprofit organizations seeking to offer the donor population a quick, secure, and cost-effective way for donating online through the Internet. (From the Web site, 5/31/00)

e501   See www.helpnetworks.com

A shopping site that offers rebates and other benefits to both schools and nonprofits; has changed its name to Helpnetworks. (11/30/99)

eBay   pages.ebay.com/charity/

The popular online auction site offers services specially designed for nonprofits to use in fundraising.

eCharity   www.echarity.com

Offers advertiser-supported facilities for accepting donations online at no charge to donor or charity (except for routine bank credit-card fees, deducted from the gift). Offers other fee-based services to assist with online and other forms of fundraising. Created a Web site to raise funds for disaster relief: www.edisaster.com.

Educate America!   www.educateamerica.org

Provides a portal site where donors can find national education charities they wish to support. Donations can be made online to any charity via check, credit card, or gift of stock. EA! is a membership organization that reviews and certifies its members annually. In addition to its Web site, EA! places its members into workplace employee fund drives, the largest being the Combined Federal Campaign for federal employees.

effinity   www.effinity.net

Their slogan on the Web site is "Reconnecting Commerce and Community. Why would you shop any other way?" Sets up malls for nonprofits and shares commissions. Offers other charity-related commerce services, including auctions. (5/2/00)

Electronic Funds Corporation   www.achnetwork.com

"Many charities, nonprofit organizations, and churches have found that accepting donations via electronic funds transfer (EFT) is not only less expensive and time-consuming but also gives a much greater dollar return than conventional old ways of receiving donations." (From a press release)

Enews.com Not-for-Profit Newsstand Network
www.enews.com/network/nn/nonprofit

Created especially for not-for-profit organizations and school groups, this Internet fundraising program enables you to offer magazine subscriptions to your supporters at low, discount prices. Choose the magazines you want to offer, include the links we provide on your Web site, and earn 21 percent on every subscription. There is no charge to participating nonprofits. (E-mail from enews.com 3/9/00)

Entango   www.entango.com

Provides fundraising services including donation processing and reporting, membership and renewal management, seminar/workshop registration, and professional outreach services.

ePromo   www.epromo.org

"You can now offer your Web visitors high-quality promotional merchandise featuring your logo/art. We create the store, link it to your site, take the orders, notify you, create the product, ship it, and send you 50 percent of the money." (E-mail advertisement 3/29/00) "The cost for setting up your epromo store is usually $99.00 and the monthly operating and management fee is $19.95." (From the Web site)

eRSVP   www.ersvp.com

An online tool that helps event planners manage invitations and guest responses. (E-mail, 7/19/00)

eTapestry.com   www.etapestry.com

eTapestry is a complete fundraising and donor management system that is run over the Internet. With access from any Internet connection, complete communications capabilities, and all maintenance and backups handled by eTapestry, it offers solutions for organizations of all types and sizes.

ewebuilder   info.ewebuilder.com

Not specific to the nonprofit sector, but worth looking into by any organization that wants to build an online store and accept credit cards at the site. (Mentioned in e-mail, 6/11/00)

eVite   www.evite.com

Online event management tools. (Announcement, 8/23/00)

Excess Access   www.excessaccess.com

"The Excess Access service links business and household item donations with nonprofit wish lists and suggested local delivery companies." (From the Web site, 12/15/99.) Other services are offered as well. There is a $5.00 registration fee every six months to participate in the surplus property exchange.

FreeToCharity   www.freetocharity.com

A Web site where people and organizations can announce items or services they are willing to give to nonprofits and nonprofits can post wish lists for things they need. (Fax announcement 6/6/00)

friendswhogive.com   www.friendswhogive.com

Charities sell magazine subscriptions via their own "Internet Newsstand" as a fundraising mechanism (template, script, etc., provided by "Friends Who Give").

Fund-Raising.Com   www.fund-raising.com

"The Source For Fund-Raising Information on the Internet." Ideas, products, resources all about fundraising. (Per NicheNet Inc, 12/12/99)

The Fundraiser   www.thefundraiser.org

"My company creates online global malls for your nonprofit's Web site. You can make money all year round with your Web site visitors purchasing items from your global mall. These malls are customized for your site—they are branded with your site's name and everything. We manage the mall for you, so you guys don't have to do anything but promote it within your organization. (From Christopher Kren, 10/2/99)

FundRaisingMegaMall   www.fundraisingmegamall.com

A project of www.cherrydale.com (E-mail, 6/23/00).

Fund$Raiser Cyberzine   www.fundsraiser.com

An online magazine bringing fundraisers how-to-hang-on ideas in fundraising.

FundRover   www.fundrover.com

Fundrover.com provides a self-service, self-administrated, online collection Web site used to accept Visa or Mastercard for donations. Nonprofit organizations can set up their customized service in minutes at no cost. Transaction fees are claimed to be lower than many of the other services.

Fund Online   www.fund-online.com

See Online Fundraising Resources Center.

GaZoom   www.gazoom.com

GaZoom is an Internet company that has developed a membership kit that charitable organizations can sell for a profit. Your supporters receive $200.00 worth of value for $20.00, and once they register online, they begin to receive "deals" relevant to their needs, which are sent directly to their home or business e-mail address.

GiftLegacy www.giftlegacy.com

Online services to support planned giving programs. Charges a fixed annual fee. (E-mail mention and Web site, 5/26/00)

GiveForChange www.giveforchange.com

GiveForChange.com gives people an easy way to make online donations to causes they care about. There are more than 280 groups on the site in 11 different categories, including the environment, children and family, human rights, and economic justice. GiveForChange.com is responding to the needs of nonprofit groups to develop new, lower-cost alternatives to expensive fundraising events or direct mail campaigns. It also puts smaller, lesser-known nonprofits on an equal footing with larger nonprofits, allowing all the same exposure and fundraising opportunities. All GiveForChange donations are processed by eGrants.org, a subsidiary of the Tides Foundation, which has a 20-year track record in supporting nonprofits working for social change. (E-mail from GiveForChange, 1/6/00)

Givenation.com www.givenation.com

Are you a nonprofit? You can add dot.com to your fundraising without adding dot.com to your name to combine the power of the Internet with what we believe is everyone's instinct to help those who really need it. (A new service, expected to be online 1/25/00. The description is from the preliminary Web site, excerpted on 1/21/00)

GivingCapital www.givingcapital.com

"GivingCapital provides a simple and secure way to donate online. We help nonprofit organizations harness the collaborative power of the Internet to acquire new donors and increase contributions. With our patent-pending technology, donors click a banner on a nonprofit organization's Web site to make their gift. From straight donations to membership campaigns, to creating a matching or challenge campaign, GivingCapital provides an array of tools to create and monitor campaigns." (E-mail, 8/4/00)

The Giving Network www.thegivingnetwork.com

An educational site dedicated specifically to nonprofit organizations in the Pacific Northwest and the people who support them.

The Giving Network offers comprehensive, analytical information about charities, original content, and local news, as well as secure online giving, donation administration services, a volunteer registry, an in-kind gift registry, and an event calendar free to qualified nonprofit organizations. The Giving Network has a database of more than 30,000 nonprofit organizations in Washington, Idaho, Oregon, and Alaska. Visitors can search for organizations by name, cause, category, or region. A transaction fee of 8 percent is collected on donations designated for participating charities. (12/1/99)

Grants Direct   www.grantsdirect.com

Provides information on Maryland foundations and grants.

GreaterGood.Com   www.greatergood.com

From a press release dated 9/29/99: "GreaterGood.com is the nation's largest cause-focused e-commerce company that helps NFP [not-for-profit] organizations tap into the year-round revenue potential of the fast-growing online shopping market. Based in Seattle, the company generates sustainable new sources of revenue for its not-for-profit partners through building, marketing, and managing e-commerce shopping villages that link from the NFPs' homepages and are branded with each not-for-profit's own name and graphic identity. The company is committed to adding a charitable giving quotient to the standard online shopping criteria of quality, convenience, and service, co-marketing with its partners via the Internet as a means to increase membership and other bases of support. For more information, visit GreaterGood.com at www.GreaterGood.com, or call 888-509-7676."

Health and Medical Research Charities of America
www.nonprofits.org/npofaq

Provides a portal site where donors can find national charities working in the fields of health issues and medical research they wish to support. Donations can be made online to any charity via check, credit card, or gift of stock. The HMRCA is a membership organization that reviews and certifies its members annually. In addition to its Web site, the HMRCA places its members into workplace employee fund drives, the largest being the Combined Federal Campaign for federal employees.

Helping.org   www.helping.org

A service of the AOL Foundation, Helping.org allows visitors to make donations to any recognized 501(c)(3) that has not opted out of their system, charges no fees (though there is a credit-card processing fee deducted from the donation en route to the recipient), and offers volunteering, technical assistance, and other links as well. The database of recognized charities is provided by Guidestar (www.guidestar.org). (PB 10/21/99.) To learn how to link an organization to the Helping.org donation-processing system, see www.helping.org/register/link.adp.

HelpNetworks   www.helpnetworks.com

Offers links to merchants that will make payments to charities or schools selected by the purchaser based on purchases. Runs shopping malls at www.helpanonprofit.com and www.helpaschool.com. (11/30/99)

Honorwalls.com   www.honorwalls.com

A "virtual venue for donor recognition." (E-mail, 7/25/00)

Human and Civil Rights Organizations of America
www.hcr.org

Provides a portal site where donors can find national human rights charities they wish to support. Donations can be made online to any charity via check, credit card, or gift of stock. The HCROA is a membership organization that reviews and certifies its members annually. In addition to its Web site, the HCROA places its members into workplace employee fund drives, the largest being the Combined Federal Campaign for federal employees.

The Hunger Site   www.thehungersite.com

Sponsored by several corporations. Every time you go to that site and click on the Donate Free Food button, one of those corporations will make a donation to feed a starving person for one day. You can do this once a day. This is a form of advertising for the sponsoring corporations. It gets their name in front of you, just the way that a television commercial does. It does not cost you anything to make this donation—everything is paid for by the sponsoring corporation.

icharity.net   www.icharity.net

Offers a variety of services to charities, including the ability to raise funds online, distribute electronic messages, and manage mailing lists.

IGaveTo   www.igaveto.com

Facilitates nonprofit clients' interactions with donors and members. (From the Web site, 9/26/00)

igive.com   www.igive.com

"Turning everyday online shopping into philanthropy." iGive has developed a processing system that may permit online shoppers (members) to take tax deductions for charitable donations based on rebates from merchants. "The salient points—it's the member's money (it's a rebate), the member is in complete control, the member chooses the cause, the deductibility is subject to the particular status of the taxpayer and the organization the money is donated to, the donation doesn't happen until we send the check, and the process we've invented to make this work on the Internet is patent-pending." (From Robert Grosshandler, CEO, October 6, 1999)

Independent Charities of America   www.independentcharities.org

ICA's highly trafficked Web site is a portal site where donors can find national charities they wish to support. Charities are categorized by type of service, and donations can be made online to any charity via check, credit card, or gift of stock. The ICA is a membership organization that reviews and certifies its members annually. In addition to its Web site, the ICA places its members into workplace employee fund drives, the largest being the Combined Federal Campaign for federal employees.

Infoweb Services   www.infowebservices.com

Our systematic approach ensures an effective Internet presence because we take time to define each client's objectives, develop the right solutions, and establish benchmarks to gauge success. The end result is improved processes for nonprofit organizations, interactive communication with their target audiences, and developing online communities of believers and members who actively support their causes. Our Web site features a collection of informative articles for nonprofits and associations, including an extensive "Nonprofit FAQ" section on developing an effective Internet Strategy. (E-mail from company, 4/5/00)

Internet Association Corporation   www.iaccorp.com

Web site developer with a claimed speciality in creating "online communities."

Internet-Fundraising   www.internet-fundraising.com

Allison Schwein, author of the *Charity-Mall Report*, offers consulting services to help nonprofits use the Internet.

Isignupnow   www.isignupnow.com

A flexible donation-processing service. (Mentioned in e-mail, 5/23/00)

kuzi.com   www.kuzi.com

Provides small ads that can be attached to the bottom of e-mail. When the ads result in a sale, the sender's chosen nonprofit organization receives a payment from the advertiser. There are also referral fees for signing up new members. (From the Web site, 6/7/00)

LitLamp   www.litlamp.com

See the Martin Resource Group.

Local Independent Charities of America   www.lic.org

Provides a portal site where donors can find local charities they wish to support. The LIC currently provides listings in 12 states, but we are eager to add more to our list. Charities are categorized by type of service, and donations can be made online to any charity via check, credit card, or gift of stock. In addition to its Web site, charities can apply to join the LIC to participate in workplace employee fund drives, the largest being the Combined Federal Campaign for federal employees.

LocalVoice   www.localvoice.com

Member-supported organizations (MSOs) spend vast amounts of resources to build relationships with donors. LocalVoice.com helps member-supported organizations build relationships with donors using a Web-based platform. Integrating e-commerce and e-communication functions, our suite of six applications enables secure online fundraising, direct e-mail marketing, member profiling, online event management, e-surveying, and online membership activation. (Adapted from e-mail, 8/10/00)

Low Country Gives   www.lowcountrygives.com

A shopping portal and consulting service focused on nonprofits in the tidewater area of North Carolina. (From Web site visit, 6/20/00)

Maguire/Maguire, Inc.   www.maguireinc.com

A marketing consulting firm that offers nonprofit association management services, workplace campaign management, and Internet services. Internet services include the Give Button, which allows a charity to use a standard or custom donation form to accept donations from their Web site. Donations can be made via check, credit card, or gifts of stock. The form includes a section for donors to offer their gifts in memory of or in honor of a special person and allows the notification letter to be sent to a third party. Donors and charities are notified immediately via e-mail of the donation. The transaction fee is 7.5 percent.

MakeADonation.com   www.makeadonation.com

Provides charities and nonprofits with a fast, easy, and secure way of accepting donations over the Internet. Through MakeADonation.com, your organization can begin accepting donations through your own Web site in less than one week. No software to purchase, no initial investment, and setup is free. Fees are based on transaction volume, not a percentage of amounts. (E-mail 4/7/00, 4/28/00)

Martin Resource Group   www.litlamp.com

Fee-based Web site for organizations seeking sponsorships for events. "A virtual sales effort that connects you directly with sponsors who are informed buyers."

Military, Veterans & Patriotic Service Organizations of America   www.mvpsoa.org

Provides a portal site where donors can find national charities with a military emphasis they wish to support. Donations can be made online to any charity via check, credit card, or gift of stock. The MVP-

SOA is a membership organization that reviews and certifies its members annually. In addition to its Web site, the MVPSOA places its members into workplace employee fund drives, the largest being the Combined Federal Campaign for federal employees.

Move On   www.moveon.org

Grassroots campaign, which began as an online effort to support the censure of President Clinton, has generated $13 million in online pledges and signed up 500,00 "volunteers" for the cause.

MyFundraisingCounsel   www.myfundraisingcounsel.com

For a monthly retainer, clients receive personalized advice about fundraising by e-mail. (From the Web site, 6/11/00)

mypersonal.com   www.mypersonal.com

"Their business model is to build a newsy homepage for groups with large constituencies, and then split the affiliate income. They already do vanity e-mail and provide online community tools. All for free. They say they are going to add online giving and other services." (Adam Corson-Finnerty in e-mail, 6/11/00)

National Car Donation Processing Center www.donateacar.com

Offers to arrange for pickup of donated vehicles and process all necessary paperwork in all 50 states. (From the Web site, 5/11/00)

Netcentives   www.netcentives.com

Offers "customer loyalty" rewards for online activities, including donations. The ClickRewards program allows participants to donate the incentives they receive for online activities to charity.

New Tithing   www.newtithing.org

Newtithing Group is a philanthropic research organization committed to increasing charitable giving, personal fulfillment, and the productivity of donations to the nonprofit sector. Our extensive financial research of IRS data and national wealth suggests that well-off individuals can comfortably afford to donate to charity hundreds of billions of additional dollars each year, while barely affecting their net worth. (From the Web page)

nextwave.com   www.nextwaveworld.com

Ten percent of sales are donated to charities they choose.

Nonprofit Advocate   www.thenonprofitadvocate.com

"My site, www.thenonprofitadvocate.com, provides information to NPOs. My newsletter, available from the site, provides direct information on how to raise money on the Web."

The Nonprofit Shopping Mall   www.npsmall.com/joinus.htm

Fourteen-page shopping malls with more than 70 merchants. Seventy percent of the total mall commissions paid to organizations. Nonbinding agreement.

Nonprofit Zone   www.nonprofitzone.com

Provides free tools and resources to help nonprofits work better, smarter, and faster.

OnLineGiving.com   www.onlinegiving.com

"Provides nonprofits with a dynamic electronic service for accepting Internet donations, one-to-one communications, and e-marketing with individual donors." (From the Web site, 5/4/00)

Parabon   www.parabon.com

Downloads and uploads problems to be worked on idle desktop computers. Offers an arrangement under which a nonprofit can be paid (approximately $5/month/computer) when supporters enroll their computers in Parabon's distributed solutions network. (E-mail, 10/24/00)

PayByCheck.com   www.paybycheck.com

PayByCheck.com is a large Internet check transaction company.

Philanthropy Center   www.philanthropycenter.org

An online information resource for charitable and nonprofit donors in peninsula and Silicon Valley (California). Sponsored by the Center for Venture Philanthropy.

PledgeMaker   www.pledgemaker.com/pmol/PMOL.htm

An online version of a fundraising software system. (E-mail, 6/8/00)

publicspirit.com   www.fund-online.com

"PublicSpirit.com is a Walnut Creek, California–based company that provides an online mechanism for people to contribute to their favorite causes while purchasing items like computer equipment and, starting in November, office products and other products. The idea is that 50 percent of the gross profit (the competitively discounted price to the shopper minus the cost of the item to PublicSpirit.com) from each sale goes to the shopper's selected organization." (From NPTalk, 10/5/99)

REACT   www.reliefinteractive.org

Portal site for emergency relief organizations announced in September 2000. (Rick Christ newsletter story, 9/21/00)

SchoolCash.com   www.schoolcash.com

"SchoolCash is a shopping site for school supporters with 150 affiliated merchants and very generous commissions. To enroll, schools should call 1-800-688-6252. In addition to online merchants, there are opportunities to buy certain items offline, such as name-brand electronics, long-distance service, and discount brokerage services. There are no fees involved and merchandise is never marked up. SchoolCash ensures supporters that their transactions will be kept completely confidential." (From David Greene of SchoolCash, 12/12/99)

SearchToHelp   www.searchtohelp.com

"A site where you can contribute to charity for free by searching the Web and signing up for various free offers. Currently, you can make an $18 contribution for free in less than 10 minutes." (E-mail, 3/20/00)

seeUthere.com   www.seeuthere.com

seeUthere.com offers special event coordination service to help nonprofit organizations by smoothing the administrative and logistical tasks of producing successful events and generating funds.

Everything in the service is totally automated. The online service includes the creation of a WEB Event Page and Web Organization Page that will create invitations that are sent through e-mail, fax, and direct mail. RSVPs are done through the Web and via telephone response. The service handles automatic reminders as well as membership management of an organization's database. seeUthere.com also provides e-commerce solutions for ticketing, online donations, and will soon include online auctions. The event coordination service is surrounded with the seeUthere.com Event Epicenter providing everything else the nonprofit coordinator may need—hotel bookings, volunteer matching, forums, employment classifieds, chat.

Shop Goodwill   www.shopgoodwill.com

Launched on August 31, 1999, by Goodwill Industries of Orange County, shopgoodwill.com earned its first $100,000 in just five months. The Santa Ana–based agency was the sole seller on the site until early December, when additional Goodwills began signing up as sellers. Seven more agencies have since posted items, and another 30 are preparing to get online.

Shop4Charity

See by ireachout.com.

ShopForChange   www.shopforchange.com or www.shop4change.com

"Any time you buy something from one of the popular merchants accessible through ShopForChange.com, we donate 5 percent of each purchase to progressive causes. We make the donation automatically— at no extra cost to you—to groups like Human Rights Watch, Friends of the Earth, and Stand for Children. You can also make your voice heard and make a difference. Throughout the year, Working Assets monitors events in the corporate world and identifies important and timely issues where citizen activism can make a difference. Each month, ShopForChange highlights one crucial corporate issue, explains what's at stake, and tells you whom to contact to voice your opinion. You can send an e-mail to our targeted decision maker right from the site." (E-mail from ShopForChange, 1/6/00)

signup4U.com   www.signup4u.com

Build customized event forms in minutes with the ability to collect fees/donations. This free cyber-programming automates Web pages and allows nonprofit organizations (United States only) to accept Visa, MasterCard, American Express, and bank checks online for a fraction of the cost of other such sites or shopping carts. This service is provided by the eServices Corporation; toll-free: (877) 866-4848.

SocialEvents   www.socialevents.com

Launched in January 2000, SocialEvents offers gift-delivery services from vendors in many countries around the world. It invites users to prepare wish lists of desired gifts that are available locally for purchase through the site by far-away friends and relatives. These wish lists may also include charitable organizations to which a gift may be made in the name of the person being honored on a birthday, bar mitzvah, retirement, or other special occasion.

TakeToAuction.com   www.taketoauction.com

An auction site that includes a feature for charities as well as selecting big-ticket items to be auctioned with part of the proceeds going to selected charitable organizations. (*NY Times*, 10/23/00)

TEN97, the Social Responsibility Network
www.ten97.com

TEN97 produces dynamic fundraising and promotional events for worthy causes. TEN97 enlists the support of socially responsible celebrities, corporate sponsors, nonprofit organizations, the media, the public, and a select team of strategic specialists. By drawing all of these resources together, TEN97 focuses diverse people, organizations, and interest groups into one team, at one place, at one time to make the difference for a worthy cause. (Adapted 8/12/99 from the TEN97 website.) (Owns CelebrityAuctions.com)

thedatabank.com   www.thedatabank.com

An online data-storage system that provides customized services for various sorts of businesses including nonprofits that maintain donor records on the Web site. (E-mail discussion, 6/7/00)

TheFundRaiser.com

See The Fundraiser.

TheRightReason   www.therightreason.com

TheRightReason.com is a community-building organization funded by helping organizations raise funds via the Internet. It also offers subscriptions for Internet access at $19.95 per month for unlimited access and rebates up to $5 per month for ongoing revenue. (From e-mail 3/10/00)

UrbanEvents.com   www.urbanevents.com

Allows event planners to announce events and sell tickets (including reserved seating and other details) online. There is no charge for the base service. The service is described as being suitable for handling everything from an in-home charity event to a full-featured cruise. (From the Web site, 1/20/00)

Virtual Foundation   www.virtualfoundation.org

We have been experimenting with online fundraising for small environmental projects initiated by local nongovernmental organizations. Information about every aspect of our project, including proposals that have been funded, projects awaiting donors, administrative procedures, and foundations supporting the project is available on our Web site.

The Virtual Foundation was begun as a model of online philanthropy and is committed to a maximum degree of transparency. We hope that others can learn from our efforts, replicate what we have developed, and give us constructive criticism so that we may improve the model.

WealthEngine.com   www.wealthengine.com

A fee-based service that simultaneously checks multiple databases for background information on individuals who are prospecting supporters of subscribing nonprofits. (Web site announced 5/11/00)

webcharity.com   www.webcharity.com

Online auction site.

Webstore America   www.webstoreamerica.com

Advertiser-supported customized e-commerce sites allow partici-pating nonprofits to receive 100 percent of payments from affiliated merchants. (The Grantsmanship Center News, Winter 2000)

WebWrights   www.web-wrights.com

A Web-design firm that offers a fixed-fee package deal to design and support a donation page to add to a charity's existing World Wide Web site. The page collects donor information but does not provide online merchant services (credit-card processing).

WeCareToo   www.wecaretoo.com

"WeCareToo offers free Web pages in its growing online directory of not-for-profit groups as well as several optional fundraising pro-grams that are structured to pay a participating group from 60 to 100 percent of all funds generated by the program." (E-mail, 8/23/00)

Women, Children & Family Service Charities
www.womenandchildren.org

Provides a portal site where donors can find national charities working to improve the lives of women and families they wish to support. Donations can be made online to any charity via check, credit card, or gift of stock. The WCFS is a membership organiza-tion that reviews and certifies its members annually. In addition to its Web site, the WCFS places its members into workplace employee fund drives, the largest being the Combined Federal Campaign for federal employees.

Glossary of Internet Terms

Note: Terms that appear underlined refer to other Glossary items.

Analog/Digital Analog is the traditional method of modulating radio signals so they can carry information. Amplitude modulation (AM) and frequency modulation (FM) are the two most common methods of analog modulation. Today, most U.S. cellular systems carry phone conversations using analog; the transition to digital transmissions is happening slowly. Digital, on the other hand, describes any system based on discontinuous data or events. Computers are digital machines because at their most basic level they can distinguish between just two values, 0 and 1, or off and on. There is no simple way to represent all the values in between, such as 0.25. All data that a computer processes must be encoded digitally, as a series of zeros and ones.

Applet Applet is a diminutive form of app (application), and it refers to simple, single-function programs that often ship with a larger product. Programs such as Windows' Calculator, File Manager, and Notepad are examples of applets.

ASP (application service provider) An online outsourcing or hosting service for software applications, typically for large businesses with hundreds of users or more. ASP users "rent" instead of buy applications, such as many back-office and e-commerce applications. Many experts expect the use of ASPs to grow quickly in the coming years, but others aren't convinced it's economical for many businesses. For now, expect ASPs to cater mostly to Fortune 500 companies.

Architecture   How components of a system are connected to, and operate with, each other. Architecture manages voice, video, data, and text—everything that travels on a <u>network</u>. Descriptions of architecture include the ability of the system to carry narrow, medium, and broadband signals. It also describes how seamlessly a system can grow—or, in other words, how much it will cost to make it grow.

Bandwidth   In a general sense, this term describes information-carrying capacity. It can apply to telephone or <u>network</u> wiring as well as system buses, radio frequency signals, and monitors. Bandwidth is most accurately measured in cycles per second, or hertz (Hz), which is the difference between the lowest and highest frequencies transmitted, but it's also common to use bits or bytes per second instead.

Beta Software   Beta versions of commercial software are work-in-progress test copies released before the full version. They're used to put the product through real-world tests and to ferret out bugs before the finished software hits the shelves. Betas often expire after a period of time, usually when the full version or the next beta is released. Originally, beta software was released only to developers, but increasingly betas are offered to the general public, usually through the manufacturer's Web site. Testing beta software can be a great way to try out a new product that you're not sure you want to buy.

Browser   A browser is your interface to the <u>World Wide Web</u>; it interprets hypertext links and lets you view sites and navigate from one <u>Internet</u> node to another. Among the companies that produce browsers are NCSA Mosaic, Netscape, and Microsoft, as well as commercial services like CompuServe, Prodigy, and America Online.

Cable Modem   Speed is something we all want on the <u>Internet</u>, and it also explains the allure of cable modems, which promise speeds of up to 80 times faster than an <u>ISDN</u> line or six times faster than a dedicated <u>T1</u> line (the type of connection most large corporations use). Because cable modems provide Internet access over cable TV networks (which rely primarily on fiber-optic or coaxial cable), they are much faster than modems that use phone lines.

Chief Information Officer   The CIO makes the computer systems go. The title is usually given to the person responsible for the computer systems, but it has come to encompass a broad range of duties, including the setting of strategic direction. A CIO makes sure a company has the right information technology to achieve its business goals.

Client-Server Architecture (two-tier architecture)   A network architecture in which each computer or process on the network is either a client or a server. Servers are powerful computers or processes dedicated to managing disk drives (file servers), printers (print servers), or network traffic (network servers). Clients are PCs or workstations on which users run applications. Clients rely on servers for resources, such as files, devices, and even processing power. On the Internet, a client is a computer that is asking or receiving information while a server (host) is a computer where the information is stored and/or presented. Another type of network architecture is known as a peer-to-peer architecture because each node has equivalent responsibilities. Both client-server and peer-to-peer architectures are widely used, and each has unique advantages and disadvantages.

Data Mining   The use of sophisticated search engines that use statistical algorithms to discover patterns and correlations in otherwise unrelated data. It's used as a way to find knowledge buried in the vast mountain of information either on the Internet or in a company's own files.

Data Vaulting   Backing up data is copying files to a second medium (usually a disk or tape) as a precaution in case the first medium fails. One of the cardinal rules in using computers is to back up your files regularly. Data vaulting is the process of sending data off-site, where it can be protected from hardware failures, theft, hackers, and other threats. Several companies now provide Web backup services that will compress, encrypt, and periodically transmit a customer's data to a remote vault. In most cases, the vaults will feature auxiliary power supplies, powerful computers, and manned security. This is also referred to as a remote backup service (RBS).

Dedicated Host   A <u>server</u> that is dedicated to the traffic to your Web site. Only very busy sites require dedicated hosting. Indeed, many companies purchase their own servers and set them up at a <u>Web-hosting</u> facility that provides fast access to the <u>Internet</u>. This practice is called *colocation*.

Dial-up   Any connection that your computer makes to another by way of a modem and phone line. It is so named because the connection is established by dialing a phone number over an <u>analog</u> phone line, usually to such services as America OnLine, CompuServe, or NetZero.

Digital Certificate   Citing concerns about <u>security</u>, many people are still wary of online transactions. In an attempt to assuage those fears, software vendors, security specialists, and online vendors have developed the concept of digital certificates. A digital certificate is a password-protected file that includes a variety of information: the name and e-mail address of the certificate holder, an <u>encryption</u> key that can be used to verify the digital signature of the holder, the name of the company issuing the certificate, and the period during which the certificate is valid. Certificate authorities (CAs) gather information about a person or company and then issue certificates. If an e-mail message or order form comes through with an attached digital certificate, the recipient can be more confident that the document is genuine.

Domain Name   The name used to identify a site on the <u>Internet</u>, and is located within the site's <u>URL</u> (e.g., the domain name of Harvard University, www.harvard.edu, is "harvard.edu"). Domain names are issued by the National Science Foundation (NSF), and they come with different extensions based on whether the domain belongs to a commercial enterprise (.com), an educational establishment (.edu), a government body (.gov), the military (.mil), a network (.net), or a nonprofit organization (.org).

DOS (disk operating system)   Refers to any <u>operating system</u> that runs on a single computer, but it is most often used as a shorthand for MS-DOS (Microsoft disk operating system). Originally developed by Microsoft for IBM, MS-DOS was the standard operating system for IBM-compatible personal computers.

DSL (digital subscriber line)   Digital subscriber lines carry data at high speeds over standard copper telephone wires. With DSL, data can be delivered at a rate of 1.5 mbps (around 30 times faster than through a 56-kbps modem). Also, DSL users can receive voice and data simultaneously; small offices can leave computers plugged into the Net without interrupting phone connections. Currently, DSL is expensive because specialized equipment—a splitter—needs to be installed at the subscriber's location. DSL Lite, the consumer-ready version of DSL, requires no such splitter and promises comparable access speeds at a cheaper rate. DSL is expected to replace ISDN in many areas and to compete with cable modems in bringing multimedia and 3-D to homes and small businesses.

Encryption   Encryption is the process of changing data into a form that can be read only by the intended receiver. To decipher the message, the receiver of the encrypted data must have the proper decryption key. In traditional encryption schemes, the sender and the receiver use the same key to encrypt and decrypt data. Public-key encryption schemes use two keys: a public key, which anyone may use, and a corresponding private key, which is possessed only by the person who created it. With this method, anyone may send a message encrypted with the owner's public key, but only the owner has the private key necessary to decrypt it. PGP (Pretty Good Privacy) and DES (data encryption standard) are two of the most popular public-key encryption schemes.

ERP (enterprise resource planning)   The use of complex applications employed by large businesses to manage inventory and integrate all the different processes of a business across multiple divisions and organizational boundaries. Used typically on an intranet, it allows different parts of vast enterprises to speak a common language and share information more readily.

Ethernet   The most popular form of local area network. Invented by Xerox Corp., it typically uses coaxial cable (as in cable modem) or other special grades of wiring that can provide high-speed communication to users on a network.

Extranet   Companies often use extranets to provide nonpublic information to a select group of people, such as business partners or customers. So while an extranet may look like an ordinary Web site, you have to enter a password or use digital <u>encryption</u> to access it. For example, Federal Express's customers can track packages on the company's extranet by simply entering a tracking number. And Bank of America's extranet lets users transfer funds or look up account balances online. Using an extranet can help companies save money by allowing customers to find information themselves, without having to call and talk to a person.

Fiber-optic Cable   Fiber-optic cables consist of thin filaments of glass (or other transparent materials), which can carry beams of light. A laser transmitter encodes frequency signals into pulses of light and sends them down the optical fiber to a receiver, which translates the light signals back into frequencies. Less susceptible to noise and interference than other kinds of cables, optical fibers can transmit data greater distances without amplification. But because the glass filaments are fragile, optical fiber must be run underground rather than overhead on telephone poles. Fiber-optic cables are far more efficient than copper (phone) lines and even coaxial cable.

Firewall   If you want to protect any networked <u>server</u> from damage (intentional or otherwise) by those who log in to it, you put up a firewall. This could be a dedicated computer equipped with <u>security</u> measures such as a dial-back feature, or it could be software-based protection called *defensive coding*. The firewall acts as a barrier between the <u>Internet</u> and an <u>intranet</u>, blocking access and certain actions past the <u>gateway</u>.

FTP (file transfer protocol)   This Internet <u>protocol</u> is used to copy files between computers, usually a client and an archive site. It's old-fashioned, it's a bit on the slow side, it doesn't support compression, and it uses cryptic <u>Unix</u> command parameters. But the good news is that you can download shareware or freeware applications that shield you from the complexities of Unix, and you can connect to FTP sites using a Web browser.

Gateway   A gateway is a program or piece of hardware that passes data between <u>networks</u>. You'll see this term most often when you either log in to an Internet site or when you're passing e-mail between different <u>servers</u>.

Gopher   Gopher is a text-based information retrieval system for the Internet. Equipped with a Gopher client, you can use Gopher <u>servers</u> to search databases around the globe for keywords or subjects. Because Web browsers include Gopher client capabilities, the Web is superseding Gopher for document retrieval. One advantage of searching with Gopher is that you can read stuff directly from the servers—no need to copy or save the files to your system first.

HTML (hypertext markup language)   HTML is a collection of formatting commands that create hypertext documents—Web pages, to be exact. When you point your Web browser to a <u>URL</u>, the browser interprets the HTML commands embedded in the page and uses them to format the page's text and graphic elements. HTML commands cover many types of text formatting (bold and italic text, lists, headline fonts in various sizes, and so on), and also have the ability to include graphics and other non-text elements.

HTTP (hypertext transfer protocol)   The protocol used to transmit and receive all data over the <u>World Wide Web</u>. When you type a <u>URL</u> into your browser, you're actually sending an HTTP request to a Web <u>server</u> for a page of information (that's why URLs all begin with http://). HTTP1.1, the latest version, is currently undergoing revisions to make it work more efficiently with <u>TCP/IP</u>.

Hub   This chunk of hardware is used to network computers together (usually over an <u>Ethernet</u> connection). It serves as a common wiring point so that information can flow through one central location to any other computer on the <u>network</u>.

Information Superhighway   A buzzword from a speech by Al Gore that refers to the Clinton/Gore administration's plan to deregulate communication services and thus widen the scope of the <u>Internet</u> by opening carriers, such as television cable, to data communication. The term is widely and loosely used to mean the Internet, and it's often shortened to I-way, the infobahn, and so on.

Internet   An internet is a <u>network</u> of computers that is freely open to all. The largest internet is known as the Internet. The Internet originated in 1969, in the midst of the Cold War, as a "nuke-proof" communications network. As you might guess, it received most of its early financing from the U.S. Defense Department. Now, however, it consists of countless <u>networks</u> and computers across the world, allowing millions of people to share information. The lines that carry most of the information are known as the Internet backbone. While the government used to run things, now major Internet service providers (<u>ISP</u>s), such as MCI, GTE, Sprint, UUNET, and ANS, own portions of the backbone. Every computer on the Internet is identified by an IP (Internet protocol) address: a string of numbers separated by periods (e.g., 123.123.23.2).

Intranet   A play on the word Internet, an intranet is a restricted-access network that works like the Web, but isn't on it. Usually owned and managed by a corporation, an intranet enables a company to share its resources with its employees without confidential information being made available to everyone with Internet access.

ISDN (integrated services digital network)   ISDN is a system for digital transmission of data over telephone copper wires. Home and business users who install an ISDN adapter (in place of a modem) can access data, including graphics-intensive Web pages, at speeds up to 128 kilobits per second. ISDN requires adapters at both ends of the transmission, so your <u>ISP</u> also needs an ISDN adapter. ISDN is generally available from the phone company in most urban areas.

ISP (internet service provider)   In the past, you could only connect to the <u>Internet</u> if you belonged to a major university or had a note from the Pentagon. Not anymore: ISPs have arrived to act as your (ideally) user-friendly front end to all the Internet offers. Most ISPs have a <u>network</u> of <u>servers</u> (mail, news, Web, and the like), <u>routers</u>, and modems attached to a permanent, high-speed Internet "backbone" connection. Subscribers can then dial into the local network to gain Internet access—without having to maintain servers, file for <u>domain names</u>, or learn <u>Unix</u>.

Java   Sun Microsystems' Java is a programming language for adding animation and other action to Web sites. The small applications (called <u>applets</u>) that Java creates can play back on any graphical system that's Web-ready, but your Web browser has to be Java-capable for you to see it. JavaScript, an easy-to-use adjunct to the Java programming language, can be added to standard HTML pages to create interactive documents. As a result, JavaScript has found considerable use in the creation of interactive Web-based forms. Most modern browsers, including those from Microsoft and Netscape, contain JavaScript support. The Java Virtual Machine (VM) is a program that interprets Java bytecodes into machine code. The VM is what makes Java portable—a vendor such as Microsoft or Sun writes a Java VM for their operating system, and any Java program can run on that VM.

Legacy   A word often bandied about by information technology consultants, *legacy* refers to an application or information system into which a company has invested a lot of time and money. For many companies to install fancy new software and hardware, it must be able to marry up to its legacy system. Legacy systems are typically viewed as an unfortunate but unavoidable impediment to large-scale upgrades.

Linux   Linus Torvalds' creation, Linux, is a freely distributed, Intel processor–based alternative to <u>Unix</u>. Linux (pronounced lih-nucks) is currently used by hundreds of thousands—and possibly millions—of people around the world. While Linux began life primarily as a hobby for programmers, the operating system has made some inroads into corporate life, particularly as an inexpensive substitute for high-priced Unix Web <u>servers</u>.

MS-Windows (MicroSoft Windows)   A family of <u>operating systems</u> for personal computers. Windows dominates the personal computer world, running, by some estimates, on 90 percent of all personal computers. The remaining 10 percent are mostly Macintosh computers. Like the Macintosh operating environment, Windows provides a graphical user interface (GUI), virtual memory management, multitasking, and support for many peripheral devices.

Mirror Server   Sometimes a Web <u>server</u> will receive more traffic than it can handle. When this happens, the server's administrator may add extra servers—containing identical data—to accommodate the flow. These duplicates are called *mirror servers*. By adding mirror servers and telling users how to access them, an administrator can keep users from receiving error messages or unacceptably slow response times when they try to access a site. Mirror servers also act as backup (see <u>data vaulting</u>) if the primary site goes down.

Network   A group of two or more computer systems linked together. There are many types of computer networks, including:

- local area networks (LANs): The computers are geographically close together (that is, in the same building).
- wide area networks (WANs): The computers are farther apart and are connected by telephone lines or radio waves.

In addition to these types, the following characteristics are also used to categorize different types of networks:

- topology: The geometric arrangement of a computer system. Common topologies include a bus, star, and ring.
- <u>protocol</u>: The protocol defines a common set of rules and signals that computers on the network use to communicate. One of the most popular protocols for LANs is called Ethernet. Another popular LAN protocol for PCs is the IBM token-ring network.
- <u>architecture</u>: Networks can be broadly classified as using either a peer-to-peer or client-server architecture.

Computers on a network are sometimes called *nodes*. Computers and devices that allocate resources for a network are called <u>servers</u>.

NOS (network operating system)   An operating system that includes special functions for connecting computers and devices into a local area network (LAN). Some operating systems, such as Unix and the Mac OS, have networking functions built in. Mac's new OS X is built specifically for <u>networks</u> and <u>servers</u>. The term

NOS, however, is generally reserved for software that enhances a basic operating system by adding networking features. For example, some popular NOSs for <u>DOS</u> and <u>MS-Windows</u> systems include <u>Novell</u> Netware, Artisoft's LANtastic, Microsoft LAN Manager, and <u>Windows NT</u>.

Novell   The world's largest network software company. Its flagship product, Netware, has been a corporate standard for building local area networks (LANs) for more than a decade.

OS (operating system)   A computer by itself is essentially dumb bits of wire and silicon. An OS knows how to talk to this hardware and can manage a computer's functions, such as allocating memory, scheduling tasks, accessing disk drives, and supplying a user interface. Without an operating system, software developers would have to write programs that directly accessed hardware, essentially reinventing the wheel with every new program.

Outsourcing   Contracting out a company's functions to outsiders. It could include everything from running a phone system to customer relations. Senior management typically likes outsourcing because it provides a level of certainty and accountability. Middle management generally dislikes it because it means, at the least, that they give up power and, at the worst, they get fired. Wired companies, conceivably, could outsource nearly everything.

Protocol   Computers can't just throw data at each other any old way. Because so many different types of computers and <u>operating systems</u> connect via modems or other connections, they have to follow communications rules called *protocols*. The <u>Internet</u> is a heterogenous collection of networked computers and is full of different protocols, including PPP, <u>TCP/IP</u>, SLIP, and <u>FTP</u>.

Proxy Server   A server that sits between a client application, such as a Web browser, and a real <u>server</u>. It intercepts all requests to the real server to see if it can fulfill the requests itself. If not, it forwards the request to the real server. Proxy servers have two main purposes: to improve performance (by storing the data that is accessed most often) and to filter requests (often for appropriateness).

Router   A device or, in some cases, software, that figures out how to send information to its destination. The router is connected to at least two <u>networks</u> and decides which way to send data based on what's going on inside the networks. Located at juncture points, routers are the traffic system of the <u>Internet</u>.

Search Engine   When a user enters text into a search form, a program called a *search engine* analyzes the text and searches for matching terms in an index file, which was created using a search indexer. The search engine returns the results of its search using a results listing.

Secure Server   A Web <u>server</u> that supports any of the major security <u>protocols</u>, that <u>encrypt</u> and decrypt messages to protect them against third-party tampering. Making purchases from a secure Web server ensures that a user's payment or personal information can be translated into a secret code that's difficult to crack. Major security protocols include SSL, SHTTP, PCT, and IPSec.

Security   Refers to techniques for ensuring that data stored in a computer cannot be read or compromised. Most security measures involve data <u>encryption</u> and passwords. Data encryption is the translation of data into a form that is unintelligible without a deciphering mechanism. A password is a secret word or phrase that gives a user access to a particular program or system.

Server   The business end of a client-server setup, a server is usually a computer that provides the information, files, Web pages, and other services to the client that logs on to it. (The word server is also used to describe the software and operating system designed to run server hardware.) The client-server setup is analogous to a restaurant with waiters and customers. Some Internet servers take this analogy to extremes and become inattentive, or even refuse to serve you.

Server Farm   A group of <u>servers</u> housed together in one location. The server farm usually functions as an off-site location where businesses store raw data, Web pages and online functions, or any combination of these. Depending on the company running the server farm and the level of service provided, the servers can have individual <u>operating systems</u> or a <u>network operating system</u>, and may also be set up to balance the load of information requests across a number of servers when demand is high.

Systems Administrator   An individual responsible for maintaining a multiuser computer system, including a local area network (LAN). Typical duties include adding and configuring new workstations, setting up user accounts, installing systemwide software, performing procedures to prevent the spread of viruses, and allocating mass storage space. The system administrator is sometimes called the "sysadmin." Small organizations may have just one system administrator, whereas larger enterprises usually have a whole team of system administrators.

T1/T3   T1 is a term coined by AT&T for a system that transfers digital signals at 1.544 megabits per second (as opposed to ISDN's mere 64 kilobits per second). When you're transferring data across a digital carrier, T3 is the premium way to go. It's not just three times the capacity of T1, as the name suggests—it's almost 30 times the capacity. It can handle 44.736 megabits of digital data per second.

TCP/IP (transmission control protocol/Internet protocol)
TCP/IP is the basic <u>protocol</u> of the <u>Internet</u>. Every computer with access to the Internet has a copy of the TCP/IP program that allows it to communicate with every other computer on the Internet—or at least every other computer that wants to send and receive messages.

Unix   Unix took off in the early 1970s as a general-purpose <u>operating system</u>. Because much of the Internet is hosted on Unix machines, the <u>OS</u> took on a new surge of popularity in the early 1990s.

URL (uniform resource locator)   URLs are the Internet equivalent of addresses. Take the URL, http://www.harvard.edu/admissions/index.html, for example. First you have the <u>protocol</u> (<u>http://</u>

and www), then the domain name (harvard.edu), and finally the directory (/admissions/) in which the file index.html resides.

Web Hosting The function of housing, serving, and maintaining files for one or more Web sites. Web hosts offer super-fast connections and easy access to the backbone of the Internet. Many ISPs, such as America Online, offer free, basic Web site hosting for members. More complex Web sites, however, are increasingly being hosted by companies such as Digex and PSINet.

Windows NT The most advanced version of the MS-Windows operating system. Windows NT (New Technology) is a 32-bit operating system that supports preemptive multitasking. There are actually two versions of Windows NT: Windows NT Server, designed to act as a server in networks, and Windows NT Workstation for stand-alone or client workstations. Windows 2000 is built on Windows NT, not on Windows 98 and DOS.

WWW (World Wide Web) Most often known simply as the Web, the World Wide Web was originally developed by CERN labs in Geneva, Switzerland. Continuing development of the Web is overseen by the World Wide Web Consortium (W3C). The Web can be described (dryly) as a client-server hypertext system (see client-server architecture) for retrieving information across the Internet. On the Web, everything is represented as hypertext (in HTML format) and is linked to other documents by their URLs. The Web encompasses its native http protocol, as well as FTP, Gopher, and Telnet.

XML (extensible markup language) XML was designed so companies could do business with each other on the World Wide Web. It creates common information formats for sharing information over the Web, and is based on HTML.

Partially taken from:

The CNet Glossary, www.cnet.com/Resources/Info/Glossary.

The Washington Post article "Glossary" by Terence O'Hara, Published on September 20, 2000 in the Wired Economy section, p. G27.

Webopedia, http://webopedia.internet.com.

Index